THE LENA GOLDFIELDS MASSACRE
AND THE CRISIS OF THE LATE TSARIST STATE

Eugenia and Hugh M. Stewart '26 Series on Eastern Europe

Stjepan Meštrović, General Editor

Series Editorial Board

Norman Cigar
Bronislaw Misztal
Sabrina P. Ramet
Vladimir Shlapentokh
Keith Tester

The Lena Goldfields Massacre and the Crisis of the Late Tsarist State

MICHAEL MELANCON

Texas A&M University Press
College Station

All photographs reprinted in this book's gallery are from *Lenskii rastrel. Al'bom,* comp. T. Takonulo (Moscow, 1932).

LIBRARY OF CONGRESS
CATALOGING-IN-PUBLICATION DATA
Melancon, Michael S., 1940-
    The Lena Goldfields massacre and the crisis of the late tsarist state / Micheal Melancon.— 1st ed.
        p. cm. — (Eugenia and Hugh M. Stewart '26 series on Eastern Europe)
    Includes bibliographical references and index.
    ISBN 1-58544-474-X (cloth : alk. paper) — ISBN 1-58544-508-8 (pbk. : alk. paper)
1. Strikes and lockouts—Gold mining—Russia (Federation)—Lena River Valley. 2. Lenskoe zolotopromyshlennoe tovarishchestvo. 3. Miners—Russia (Federation)—Lena River Valley. I. Title. II. Series.
    HD5396.M732M45 2006
    957'.5—dc22
                        2005016382

Contents

List of Illustrations

following page 114

I. N. Belozerov

Member of the Imperial State Council and V. I. Timiriazev

Alfred Ginzburg

Work proceeds under the observation of guards

Workers' summer living quarters

Andreevsk mine

Workers meeting

Members of the Strike Bureau, Strike Committee,
   and the Barracks' elders

N. V. Treshchenkov

Workers' March to Nadezhdenski mine

Detail from an artistic representation of the Lena shooting

Photograph of bodies after the shooting

Another view, bodies after the shooting

Demonstration at mass grave of the Lena workers

Wives and children of massacred workers

The Committee of Workers' Deputies

Workers discuss governor's suggestion to return to work
   after shooting

Workers leaving the Aleksandrovsk mine

Workers embark on barges

MAPS

Tables

Acknowledgments

The resources of the State Archive of the Russian Federation (Moscow), Hoover Institution, New York Public Library, Institute of Social Sciences Library (Moscow), the Russian State Library (Moscow), Moscow State University Library, and Indiana University Library have provided the historical data on which this manuscript is based. Funding for travel and research came from Auburn University Humanities Fund, Research Grants-in-Aid, and the History Department. Special thanks go to Larry Gerber of the Auburn University History Department for reading the manuscript and making many useful suggestions.

THE LENA GOLDFIELDS MASSACRE
AND THE CRISIS OF THE LATE TSARIST STATE

Introduction

The Lena goldfields massacre of 4 April 1912 marked a turning point in post-1905 Russian history. Reaction to news of the shooting was fierce and prolonged, quite similar to that of Bloody Sunday, 9 January 1905, which helped spur the 1905 Revolution. Strikes and demonstrations swept the country; public opinion rose in outraged voice; and socialists as one inveighed against the evil tsarist-capitalist regime. Social Democratic and Socialist Revolutionary leaders in Paris issued a joint proclamation in protest of the massacre. In the State Duma, the Social Democrats and the Trudoviks (peasant-oriented deputies) jointly demanded that the government account for its actions.[1] Vociferous debate flared in the Duma, as even conservatives accused the government of malfeasance.[2] In the long run, revolutionaries put to use in their propaganda the symbolism of workers' lives sacrificed for capitalist gold. Each year until the fall of the old regime, strikes and demonstrations marked the shooting's anniversary. The Lena events entered the realm of revolutionary lore, as when during October 1914 the Moscow Group of Socialist Revolutionaries issued an antiwar leaflet that stated: "On the distant Lena and in the capitals of Russia, [the proletariat] ever demonstrates its readiness to continue the struggle."[3] As regards its immediate effects, historians of the period such as Leopold Haimson, Timothy McDaniel, Victoria Bonnell, Robert McKean, G. A. Arutiunov, Rose Glickman, and many others agree that the massacre shocked society and helped renew the workers' movement after its post-1905 doldrums. "News of the massacre," wrote Haimson, "provoked a great outburst of public protest and . . . a veritable explosion in the Russian working class."[4]

Even so, the Lena events have received minimal scholarly attention.[5] Without consulting primary sources, the scholar or interested layperson will find it impossible to find out much about the general context of the strike or obtain a substantive account of societal responses to the massacre. In order to redress the historiographical neglect, this book explores all these and other related matters under the rubric "anatomy of a massacre." In a sense, the term "anatomy," with its physical and investigative associations, aptly fits the massacre to which it applies. Here it will have a broader definition to signify a thoroughgoing examination of a single set of time-bound events—a well-known strike and shooting at a crucial point in late imperial history—within much broader contexts that in turn raise a series of weighty questions. Among the matters discussed in some detail are Siberian economic development, with special reference to gold mining; tsarist legislation about mining and especially about mining labor; the history of Lena gold mining; and the specific attributes of the region's eventual monopolistic proprietor, Lenzoto. (Lenzoto was the commonly used Russian acronym for Lenskoe zolotopromyshlennoe tovarichestvo, which translates Lena Gold-Mining Company). On a broader level, the analysis addresses a series of questions about state and society in late tsarist Russia. These include the role of the state in economic development, state-labor and society-labor relations, and the labor and socialist movements in the regions and in the nation as a whole. As one aspect of this web of significance, this study fully recounts and analyzes Russian society's furious reaction to the shooting, a matter worthy of attention in its own right.[6] The various aspects of the multiple stories recounted here represent a thorough intertwining of local, regional, and national histories.

The book is informally divided into three parts. The long-term context or early history of the strike and massacre, the first part, is vital to comprehending the fateful events themselves. Chapters 1 through 3 examine the history of regional conditions and developments that foregrounded and led to the strike. Taken together, these describe the central events' general setting, that is, the physical surroundings (the Lena region of Eastern Siberia) and the industry (gold mining). They also develop the events' specific setting and, in a sense, moving cause, that is, the history of the company involved (Lenzoto), with special emphasis on labor relations.

The strike, shooting, and immediate aftermath are the second and central part of the story, the tragic episode that galvanizes attention and provides the thread tying the whole together. Chapters 4 and 5 examine the events themselves, with the government's role as a constant subtheme. One chapter details the conduct of the strike, the shooting, and its immediate aftermath; the other focuses on the strike's political character, with special attention to socialist involvement. These first five chapters constitute the study's empirical basis and central narrative.

Chapter 6, the third and concluding part of the story, analyzes society's turbulent response to the shooting and to the government's involvement. This chapter underscores the reasons the Lena events merit broad and close scrutiny in the first place. Of note throughout as principal theme underlying and informing the narrative is the evolving relationship of the late tsarist state to society and labor.

The goal of this book, therefore, is not just to recount the story of a tragedy, in this case, a history of a shooting of striking workers, as compelling as that may be. Its goal is to place the tragedy within a broad context in order to tell a story of even greater historical significance. Each part of the "anatomy" reveals something in its own right. Each constitutes a small history quite worthy of attention. Together the three parts of the story, each pursued at some length, provide a deeper understanding of the specific event. They also enable one to measure and evaluate Russia's development and prospects during the last decades of the old regime's existence. The final analytical results do not always fit neatly into existing interpretations of late tsarist Russia.

This study uses archival sources, including the holdings of the official Manukhin investigative commission, police files, and Ministry of Justice documents. In addition, it employs memoirs, contemporary newspapers and journals, several excellent pre-1917 and early Soviet document collections, and various Soviet-era studies. Most of the chapter titles and subheadings are straightforward and self-explanatory, constituting the study's primarily empirical and narrative structure. Running through the book, however, is a thread of analysis with theoretical underpinnings. This refers to "voices" and "discourses," matters that require additional commentary. First and foremost, contemporary materials from several viewpoints about the strike and shooting suggested the fruitfulness of pursuing opposing interpretational strands, or discourses. An additional inspiration comes from the famous Akira Kurosawa film *Rashomon* (1951), in which several individuals traveling on a road witness a murder. In their later renditions to the authorities, it gradually becomes clear that they "saw" different things while witnessing the same event. A final inspiration arose from the thinking of Mikhail Bakhtin, the Russian literary critic and philosopher, about polyphonic voices as vital constituents of all events, without which a version of an event, in his view, becomes a lifeless abstraction.[7] Bakhtin insists that the voices of all chief participants in an event be reproduced in any subsequent reconstruction of the event. Bakhtin's ideas, like those expressed in Kurosawa's film, find their way into this study's analysis in an inspirational rather than rigorous way.

A brief, concrete examination of the abstract approach will demystify it. From the Bodaibo mines to St. Petersburg stretched a network of company and state officials who constituted the entrepreneurial-state administrative control of the Siberian gold-mining industry as concentrated in the Lenzoto mines on upper Lena River branches. These individuals knew one another and transmitted information and orders up and down the vertical-horizontal lines of communication. They also reached and carried out decisions based on the information they transmitted and received. Before, during, and after the strike these people "comprehended" everything pertaining to the strike according to certain discursive patterns and lingoes that characterized their communications. A second network coexisted alongside the first one. This consisted of worker leaders, certain mining inspectors and administrators, and even the Irkutsk governor, all of whom also exchanged information and achieved a "comprehension" of what happened, albeit one different from the first group. These coexisting phenomena reflect what might be called the Bakhtin effect.

The two "comprehensions" were at stark variance: crudely put, one was antiworker and procompany; the other, proworker and anticompany. People living in the two interpretative worlds saw and experienced the same things differently (the *Rashomon* effect), reached different decisions, and, naturally, acted differently. This observation, which in common parlance might be reduced to "everything depends on one's point of view," is not intended to preempt the possibility of deliberate misinterpretation and exaggeration on the part of one or the other group. Human beings are sometimes guilty of bad faith, on which basis they make genuinely bad decisions with poor, even tragic, results. Still, the use of the dual discourses narrows somewhat the scope of the deliberately "bad," in that people living and working in different discursive worlds indisputably process and interpret information differently.

This multivoiced line of analysis, the *Rashomon*-Bakhtin approach, in this case finds its most direct basis in four substantial volumes (documents, firsthand accounts, statistics, and evaluation) about the Lena events, all published within a year or so of the events themselves. All these, along with the archival and other sources, are used in this book. The first of these volumes is P. N. Batashev, *Pravda o lenskikh sobytiiakh* (The Truth about the Lena Events), which consists of documents collected by the Lena workers and spirited to St. Petersburg in 1912. It also contains additional materials assembled by Alexander Kerensky and other socialist advocates who visited the area shortly after the shooting. Its compilers, Kerensky, G. B. Patushinskii, A. A. Tiushevskii, A. M. Nikitin, and S. A. Kobiakov, used Batashev's name (he was one of the strike leaders) as a symbolic gesture.

The second volume, S. Manukhin, *Vsepoddanneishii otchet chlena Gosudarstvennogo soveta, senatora tainogo sovetnika Manukhina* (Most Humble Report of State Council Member, Senator, and Secret Advisor Manukhin), represents the results of the tsarist government's on-the-spot investigative commission. The third and fourth—G. Kvasha, *Statistiko-sravnitel'nye svedeniia o material'nom polozhenii rabochikh na priiskakh Lensko-zolotopromyshlennogo tovarishchestva* (Statistical-Comparative Evidence about the Workers' Material Situation at the Lena Gold-

Mining Association Mines), published by Lenzoto, and A. Nevskii, *Lenskie sobytiia i ikh prichiny* (The Lena Events and Their Causes)—portrayed Lenzoto's relations with its workers in a favorable light.[8] Thus within a year or so of the shooting, voluminous document collections and evaluations had appeared from three different viewpoints.

The Batashev collection was proworker, anti-Lenzoto, and antigovernment (in other words, it expounded the worker-socialist viewpoint). Despite its official nature, the Manukhin collection and commentary turned out to be a circumspect variant of the first, minus blatant antigovernment rhetoric and support for socialism. One might call this the humanist, reforming bureaucrat viewpoint, not very distant from the liberal-progressive one that achieved wide currency in Russian society in response to the shooting. The statistical data issued by Kvasha, a company mining engineer, and the Nevskii volume were procompany and antiworker. Their (and Lenzoto's) viewpoint was shared by the autocracy. Readers familiar with Russia's history during that era may recall Minister of the Interior N. E. Makarov's reprise of the shooting during his speech to the Duma: "Thus it has always been; thus it will always be."

The earliest published sources about the Lena massacre raised quite sharply the question of the various discourses involved in the events and their evaluation. One could read any one evaluation and come away convinced of its probity and accuracy, until one read the others. The archival sources provide a heady expansion of the theme: one finds detailed worker commentaries, socialists' remarks and tracts, company documents from both local and St. Petersburg offices, local, midlevel, and central government and police accounts, local church chronicles, bystanders' recollections, and so forth. They all center on the same things, but with a spin, they fly apart into individual voices or sets of voices, each with its own background, outlook, and understanding. Nudge them a bit and they finally begin to coalesce into two main lines of evaluation: the workers were at fault or the company and state were at fault. The interest lies in all the waypoints along the road to those two basic conclusions.

This study eschews relativism. It does not proclaim all viewpoints equal, nor does it doubt for a moment the utter primacy of the act (not the discourse). Discourse itself may be an act and help determine other acts. Still, strikes, shootings, grievous wounds, and deaths are best understood and accepted as nonlinguistic facts. Blood, wounds, pain, and death occur in a more basic realm than mere words. The linguistic formulations, no matter how eloquent, used to describe and comprehend the phenomena are still just words. The (f)act underlies and antedates the word. In the human world, acts entail a moral component. In other words, this study discloses the various voices and discourses that thread their way through, help shape, and then characterize the events. It also stands on reasonably established facts and unhesitatingly reaches judgments.

This study joins several others that seek to elucidate aspects of Russian or Soviet reality by minutely dissecting telling episodes such as major strikes, political demonstrations, and their repression. Among these are Reginald Zelnik's book about the 1872 Kreenholm strike, Gerry Surh's extended analysis of Bloody Sunday, and Samuel Baron's investigation of the 1962 Novocherkassk strike and shooting. Of related interest is Koenker and Rosenberg's examination of the role of strikes during 1917.[9] Although no single conceptual model suffices for comprehending these disparate events, their very choice suggests the usefulness of what might be called crisis-point analysis. The initiating actions and the corresponding reactions profoundly disclose the political culture at a certain juncture in time.

The primary reason for exploring the Lena goldfields massacre is its influence on Russian pre–World War I history. It revivified the workers' and revolutionary movements, sharply worsened state-society relations, and, more unexpectedly, further promoted an already waxing society-wide consensus that Russia's laborers deserved a fairer shake than they were getting. The evidence about the strike and shooting reveals other compelling aspects as well. The entire situation around the distant mines, the strike, and the shooting comprised a kind of microcosm of the late tsarist polity. Workers, socialists, state and entrepreneurial administrators, and people at the middle and highest levels of Russian society (government ministers, influential business leaders, famous names) all became involved in an interaction replicated many times over, with various nuances and outcomes, all over Russia during the nation's industrialization. One way of understanding the events is as a checkpoint, among many others, in late nineteenth- and early twentieth-century Russian modernization. Later observers can employ the Lena events, which themselves produced significant effects, to measure and evaluate the interrelations between state, society, business, and intelligentsia at a certain compelling moment in time.

The Early History of Lena Gold Mining

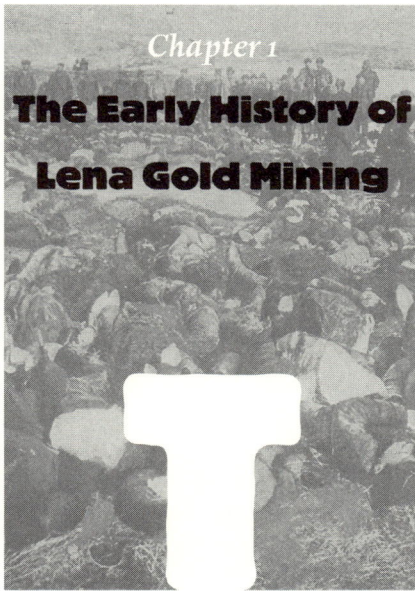

The Lena river basin first opened to Russian history when the commander (*sotnik*) Peter Beketov established a prison-fortress (*ostrog*) at Iakutsk in 1632. The Lena and its numerous upper branches served as pathways of exploration to the Amur area and what later became the Russian Far East. The Lena area was sparsely populated by Iakut settlers along the river courses and by Tunguz nomads who penetrated deep into the taiga. Russia's contact with the area was sporadic, aimed more at general control for travel than at settlement or exploitation of the vast mineral resources. These remained largely unknown to Russians passing through the harsh environment during the seventeenth and eighteenth centuries. The nature of the empire's involvement with the Lena river basin throughout the early era is captured by half-mythological stories passed down among the Iakut inhabitants about the early white-skinned explorers and their destructive firearms. "What is this?" went one saying reflecting hapless Iakut attempts to resist early Russian incursions with firearms into their territory. "A fly comes, bites, and a person dies?"[1]

THE LAND OF COLD AND GOLD

The Lena River originates to the west of Lake Baikal and sweeps more than fifteen hundred miles first north and then east of the lake on the way to Iakutsk. Along this stretch, two enormous river systems, the Vitim and Olekma, whose own upper reaches extend south deep into the East Asian land mass east of Lake Baikal and to the north of the Amur River and China, feed into the Lena.[2] It was along the numerous rivers and streams of the Vitim and Olekma systems that Russia's richest gold sources were located and where this story unfolds. The Lena and all its grandiose main tributaries, the Vitim, the Olekma, and to the east and the north, the Aldan and the Vilyuy, drain an area roughly equal to European Russia before flowing northward into the Arctic Ocean in the area of the Laptev Sea. The size and water volume of the Aldan alone equals that of the Volga. As the Vitim and Olekma flow from south to north they collect the waters from the endless systems of snow-covered mountains that characterize Eastern Siberia around the Baikal. This territory covers a hundred thousand square miles. In altitude it ranges from about 1,300 feet along the banks of the Lena up to 5,775 feet, the height of the tallest peak, the granite Teptorgo. The Nygra River, a branch of the Olekma, where gold was found early on, is situated at 2,000 feet above sea level, and the Vitim River, where later discoveries were made, is 890 feet above sea level. The vast Vitim and Olekma systems are geologically identical and quite similar in appearance. Both contained mineral wealth in abundance. In their entirety, these two river systems constituted two districts (*okrug*) of Irkutsk province (*guberniia*) and much of Iakutsk province. The Olekminsk okrug (Iakutsk province) alone equaled in size the entire Austro-Hungarian Empire.

The region is at one and the same time compelling and daunting. The recent volcanic origin of the area is revealed by numerous perfect cone-shaped peaks, with their heights uniformly covered with year-round snow and ice. Along the Bodaibo River (tributary to the Vitim), where the principal events of this history occurred, the mountains were uniformly rounded rather than peaked, as elsewhere in the Olekma-Vitim systems. The predominance of soft shale along the Bodaibo River gave the area a rather nondescript appearance (as indicated by photographs of the area at the time of the 1912 massacre), in sharp contrast to the region's usual spectacular views. The smaller rivers and streams that descend from the mountains of the entire system carve out countless broadening valleys. Before mining damaged the region's ecology, the mountains and slopes that edged the waterways were covered with luxuriant, greenish blue coniferous forests—spruce, fir, pine, and cedar—interspersed with occasional strips of lighter green arctic birch. During the summer, patches of grass appeared. The larger rivers in the system, especially in their lower reaches, carry enormous water flows that cut deeply into the earth and stone, creating steep banks that offer little refuge for habitation, agriculture, or even landing. The swiftness and deepness of the rivers themselves are legendary. The Lena had innumerable sharp turns, stone islands, and rocky banks. Here and there the swift water and ice had recently washed over a bank and eaten it

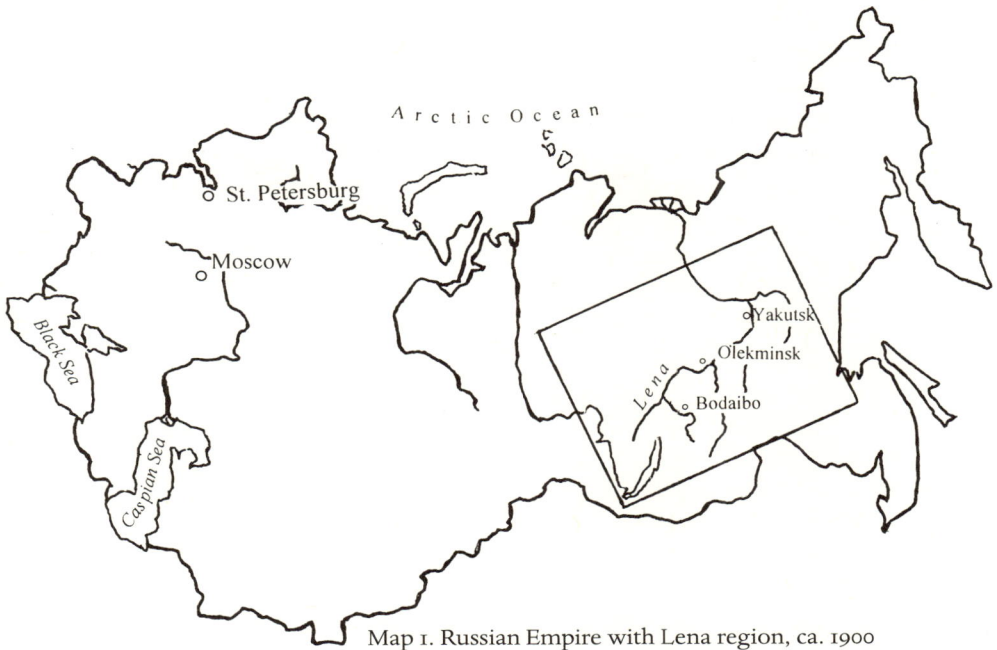

Map 1. Russian Empire with Lena region, ca. 1900

away to fell trees and expose new rock, creating a picture of devastation until, after years had passed, things settled into place and flora again thrived. The deep swift water itself shone like a mirror. Russian settlers described the timeless realities of the Lena as follows: "What kind of river is this? To the right and left, mountains, below water, and above— emptiness." Another commentator noted that the Lena area created the ineradicable impression of a wasteland; a third called it "terra incerta et incognita." Indeed, this was not the nurturing Matiushka-Volga.

The climate did not encourage easy settlement. The winters are long, with freezes settling in by October and thaws not complete until mid-May. During June and early July, light steady rains often occur and nighttime temperatures usually fall below freezing. During July and August real summer sets in, with days (and sometimes nights) pleasingly warm and the daytime skies clear blue; more often than not, nighttime temperatures hover near freezing. Temperatures of sixty-eight degrees Fahrenheit or more are common. During the deep winter, air temperature falls to minus forty degrees Fahrenheit or below; on the Olekma, temperatures have reached below minus ninety degrees. Although the temperature changes only gradually from winter to summer and back again to winter, daily temperatures alter precipitately and drastically. For example, during March the air can reach minus forty just before sunrise, whereas by midday the snows begin to

Early History of Lena Gold Mining

melt, marking an alteration of seventy degrees or more within a few hours. The overall average temperature along the Vitim and Olekma systems is about twenty-five degrees Fahrenheit.

Permafrost characterizes the entire region. Even in summer the thawed layer of earth is only about five feet deep, below which lurks the eternally frozen depths; only in a few places are conditions such that the permafrost lies deeper beneath the surface. This factor shapes the flora of the entire region, since root development occurs only in the thin warm layer of soil above the permafrost. Perhaps the most striking meteorological characteristic of the region, besides the cold, is the dryness of the climate. Even in deepest winter, snow falls are light, and strong winds blow much of it off the ground into drifts, so that in open places a cover of only a few inches is the rule. Total precipitation averages only about seventy-one inches, with 70 percent coming during the four warmest months (June–September) and the balance coming as steady light snowfall during the winter. Remarkably, during the 1880s one commentator who wished to encourage local agriculture referred to the climate in the Vitim-Olekma systems as "moderate." This was clearly an exaggeration, but with proper care agriculture could thrive, doubtless aided by the steady summer rains that watered an otherwise dry region precisely during the growing season.

Along the tributary river systems, during the spring thaws enormous ice barriers form in certain places, forcing the water to seek its path among the blocks of ice or by burrowing right through them. On the smoother, frozen Lena, people often traveled by troika, moving along at high speed on the slick ice. The exhilarating ride could suddenly turn hazardous when the ice cover in places became so thick that for a third of a mile or more the subterranean water escaped to flow on the surface of the ice to a considerable depth. Panic-stricken drivers struggled with the careening, skidding troikas to stop their forward motion before they slid into the icy water.

A plenitude of wildlife inhabited the entire landscape in the recent historical period. Fur-bearing animals—sable, polar fox, black and gray squirrel, red fox, and others—abounded, as did stately elk and enormous black bears. The light snow cover offered ready forage even in the deepest winter for the elk and the hardy long-horned cattle kept by the Iakut and other early settlers. During the summer, hordes of voracious Siberian mosquitoes so plagued the elk, even threatening their lives, that the beasts withdrew into the swamps and immersed themselves to their necks to protect their bodies. Humans covered themselves with clothing, gauze, netting, and gloves. The lakes and rivers were filled with fish, some indigenous and some that swam the river systems all the way from the Arctic Sea to spawn, by which time these specific breeds, denuded of fat and flesh by the twelve-hundred-mile watery trek, were virtually unfit for consumption. Still the rivers were a veritable cornucopia of edible fish, desired both for their flesh and their caviar, a considerable part of the livelihood of man and beast. In the modern era, human settlement and mining pushed the forest cover farther and farther back from the rivers, so that much of the wildlife withdrew deeper into the taiga. Discussions of life in the Lena region during the nineteenth century make limited mention of trapping, except among the Iakut tribespeople. Perhaps a richer lure than furs mesmerized commentators.

The Iakut and Tunguz peoples who originally inhabited the Vitim-Olekma systems, the first settling along the rivers and the second constantly traveling the trackless forests and mountains of the deep taiga, totaled no more than 250,000 people by mid-nineteenth century. The already-settled Iakut people adapted quickly to the new conditions of life after the arrival of Europeans, whereas the Tunguz nomads avoided contact with outsiders. Both groups spoke languages of the Turkic group, although physically they resembled the peoples of Mongolia (a small Buriat-Mongol population inhabited the extreme southern reaches of the river systems, near the Amur). Tatars politically exiled to the region found that within a few weeks they could understand and converse in the Iakut and Tunguz languages rather freely, which according to one commentator, had roughly the same relationship to one another as Polish and Russian. By the time of significant contact between Russians and the Iakut peoples, the latter utilized a vocabulary of roughly three thousand words, augmented by numerous Russian words. Since the Iakut language has no sound for *v* (the Russian *b*), borrowed common words come out as follows: *bilka* for *vilka* (fork) and *samobar* for *samovar* (and, presumably, *bodka* for *vodka*).

Some commentators felt that the relatively small active vocabulary of the Iakutsk language, which at the time had no written version, reflected the impoverishment of the life and culture. Others pointed out the complex mythologies handed down by word of mouth, reflecting the rich traditions of both the Turkish and Mongol heritages. Still others felt that, if anything, the Iakut culture was "stronger" as demonstrated by the tendency of Russians who settled in the area and married Iakut women to "go native," a phenomenon referred to as *obiakutenie* (Iakutization). Soon they wore Iakut clothes, spoke Iakut, and, except for their white skin and different stature, appeared as full-blown Iakut tribespeople. The necessity of adopting methods of life suitable to the harsh conditions had more to do with this adaptation than the dominance of one culture or another. In truth, the traditional Iakut way of life was already passing within a few decades of the discovery of gold and other mineral wealth in the tributaries of the Lena. Inhabitants of the small, sparse Iakut settlements along the rivers lived by fishing, hunting, small-scale farming, and keeping their traditional horned cattle, which survived the winters solely by foraging in the shallow snow. On their cultivated plots, the Iakut settlers raised rye, wheat, potatoes, and oats, which supplemented their heavy meat diets. Iakut women had developed the curing and sewing of the rich indigenous furs to a high skill. They also sewed and fashioned mammoth skins retrieved from the frozen taiga to make shoes and other objects. In recent times, Iakut men also acted as traveling merchants throughout the region, purchasing goods at Russian fairs and distributing them to distant places. By the latter decades of the nineteenth century, most Iakut peoples along the river systems were baptized, although some maintained their native religions. Commentators noted their deep spirituality.

By the late eighteenth and early nineteenth century a very tiny element of Russians and other ethnic groups from the huge empire had filtered into the area. By definition, these were undesirables: desperadoes, murderers, and bandits, either fugitives from justice bent on burying their past identities and misdeeds or actual escapees from hard labor and exile. Both sought out the anonymity of the deep Siberian taiga, far from the reach of tsarist authorities. They either married Iakut women or eked out a hermitlike, impoverished existence. Such population elements from European Russia were incapable of bringing about any improvements or introducing even the rudiments of civilized life. If anything, they were a detriment to the way of life in the region.

The discovery of gold in Eastern Siberia dates to the early decades of the nineteenth century. The earliest imperial legislation pertaining to Siberian gold mining came in 1826, followed every few years thereafter by additional laws, regulations, and adjustments. By the mid-1840s, various rich East Siberian fields plus gradually expanding Urals gold production had made Russia the leading gold producer in the world, responsible for fully 45 percent of world production. Toward the end of the decade, falling Siberian yields and famous gold strikes in California and Australia permanently removed Russia's status as top producer. Even so, new discoveries throughout the following decades, primarily in Eastern Siberia, maintained the Russian gold industry as a significant contributor in the world market. The first discoveries in the Lena system occurred during the early 1840s along the Olekma River. The result was something akin, on a minor scale, to the California gold rush a few years later. Prospectors and entrepreneurs gravitated toward the region. Settlements of people from the European sections of the empire arose. For example, the villages of Olekminsk and the ill-

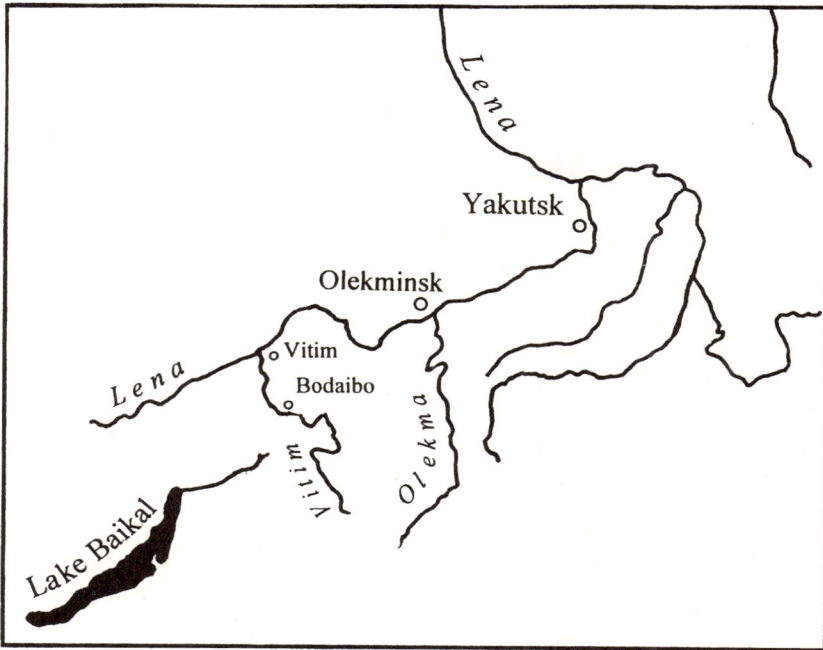

Map 2. Lena Region

reputed Vitim grew up near the conjunctions of those rivers with the Lena. Transportation networks, at first fragile and sparse, gradually took shape in the form of stations situated at various places along the Vitim and Olekma rivers. Even so, the remoteness and the desolate environment, far from encouraging real societal development, led instead to something rather different. Most of those who came had no wish to stay. Whether as individual prospectors or as part of some entrepreneurial effort, the gold-mining population saw the area as a place to exploit, to make a fortune if possible, and then, leaving nothing behind but the mostly unpleasant traces of their activities, to abandon the place once and for all. In any case, the idea of striking it rich through discoveries of gold hardly attracted savory elements.

Once discovered, the gold proved abundant. The rivers and mines of the Vitim-Olekma systems soon produced a third of all Siberian production. Prospectors claimed that "there's gold everywhere here where you find pyrite or quartz," two locally common minerals. The biggest problem was that the richest sources were located hundreds of miles from any transportation. Small prospectors could not exploit the discoveries they made. The gold ore came in three varieties: yellow, red, and black, the last of which was the best since it signified an admixture of silver and gold, whereas the other two mixed gold with nonvaluable minerals. In addition to gold, the area had silver, platinum, and a range of precious and semiprecious stones. Other minerals of potential value were also present. Explorers reported a common occurrence when they walked near certain mountains: the magnetic pull was so great that their compasses pointed only there. This, of course, indicated large amounts of iron. By the later decades of the nineteenth century "Iakutsk iron," of such high grade that it was semisteel without additional processing, was being exploited. By the 1880s oil had been discovered in the Olekminsk region. In addition, the region boasted high quality clay for porcelain, salt in enormous quantities, and mineral water from springs, hot springs, and gushers. During the 1890s one writer called the region "our Russian California," a status it could certainly not attain because of its climate and remoteness.

Toward the middle of the nineteenth century, some population elements from other parts of the empire began to filter into the region for reasons having nothing to do with gold mining. Sources speak of a sparse local Russian peasantry, supporting itself in part by agriculture and cattle raising and in part by small government subsidies. No more than a very few thousand occupied the entire Vitim-Olekminsk region. This newly indigenous peasantry represented individuals resettled in Siberia as part of well-known programs designed to relieve European Russian land shortages and develop Siberia. This population settled along the Lena and the lower reaches of the Vitim and Olekma in those few places where low banks extended back from the rivers, rendering possible the clearing of the forests for agriculture. The land was worked by means of the "Iakut plow," a simple metal triangle forged by local peasant or Iakut blacksmiths and attached to wooden shafts for handles. No other technology was available, and the peasants displayed little tendency toward agricultural improvements. Wheat, barley, potatoes, and onions were the principal crops. Except near the existing towns, grain and vegetable plots were small, and the peasants concentrated their efforts on cattle for milk, cheese, and meat. Only small quantities of hay were grown, leaving the cattle for the most part to their own devices during winter. According to some observers, the local peasantry lived under the thumb of kulaks, rich peasants, who dominated the river transport of grain and the grain market in general. The peasant population was not distinguished for its diligence, yet despite this—and despite the short growing season and limited technology— their return on grain crops was as much as twentyfold (Iakut farmers got an eightfold return), superior to that in much of European Russia. When questioned about their relatively small plantings and large cattle herds, most peasants replied that this was simply their custom. Perhaps it had to do with the relative ease of cattle grazing, winter and summer, as opposed to the risks and onerous labor of grain cultivation. It certainly represented a continuation of Iakut tradition, an aspect of "Iakutization."

Bread was occasionally available to travelers along the river systems, but at exorbitant prices. The exception was bread, pastries, and other baked goods readily available at decent prices from communities of the *skoptsy* (a persecuted religious sect of Russian Orthodoxy that practiced castration and abstinence from sexual relations). The main such community in the region was the Spasskii district of Olekminsk, at the juncture of the Olekma and the Lena, where the skoptsy population reached several hundred. Until the mid-nineteenth century, this particular skoptsy population had lived on the Alan Islands off the Crimea. Having been captured by the English, who temporarily occupied the islands during the Crimean War, and having chosen repatriation, they nevertheless received harsh treatment from the Russian authorities, who sent them to hard labor (*katorga*) at the Iakutsk prison. After numerous pleas and lengthy negotiations, the governor-general of Eastern Siberia had allowed them to settle in Iakutsk province after their prison labor had ended.

Here they had established model communities, such as the Spasskii suburb of Olekminsk, notable for its solid houses, reminiscent of rich peasants' dwellings back in Russia. The homes were decorated with Russian motifs and had solid roofs and courtyards protected by strong gates. Invariably, a large chained dog that barked menacingly at strangers provided further protection for each courtyard. Within, everything was cleanliness, order, and prosperity. The wealth received yet one more safeguard in the form of a prominently displayed revolver in the guest room of each home. Although the skoptsy were prevented on religious grounds from using firearms, presumably visitors would not be aware of the ban. The backbone of skoptsy prosperity was their superb agriculture. By dint of the hardest labor, they had drained the swamp and cleared the forest that had formerly constituted the Spasskii site. Here they planted grain that often yielded fortyfold crops, virtually unheard of elsewhere. Additionally, they grew melons, watermelons (on the latitude of St. Petersburg!), onions, potatoes, and other crops. Their cattle were well fed and yielded superb supplies of milk. When early freezes occasionally destroyed the year's grain crop, they did not suffer, having invariably set aside surpluses from previous years. Their fields even seemed immune to the depredations of Siberian locusts that often threatened the grain crops of the other peasants, leading the peasants to suggest that the skoptsy used some kind of spell against the insects (perhaps they had devised an organic repellent). In any case, all along the river courses conversations arose about the excellent bread and pastries available only at the skoptsy communities. Yet another cornerstone in the foundation of skoptsy prosperity were the artisanal skills displayed in their nonagricultural time. Every adult member of the community, most of whom were literate, engaged in smithing, carving, and building, and in addition, traded the quality goods their industry produced. For some observers, these gentle, industrious religious sectarians served as veritable models for a balanced economic development in Eastern Siberia.

A significant aspect of the indigenous economy and society was the fishing industry, pursued by the Iakut inhabitants on the basis of *arteli* (work cooperatives). The fish sought by the arteli were *nel'ma* (white salmon), *taimen'* (described by one commentator as "river shark"), *moksun'* (a fish similar to *nel'ma* with certain distinguishing characteristics and that was much rarer in the Lena system than in other Siberian rivers), and *omul'* (no translation available). The river also teemed with several smaller edible fish renowned for a fat content so high that they could be fried whole without oil. For some reason, in any given year either the *omul'* or *nel'ma* predominated to the exclusion of the other. These two and *taimen'* were all considered delicacies and figured in numerous local dishes, including a famous fish pie (*pirog*).

The area's arteli were quite small, numbering no more than six people. The normally narrow banks of the rivers and the relative shortness of their navigable length permitted the use of only small throw-nets, thus accounting for the smallness of the cooperative efforts. Normally, one individual owned the throw-net and was the master of the artel'. At the end of the catch, the fish were divided up among the participants, with the master receiving an extra share for providing the net. When net owners did not participate in the fishing, they received only one share of the fish. Some Russian commentators felt that this marked a sizable undercompensation for the ownership of the means of production. One analysis figured, however, that the cost of purchasing a net roughly equaled the profit of a single individual's labor (compensated for by selling the allotted fish) for three years, indicating a very fine calculation of cost and profit in figuring the net owner's share. Arteli came together on the basis of personal acquaintance and compatibility, a necessary precondition under circumstances that required close coordination, extreme patience, and hard labor: whole weeks could produce little or nothing and then suddenly a single day could yield a veritable fortune from the river. Although in European Russia the peasantry commonly used various artel' systems for productive and hiring-out functions, one commentator felt that the regional fishing arteli represented Iakut rather than Russian custom.

All long-term residents of Eastern Siberia lived under the threat of the debilitating nerve disease *meriachestvo*. Although the incidence was not high, the consequences for those infected by this indigenous viral disease of the nervous system could be severe. During the last century the disease was often called "an illness of healthy people" since victims during the lengthy early stages showed no signs of ill health except seizures similar to those of epileptics. A significant difference in the symptoms is that epileptics have no recollection of the period during the seizures whereas *meriaki* (those suffering from the disease) are fully aware of their surroundings and experiences. People afflicted often engage in involuntary extreme movements of the arms, leading them unexpectedly and unintentionally to strike people within an arm's length. This sometimes led to awkward results, as when a newly arrived (and uninformed) officer or senior bureaucrat would suddenly find himself struck by a hapless subordinate. Another symptom was the compulsive, loud repetition of words and phrases heard by afflicted people, creating bizarre effects in official or social situations. As the disease progressed, people became physically debilitated and eventually bedridden. Since even the etiology was unsuspected, nothing approaching treatment or relief from symptoms was available. For some reason, discussions of health problems among gold miners and officials within the Vitim-Olekma systems during the late nineteenth and early twentieth century do not mention *meriachestvo*. None of the sources consulted provide any statistical data for the occurrence of the disease, and presumably none had as yet been collected. It may be that the incidence of the malady was sufficiently small in any given population and its progress so slow that it simply did not emerge until later among the predominantly transient gold-mining segments of Eastern Siberian society.

EARLY LENA GOLD MINING AND ITS LEGISLATION

According to most reports, gold was first discovered along a branch of the Olekma River in 1843.[3] The actual pioneers of the discovery were independent prospectors or, in the parlance of the day, *khishchniki* (crook, or crafty, dishonest person), who defied tsarist legislation restricting the new Siberian gold mining industry to nobles and merchants. This legislation reflected the state monopoly on gold and other precious metals and minerals, a situation that provided scant lawful scope for the hardy prospector who set out into the wilds to strike it rich on his own. Indeed, some of the early prospectors were real outlaws who were seeking their fortune after having escaped from political exile or hard labor, factors that doubtless contributed to their not entirely undeserved bad reputations. Still, in a real sense the Siberian mining codes constructed this disreputable social identity. Any prospector of humble circumstance violated the law the moment he discovered gold since the law forbade people outside the designated elite categories from doing so. In any case, investment entrepreneurs, who lived within the law or knew better how to skirt it without dire criminal consequences, soon followed.

During the 1850s the entrepreneurial pioneers who exploited the first strikes along the Olekma River were certain Irkutsk merchants who plunged capital into this inherently risky business. Among them were K. Trapeznikov, I. Solov'ev, and A. Sibiriakov, the first of whom opened the earliest Olekma mining concern during the 1840s. The Trapeznikov and Sibiriakov companies played a long-time role in Siberian mining, although, over time, the nature of these and other firms engaged in the Lena gold industry changed drastically. As true venture capitalists, the Irkutsk merchants dispatched well-equipped prospecting parties, which then began to work the gold sites discovered in the sands along certain Olekma river courses. In disappointing reality, only occasional gold-mining claims over widely dispersed areas with minuscule returns characterized the first inauspicious decade of Olekma gold mining. The first three years of mining produced less than five pounds of gold, total. Several rich finds during the mid-1850s altered the picture forever. The mining firms of Trapeznikov, Solov'ev, Sibiriakov, and several others began to yield tens of pounds of gold annually, returns that amply rewarded the capital investments. During this pioneering era, the white-collar employees hired by the gold firms consisted entirely of political exiles of intelligentsia background, no other suitable personnel being available in the vast region.

One later commentator, A. Blek, characterized the era's gold mining as strictly "exploitative," having the sole aim of the quickest return on invested capital, without any thought of future development. F. V. Boltunov, a railroad engineer who visited the area during the early twentieth century, described the tendency of early entrepreneurs to jump great distances from one site to another. Early investors concentrated only on the very richest surface areas, abandoning half-used or less-productive areas to smaller entrepreneurs. Susan McCaffray notes that the first Donets Basin coal-mining entrepreneurs, many of whom also went into operation between 1820 and 1870, displayed similar short-term attitudes toward their enterprises.[4] The outlooks and methods of the first two decades of the Lena gold mining therefore resulted in no solid construction or rational, permanent development of the mining industry. Nor did the industry of this period leave any trace of infrastructure or improvement in the region. Instead, riverbanks were de-

forested, as huge amounts of wood were consumed for fuel, for housing and administrative structures, and for mining procedures. Additionally, huge quantities of sand, gravel, and broken stone began to
accumulate on the banks of the rivers near gold sites, industrial flotsam
and jetsam that, along with deforestation, changed the appearance and
nature of the region.

Even as the government struggled to exert its sway over the Siberian gold industry, prosperous and respectable Irkutsk merchants hastened to extract quick, huge profits from the richest and most easily
mined veins of gold on or near the surface of the river sands. They were
perhaps worse khishchniki than the lowly independent prospectors.
Alongside their legitimate operations, the entrepreneurs encouraged
and rewarded the discoveries of the half-legal or illegal prospectors,
used their well-financed teams to purloin the gold from undeclared
sites, and disposed of it outside the legally imposed channels into the
state treasury. This explains the government's ever-expanding network
of officials and authorities and meticulous and detailed regulations, not
to mention direr threats of fines or imprisonment. The laws' wording
leaves no doubt that the legislation was aimed at entrepreneurs. Certainly early investors of this type hardly held the rights and well-being
of workers uppermost in their minds, despite the government's paternalistic but not always humane efforts on the laborers' behalf. The unfortunate character of early Lena gold mining, including the hasty
nonpermanent character of the industrial works and infrastructure,
stamped itself indelibly on the local industry. The oddly unpleasant atmosphere survived even into the early decades of the next century,
when the Lena workers struck in 1912 and met a harsh response.

Early legislation about Siberian gold mining had the dual goals of
promoting and regulating the new industry. For example, an 1826 decree extended to private individuals the right to locate and exploit gold
in Western and Eastern Siberia. In 1831 new decrees created Siberian
mining administration offices under the auspices of the governors-
general of Western and Eastern Siberia for "close and alert supervision" in order to prevent "abuses." Although "claim-jumping" was the
primary abuse mentioned, laws controlled every imaginable aspect of
Siberian prospecting and mining on both private and state lands. It so
happened that all lands where gold mining developed in the Lena system belonged to the state. The first statutes that applied to labor in the
region, this study's primary concern, appeared in 1837. In 1838 the earlier piecemeal legislation received codification and amplification in
detailed gold-mining regulations that constituted the urcode of Siberian mining. The new statutes pertained specifically to labor and gold-
mining procedures in Eastern Siberia, where, in fact, most new claims

occurred.[5] On the labor question, 1837–38 statutes ordered that gold miners who were political exiles (free workers in the area still being a rarity) and who were charged with any violations be turned over to military courts. The 1845 general tsarist criminal code penalized with fifteen to twenty years at hard labor any collective resistance on the part of unfree workers anywhere in the empire. Free workers charged with similar activities received incarceration from one week to three months. In effect, the era's general tsarist and Siberian law codes criminalized all organized defensive worker activity.[6] Thus even before the first discovery of gold in the Olekma region, the legal bases for the exploitation of the valuable mineral there had taken shape.

Detailed provisions from the 1838 code about the hiring and administration of workers in the mines reveal much about East Siberian gold mining and about labor in preemancipation Russia. Political exiles and a growing category of free laborers, characterized as Siberian residents, both required appropriate documents from local authorities. One-year work contracts were the standard. Aside from individual contracts, family heads and artel' leaders had the right to sign for their collectives, a practice that led to abuses. Work contracts conformed to Siberian labor regulations, which, with modifications, reflected imperial labor laws. Work conditions constituted a major part of the contract. By law, contracts had to specify the exact place and period of work, the number of hours a day, and the number of days a week. In effect, existing laws allowed a fifteen-hour workday, six days a week, which became the Siberian norm. Contracts also specified pay rates, provisions for food and housing, rates for fines and docked time for illness, and regulations about private prospecting. Even the slightest concealment (*utaika*) of gold, silver, and gems by workers resulted in prosecution in the military courts.

The laws also imposed certain restrictions on the workers and the employers. For instance, employers could not inflate the cost of provisions they provided and were obliged to inform the authorities if they fired a worker. Workers could not quit before the contracted time nor could other employers hire such people. Such restrictions were the bane of Siberian gold miners' existence well into the twentieth century. Not even a serf-owner could recall a worker from the mines prior to the end of the contracted period, a reminder that before the emancipation both serfs and state peasants commonly worked off the land. In addition to restrictions, the 1838 law also outlined mutual responsibilities. Contracted workers should "behave honestly, respect the owner and his staff, in no case get drunk, go nowhere willfully, but be responsible, not rude, not stubborn, and do not contradict [superiors] or else the employer will have the right to satisfaction for the infraction." Employers had to fulfill all contracted conditions to the letter, ensure the quality of food, and pay off salaries at the end of the work period. In language mirroring the exhortation to workers, the regulations urged employers to "maintain humane relations with the hired persons without insult [or] pressure," and refrain from "inflicting on him heavy beatings" or subjecting him to anything "dangerous to his health."[7]

Rather than significantly limit workers' exploitation, the 1838 code merely forced employers to observe certain formalities. Aside from the six-day workweek, the fifteen-hour workday, the ultimate salary payoff, and several other restrictions, without which neither work nor life would long continue at the mines, employers fulfilled the law simply by correctly formulating the hiring contract. The law required nothing of the employers—not a fair wage, not food or housing nor anything else—as long as the contracts laid out the conditions of hire in these respects. In reality, employers invariably provided food and housing of sorts since neither were available in the taiga. In addition, unrestricted child and female labor in the Siberian mines existed until the 1880s and under certain restrictions until the 1912 massacre. For all their harshness, significant aspects of the 1838 work conditions remained in the Eastern Siberian gold industry until the era of the Lena strike and massacre.

The 1838 law also created the basic administrative structures and procedures that prevailed in Siberian gold mining until 1917. The statutes established multiple oversight over private gold mining on the part of local officials of the Ministries of the Interior, Finance, and State Domains (later Trade and Industry). The first had primary responsibilities for the workers and the second two for the mining entrepreneurs. Special mining inspectorates, with deputies from the Ministry of Finance and the Chief Mining Administration (Ministry of State Domains), operated under the direct subordination of the East Siberian governor-general and the Mining Administration. The inspectors acted as mediators in disputes between mining entrepreneurs, ensured the enforcement of the rather detailed regulations, prevented illegal transactions involving gold, and had the general charge of bringing about the "success of private gold mining." One article precluded conflicts of interest by forbidding these officials from engaging in gold mining.[8]

This bureaucratic intertwining, which endured in Siberian gold mining until the 1917 revolution, had the goal of establishing government control of the gold industry and achieving maximum gain for the treasury. Clearly, the government was convinced that only private mining could attain maximum profit for the treasury, requiring special efforts to impose government control. The history of gold mining in Eastern Siberia from the 1820s on constitutes the state's rejection of the formerly predominant concept of state-owned mining with attached (unfree) labor forces. Even so, forcing private entrepreneurs and privately hired workers to conform to government priorities was a more arduous business than doing the same with formally compliant but indolent state-owned concerns. Such enterprises, run by bureaucrats and manned by possessional labor (state serfs) or political exiles, formally complied with directives but were not productive. Unfortunately, rather than the unified control of private concerns envisioned by the state, the new legislation led to mixed signals, bureaucratic infighting, and blatant working at cross-purposes. As Daniel Orlovsky has commented about late tsarist bureaucratic management of the economy, "there was a welter of competing jurisdictions, overlapping competencies, and confusion."[9]

Mining legislation of the decades before emancipation reflects the realities of life and labor in the Siberian gold industry.[10] The early 1840s statutes that allowed the transfer of possessional labor (in this case, serfs) to Siberian gold mines suggests labor shortages in an industry where most workers had been political exiles. In any case, possessional labor in Russia was already yielding to more productive free labor. The 1861 abolition of serfdom rendered the question moot.[11] An 1841 statute established a gendarme staff officer with the responsibility of maintaining "order in private Siberian gold mines," a measure that hints at strikes, disorders, and outright uprisings, the patriarchal care of the government notwithstanding. Other statutes further regulated work documents and the status of free and unfree (political exile) workers who were fired.[12]

All early regulatory statutes had assumed that Siberian gold miners were more or less permanent residents, whether rare indigenous citizens, political exiles, or transferred possessional workers. This situation changed drastically with the 1853 laws, which for the first time laid down the conditions for hiring workers from the "Great Russian provinces." This previously unheard of practice demarcated a sea change in the hiring practices of a burgeoning industry that required greater labor sources than were easily available in Eastern Siberia. The new regulations required that workers hired from European Russia travel in arteli and entrust their documents to the elected elder (*starshina*), who was empowered to maintain order. Other provisions established joint responsibility (*krugovaia porukha*) for criminal actions and specified that all such work groups check in with the police at designated places along the travel routes. These and other draconian measures reflected the tendency of European Russian workers to engage in wild rampages en route to the arduous and sometimes dangerous East Siberian labor that awaited them. The new laws also established strict regulations for off-time prospecting for hired mine workers. This single exception to the restrictions on gold-mining entrepreneurship probably constituted the chief lure for European Russian workers to accept work in the distant and forbidding East Siberian mines. The minute regulation of these activities reveal the government's positive obsession with channeling to the state treasury all gold and other rare minerals.[13] An 1855 administrative decree for the first time specifically mentioned the Olekminsk (Lena) gold-mining region, which later would loom ever larger in the picture of Russian gold mining.[14]

The new 1857 imperial law code contained extensive sections on the mining and textile industries, the empire's two largest sectors of production. One statute from the Siberian mining codes ordered that advance travel money paid to workers could not exceed the entire pay of the contracted work period, a provision that suggests horrendous past abuses.[15] The 1857 laws provided workers in privately owned mines the right to complain to the state mining administration about the quality or quantity of food, a matter that remained at the heart of worker-entrepreneur conflict in Eastern Siberia.[16] Complaints about food kicked off the strike that led to the 1912 Lena massacre.

Tsarist legislation about Siberian gold mining and labor prior to the great reforms suggests that the government, hungry for the mineral wealth of the Siberian taiga, was quite willing to favor private mining over previously predominant state enterprises. Likewise, the government's approach acquiesced in and helped open the way for hiring free labor from Siberia and European Russia, as opposed to the earlier unfree labor. The tsarist state indisputably adopted a free market approach to the Siberian gold industry. The limits to tsarism's economic liberalism is suggested, however, by the law's increasingly stern, exactingly detailed supervision of an industry that channeled the precious metal exclusively into the state treasury. The restrictions on workers' movement, the immediate police presence and authority, the frequent references in the codes to "maintaining order," and certain protective measures for workers all reflect the autocratic state's direct paternalistic relationship to the empire's laboring peoples. They also eloquently testify to the onerous working environment and the workers' attempts to shake free from it, a matter of direct concern as late as 1912. For all the considerable changes that occurred in labor laws and, for that matter, in the gold-mining business and in technology after the emancipation, many of the conditions facing East Siberian miners at the time of the 1912 Lena strike and shooting were reminiscent of the preemancipation era.

Modern Lena Gold Mining, Lenzoto, and the Workers, 1861–1912

The history of Lena (Olekminsk) gold mining during the second half of the nineteenth and the early twentieth century constitutes the long-term context of the 1912 Lena strike and massacre. This was an era of rapid transformation in the global and Russian economy. As a striking example, regional gold mining evolved into a monopoly of one industrial giant. Beginning during the 1880s, imperial labor legislation underwent extraordinary alterations, including the introduction of a factory inspectorate, restrictions on work hours, and limitations on women's and children's labor. Overall these legislative reforms lay surprisingly lightly on the lives and work of Lena gold miners. The following account bears upon life and economic modernization in Siberia. It also sheds a piercing light on the interactions between the Russian state, Russian legislation, entrepreneurs, and, of course, workers.

LENA GOLD MINING, LAWS, AND LABOR AFTER THE EMANCIPATION, 1861–1900

Beginning in the early 1860s, gold mining in the Olekma-Vitim systems underwent significant alterations precisely when serf emancipation wrought changes for labor. Symbolic of these alterations was the founding in 1861 of a new type of enterprise in the region, the Lena Shares Company (Lenskoe Paevoe Tovarishchestvo), the parent company of Lenzoto, against which workers struck during 1912. The exhaustion by the late 1850s of the easily found and exploited surface gold along the Olekma River created the need for new endeavors. The early merchant investors had reaped rich rewards, but to continue doing so would require heavy new financial outlays. Older merchant firms such as the Trapeznikov and Sibiriakov concerns, as well as the new Lena Shares Company, offered shares or became joint stock companies. Their goal was to raise the capital needed to exploit the more expensive, but much more profitable, veins of gold just beneath the surface of the various Lena river systems. The new capital-intensive gold mining made its debut in the Olekma river system, primarily on the Nygra River, where the Lena Shares Company began operations during the early 1860s, and very shortly thereafter expanded to the Vitim River.

The 1863 discovery of deep, extraordinarily rich veins of gold on the Nagatami River, an upper branch of the Bodaibo River in the Vitim system, spurred a gradual but permanent transfer of new capital from the Olekma to the Vitim. This occurred while the Olekma River holdings were still being exploited. With mines along both river systems in full production, the annual gold yield reached unheard of quantities for Siberia, although gold discoveries in other parts of the world reduced Russia's share of global production. Steamship lines, with networks of stations, went into operation along the crucial river courses and, where possible, new roads connected mining sites.[1] Enormous distances were involved in transporting people, supplies, and equipment in one direction and the same people, gold, and other valuables in the other. Even so, regularized transport significantly lowered the cost of supplying the gold-mining region. During the 1860s and 1870s, the richest mines yielded astounding quantities of gold-bearing sand and, after processing, gold. Investors quickly recouped their investments. The last of the old-fashioned Irkutsk merchants, having made fortunes beyond their imagining, left the business, leaving gold mining entirely in the hands of the new shares companies. Many companies avoided costly new explorations in favor of exploiting existing sites to the end of their profitability. The process of capital concentration continued and by the 1870s large investment-oriented companies, such as the Pribrezhno-Vitimsk Company, the Bodaibo Company, and the Industrial Company (Kompaniia Promyshlennosti), supplanted most of the partnerships and joint stock companies. This represented the third generation of the Lena gold-mining industry in its transformation from individually owned firms, to partnerships and small shares companies, and finally into the realm of big investment capital. In size and income, the newest firms also left in their wake Lenzoto's parent company, the Lena Shares Company, which had inopportunely settled on the Olekma River just as the Vitim system began its surge to predominance.[2] By the 1880s an entrepreneurial equilibrium had been reached, which led to a distinct stagnation in the Lena gold industry.

Tsarist mining legislation mirrored these changes. The 1870 mining codes, the first after emancipation, largely reflected the 1838 laws, plus subsequent alterations. New statutes of the 1870 codes aimed at strengthening oversight of an already highly controlled industry. One article created "special mining police (*gornye ispravniki*) . . . to preserve social order and safety" at important mining sites, an expansion over the existing regional mining gendarmes. The articles of the 1870 code aimed at enabling a waxing network of state officials to enforce regulations about the prospecting, mining, measuring, and shipping of gold.[3] They reflected the government's abiding interest in exerting absolute control over precious metals and stones.

With regard to the hiring of workers, one postemancipation statute asserted the absolute right of the individual to sign work contracts. In Eastern Siberia, this new absolute right remained on paper only, since family heads and artel' leaders continued to sign work contracts for their collectives. Various provisions of the new codes raise sharp questions about the workers' status and rights. For example, when workers reported to their work site, they were obliged to surrender their passports until the end of the contract. For growing cadres of non-Siberian workers, the law imposed a seven-year contract, whereas Siberian workers continued to get one-year contracts. Since workers still had no legal right to quit, over the years thousands of European Russian workers found themselves serving seven-year terms of enforced servitude, unless, of course, they were fired. Workers now could not even leave the work site without the mining administration's written permission, an arrangement reminiscent of serfdom. The 1870 code also dropped the earlier humane restrictions on the workday to fifteen hours and the workweek to six days.[4] Employer's now had absolute discretion as long as the contract stated the conditions, to which prospective employees could agree or not.

Some statutes were improvements over old ones. For example, employers could not dock workers' pay when illness or transportation snags delayed their contracted arrival date at the mines. In cases of work-related death or disabling injury, the entrepreneur was obliged to pay a monetary compensation equal to triple the agreed-upon annual wage. In cases of light injury, workers received free treatment in a clinic with no pay deductions. Management now assigned all miners to work parties, which elected elders and deputies empowered to negotiate with management and to impose penalties for certain infractions. The latter included up to twenty lashes with rods (*rozgi*), a rough sort of democracy.[5] On the whole, the weakening of protections with regard to the workday, hours, and the contract period outweighed the by-no-means-insignificant improvements. Workers from distant regions had no way to prejudge the adequacy of the listed conditions. Once they signed, they were tied for the full term of the contract, which for workers from European Russia fell to five years only in 1886. The new code also observed eloquent silence about pay rates. Additionally, as one early commentator pointed out, the 1870 code entirely ignored the question of women's and children's labor.[6] Articles specifying physical punishment were positively ominous. Although general tsarist penal codes allowed physical punishment, this new inclusion constituted an enabling statute for the Siberian mines that ensured application. Overall, the 1870 mining code eliminated some abuses, tightened control over workers, and actually intensified workers' exploitation. One disappointed Siberian mining engineer commented that it "provided the mine owners full arbitrary power [over workers]."[7]

How to interpret these developments? The key was in the wording of new statutes on fines for worker infractions that "violate[d] the economic interests of the gold-mining entrepreneur." From the outset, the government promoted private enterprise, although certainly not laissez-faire, in East Siberian gold mining. Laissez-faire ran afoul of the state's desire to control precious metals and to exercise paternalism toward laborers. By 1870 the arrival of big capital on the gold mining scene promised a heady expansion of the state's gold reserves, the sine qua non of which, however, was heavy state-guaranteed profits for the entrepreneurs. Thus the government edged toward laissez-faire in industry-worker relations. In this calculation, entrepreneurial economic interests outweighed workers' welfare.

During the 1880s, when imperial labor legislation offered real structural change by creating a factory inspectorate, regulating child labor, and introducing other innovations, East Siberian mining legislation tended merely toward rationalization and empirewide administrative consistency. For example, one mid-1880s regulation aligned the work year in the Lena (Olekminsk) and Far Eastern (Amur and Primor'e) mining regions. Of real benefit for miners was the 1887 ban on physical punishment.[8] Reform of work contracts, the terms of which inspired virtual horror in observers, did not occur. As Mining Engineer L. A. Karpinskii reported to the East Siberian Department of the Imperial Geographical Society in 1886, the contracts were "one-sided" and imposed "heavy conditions" on workers.[9]

The question arises as to why imperial labor legislation as sweeping as that of the 1880s had so little effect on East Siberian gold mining. For one thing, the new factory inspectorate did not apply anywhere to mining, which fell under the separate jurisdiction of the Ministry of State Domains. Furthermore, by the 1830s Siberian mining already had an inspectorate system. Thereafter, *nadzor* (oversight) and *reviziia* (inspection), whatever their actual effect, were constant subjects of discussion in commentary about the regions' mines. In this respect, Siberian mining was decades ahead of Russian industry elsewhere, a circumstance that reflected the state's response to the tumultuous history of abuses and resulting disorders in Urals and Siberian mining. Another factor was the question of enabling decrees, without which local officials and employers would studiously ignore general laws. If an imperial law did not provide detailed sanctions and regulations that applied to a certain region or industry, the law remained in local abeyance. Finally and perhaps most tragically, a constant refrain in imperial law codes about industry was that this or that law applied to the entire empire "except for the Siberian gold-mining industry."[10] State-sponsored Siberian gold-mining exceptionalism was the real culprit.

In truth, Lena mining workers faced an unusual array of problems. For example, newly hired workers had to overcome truly daunting difficulties just to get to and from the mining region. The discovery of rich deposits on the Bodaibo River, a lower branch of the Vitim, eventually resulted in the concentration of most Lena gold mining in that area. Workers hired in relatively nearby Irkutsk traveled no fewer than one hundred days covering almost 1,553 miles to get to the mines. The last leg of this trek, from the town of Vitim at the Lena-Vitim conjunction to the Bodaibo area mines, covered 124 miles along the largely uninhabited banks of the Vitim. Workers hired in more distant parts of Siberia or in European Russia made much longer journeys. By the early 1900s the company town of Bodaibo at the Bodaibo-Vitim conjunction provided at least a hint of civilization toward the end of the trek. Prior to that, nothing interrupted the wilderness between the ill-appointed town of Vitim at the Vitim-Lena conjunction and the mines.[11] Workers covered this distance by foot along rough riverside paths or, if they could afford it, by water transport. On completion of their work, they undertook the reverse, no less arduous trip. Gradually, a sparse network of privately owned stores and services arose along the entire route to fulfill the workers' needs. Some observers felt that their real purpose was to extract from the hapless miner, coming and going, every kopeck he had.

This was all akin to running the gauntlet twice, with hard labor in between. One commentator spoke of the workers' outright "physical suffering" en route to the mines and doubted that people from distant areas "would willingly come if they had any idea what awaited them."[12] Special agents, who were not averse to deceptive accounts about Lena mining work, did the hiring for eight rubles per head.[13] One of the agents' functions was to issue advances to newly hired workers to enable them to pay off debts, take care of their families, and reach the mines. During the 1870s and 1880s, the advances ran between sixty and one hundred rubles. It was perhaps characteristic of the problem that this seemingly humane arrangement also became a subject of gross abuse. It signified that the entire cost of reaching the distant mines was laid on the hirees, who then had to labor for months to pay off the initial debt. All too often inexperienced workers found themselves bilked or simply robbed by crooks along the route; others succumbed to temptation by disappearing with the advance money.[14]

During these decades eyewitnesses invariably framed their testimony in terms of outright hardship for Lena miners and the need to do something to correct it. The mining engineer Karpinskii had complained about the harsh conditions imposed by the "one-sided" work contracts. A later commentator described the "patriarchal regime" at the mines, which eventually necessitated government intervention to impose some limits on the employers' arbitrariness. Observers regularly raised probing, indeed accusatory, questions about the living quarters, food, pay, and the "utter dependence" of the workers on the companies for their very survival at the distant mining sites. Most workers filled out their meager pay by working long hours on holidays, a further hardship. Visitors noted that there were "no holidays" at the mines. "Few workers," continued one observer, "had well-built habitations." Another described the barracks as "cramped, low, and dirty" with "bad air" and, he continued, "only the unspoiled Russian *muzhichek* [strong little peasant] is capable of surviving this environment." In this regard, by the 1890s hiring agents focused heavily on West Siberian and Urals/Volga Russian peasants, distinguished for their strength and fortitude.

Commentaries of the 1870s through the 1890s found the food issued by the mining companies to be quantitatively adequate but nutritionally poor for the extraordinary exertions of mine work. Consequently, the miners resorted to cash or credit outlays for high-priced meat, tea, and sugar at company and private stores, which led to indebtedness. The long work hours under especially arduous Siberian conditions were "hard on the [workers'] organisms."[15] Health facilities were available but limited in quantity. By 1889 the region's twenty-eight medical clinics had a total of four doctors and twenty-six *feldshers* (medical assistants). An 1892 evaluation attributed the "quite significant illnesses and deaths at the mines" to the onerous nature of the work, the extreme climate, the workers' carelessness, and the inadequate medical personnel.[16] Housing provided by the industry was grossly substandard. Makeshift wooden structures with clay floors housed married and unmarried men, women, and children. The imbalance between numbers of men and women caused another kind of problem. Sexually starved workers went on famed rampages when they reached populated areas such as Vitim. Syphilis was endemic. Furthermore, deprived of other sexual outlets, workers widely engaged in "unnatural vices," as one report put the matter. Another called the mines "the grave of family life."[17] All of this is indicative of what one person called the "evil side" of Lena gold mining.

This lurid characterization is entirely appropriate for aspects of the Lena experience. For hundreds of miles along the rivers, no government or police agents watched over the miners on the way to and from the mines. In the trackless taiga, unscrupulous individuals waylaid them, got them drunk, robbed them, and sometimes murdered them. Observers spoke of bodies quietly floating down the rivers.[18] The village of Vitim at the Lena-Vitim juncture stood out as the most exquisite example of this moral dissoluteness. Originally a farming village of 128 families, by the 1870s its very existence centered on the sale of spirits to passing mine workers. At the beginning of that decade, Governor-General N. P. Sinel'nikov reported that the local peasant families "hardly bother to engage in agriculture." Another commentator from the 1890s claimed that every house served as a tavern with cash or illegal gold as tender. I. Angarskii's 1889 report described tiny Vitim, whose population swelled at peak travel seasons to four thousand, in terms reminiscent of nothing so much as the American Wild West. Gambling, drunkenness, and prostitution were the occupations, knives and guns common currency, tempers short, shoot-outs and theft the rule, and the law usually absent. For the year 1886 alone, this tiny hamlet was the scene of four murders, two attempted murders, two suicides and one attempted suicide, two break-in robberies and four robberies without break-in, various deaths from overconsumption of alcohol, five unaccountable dead bodies, and two drowning victims. These statistics, according to Angarskii, did not cover "those deaths and misdeeds concealed forever by *matiushka* [little mother] Lena and the dark summer night." A mid-1880s government report had forecast Angarskii's findings when it claimed that "workers arriving here succumb to drunkenness and debauchery without any restraint, and calculating people, putting aside all conscience and humanity, cast out the nets to strip the workers of their funds. . . . Human life counts for nothing here. The Lena bears away workers' bodies by the tens."[19] After the turn of the century, state and company control and discipline finally arrived. Vitim dropped out of sight, and Bodaibo up the Vitim River was a true company town. Exploitation of gold and workers took on a different hue.

The hair-raising criticisms that dotted the pages of Siberian newspapers and journals did have an effect. Beginning in the 1870s, a series of Siberian governors-general, including N. P. Sinel'nikov (1870–74), D. G. Anukhin (1879–85), and A. D. Goremykin (1891–95), genuinely strove to improve the workers' lot. Because of their far-reaching juridical mandates and their financial independence, only the governors had sufficient autonomy to intervene. Intervening and actually solving problems were, however, two different things. As the historian of Siberian industry V. I. Semevskii wrote during the late 1890s, "if the [governors'] efforts . . . were naive, [they] at least had the workers' interests at heart." Sinel'nikov, Anukhin, and others waged a virtual war against the illegal sale of spirits to miners. One governor-general suggested legally sanctioning the issue of "wine portions," actually spirits, by the companies to subvert the illegal trade. Sinel'nikov wanted supervised networks of institutions along the travel routes to cater to workers in an orderly fashion, an idea that foundered on the expense involved. All the governors attempted to enforce the 1848 decree against illegal sales of spirits to miners. The ongoing commentary does not indicate success in the gubernatorial struggles against worker drunkenness.[20] Although corruption entered the picture (the spirits trade involved money and gold), the real problem was that 150- to 200-mile stretches of taiga roads and river pathways had no police whatsoever.[21]

The governors-general issued directive after directive aimed at improving conditions for workers in other ways. They tried to regulate food, work contracts, health care, and living quarters. They attempted to limit or eliminate corporal punishment. They strove to prevent the rehiring of workers in debt to the mining companies, a practice the governors equated to indebted servitude (kabal). As regards the last practice, an official 1874 report suggested that the companies created fraudulent indebtedness by inflating fines against workers. The Tomsk Provincial Council's extensive 1882 recommendations about improving the gold miners' situation "had no effect" because, according to Semevskii, news had recently come from above about impending substantive mining legislation, which also never appeared.[22]

In one area, the gubernatorial efforts may have worked. In 1880, at Governor-General Anukhin's urging, the East Siberian administration forbade below-surface mining for children under fourteen and for all females and forbade work after 9 P.M. for boys under ten and for all females. These and other new regulations improved things for women and child laborers until the 1892 mining laws specifically extended imperial labor legislation about women and children to the Siberian gold mines. Even so, the wording of the 1880 directives clearly permitted mining companies to hire children, even those under ten years old, as long as the contract stated the basic conditions and observed the new directives.[23]

Unfortunately, the governors' efforts played out against a counter-vailing backdrop of overt government sponsorship of the big gold-mining companies. As M. Orfanov commented in an 1883 publication, "the gold-mining industry has always operated under the special protection of the government." Furthermore, continued Orfanov, the companies, through illegal payments, "have bought out the only [local] authorities to whom the workers . . . could turn," as a consequence of which the "gold-mining industrialists do not stand on ceremony with the workers."[24] Numerous contemporaries supported this view. The highest government circles (the ministries in St. Petersburg) and the lowest (the local mining and police officials) established an unholy alliance with the entrepreneurs, with results inimical to interests of the workers and, for that matter, the local Siberian population. Resistance was costly. Sinel'nikov, for instance, believed that his efforts to improve conditions for the miners led to his removal from his post.[25]

Sinel'nikov's well-intentioned interventions wrought at least one outright evil effect. The governor originated the idea of sending "the most incorrigible hard-labor prisoners" to private gold mines such as those in the Olekminsk region. He hoped that productive salaried labor would rehabilitate these individuals. Their gainful employment would also relieve a financial burden on the treasury (by workers' paying for their own upkeep) and offer certain economic benefits (lower-paid workers) to the mining companies. His arguments persuaded the emperor, who issued the imperial decree of 16 August 1872 that put the program into action. Eventually many hundreds of hard-labor prisoners received employment in the Lena mines, where they mixed in the barracks with the other miners and their wives and children. Initial reports prematurely proclaimed the results "satisfactory." In reality, most hard-labor prisoners could not cope physically with mining work. By the end of one year, of 260 hard-labor prisoners reporting to one mining company, only 184 remained. The balance had died, fled, been shipped out for "unreliability," or become severely ill, for an attrition rate of 35 percent. The three-year attrition was more than 50 percent.[26] Other companies had similar experiences. In addition, the integration of hard-labor prisoners, often hardened criminals, into the working population led to a crime wave around the mines. The constant infliction of corporal punishment and other harsh control measures for the hard-labor miners thoroughly demoralized the rest of the labor force. Neither in terms of efficiency nor of human consequences were these results remotely satisfactory. By the early 1880s, this unfortunate practice was on the wane, though hiring political exiles still maintained its economic viability (see table 2.1).

It was common coin among commentators that the government

Table 2.1

DISTRIBUTION OF TYPES OF LABORERS IN THE OLEKMA SYSTEM

Year	Political exiles (% of workers)	Hard-labor prisoners (% of workers)	Peasant-urban workers (% of workers)	Total workers
1880	4,150 (38)	303 (3)	6,345 (59)	10,798
1881	4,370 (41.4)	171 (1.6)	6,002 (57)	10,543
1882	4,188 (39)	95 (1)	6,429 (60)	10,712
1883	4,262 (39)	76 (0.7)	6,497 (60.3)	10,835
1884	4,423 (37)	24 (0.2)	7,490 (62.8)	11,937
1887	5,178 (46)	0	6,078 (54)	11,256

Source: Semevskii, *Rabochie na Sibirskikh zolotykh promyslakh*, 863, 869.

heavily favored large-scale and even monopolistic capitalist exploitation of Eastern Siberia's gold.[27] If sizable operations opened even in remote regions, the government quickly built way stations and post offices at great expense and stationed Cossacks (later regular army units) at strategic locations for control purposes. In the matter of troops, the government expected illegal company subsidies for their upkeep. The laws made it impossible for small and medium operators to thrive since most could not obtain proper licenses or bear the huge start-up costs. The web of state policies reflects the government's ongoing priority of controlling gold. In other words, high-level policy took total precedence over the benefit of local Siberian communities, an analytical tendency that closely fits Steven Marks's interpretation of the construction of the Trans-Siberian Railroad.[28]

Close collusion between central government ministries and large entrepreneurs further exaggerated these tendencies. For example, rules prevented the sale of wheat and other foodstuffs near the mines, in favor of large company-controlled shipments of Irkutsk grain and Iakutsk meat, the latter of notoriously poor quality. The resulting low prices fit the big companies' financial requirements quite well. Yet, as many commentators pointed out, high-quality grain and meat were available locally. The purchase of these higher-priced foodstuffs would have provided an enormous spur to local agriculture, which was quite productive. The result would have been a prosperous peasantry and, as local peasants responded to economic stimuli, lower prices. Instead, only the immediate convenience of the big companies counted. The shipments from great distances also pleased the kulaks (wealthy peasants) and merchants who controlled both river transport and the wholesale food market. Firsthand witnesses of the local economy insisted

Modern Lena Gold Mining

that simply legalizing private gold transactions alone would have spurred the region's economy. Instead, all gold had to be channeled directly to the government by companies of considerable scale. No gold except illegal gold had any local impact.

From the early 1860s on, the mining industry underwent gradual transformation into investment companies owned in St. Petersburg, Moscow, and, later, abroad. The mines also shipped in labor from farther and farther away. During the 1890s the entrepreneurs gradually exerted their control over local commerce as well. This system ensured dual malign results. Exactly nothing legally accrued to the local economy, and the workforce experienced the heaviest possible exploitation. Nevertheless, a colossal underground economy in spirits, all manner of vices, and legitimate goods flourished with illegal gold as the tender. In all likelihood, this deprived the state treasury of more gold than under full legalization, since illegal gold channeled its way to China and elsewhere. As many commentators noted, the experience of the Amur gold industry suggested other possibilities, far more favorable to local economies and more humane to workers.[29] In any case, by the 1880s and 1890s many observers felt that by legalizing gold transactions and taking other measures that would have spurred local economies, the government could have created thriving regional economies in all Siberian gold-bearing areas. Commentators also felt that the economic success of the Lena region's skoptsy further validated the potential for general prosperity. As late as 1911, in connection with a planned Irkutsk-Bodaibo-Amur railroad line, the railroad engineer F. Boltunov argued for improving the region's economy by opening gold mining to the entrepreneurship of workers' arteli.[30] This, however, was not the path chosen, setting the stage for the modern era of Siberian gold mining and, by the turn of the century, the rise of a single investment giant that proceeded to monopolize the entire Olekminsk region.

During the early 1870s the mining engineer A. Loranskii wrote an account that captures the essential problem for workers of Lena gold mining:

> In the taiga, thousands of [miles] not only from cities . . . but even from simple living places, far from judicial institutions, the workers exist in full dependence on the employer and must fulfill his every whim and obey his arbitrary will. At a factory or plant situated [in settled areas], when employers violate the contract or otherwise oppress [workers], the [workers] can easily find jobs elsewhere and, furthermore, gain more or less rapid satisfaction in the courts. In the distant taiga . . . the worker cannot easily abandon the mines and seek other work. That would re-

quire financial means and energy [not to mention that quitting was illegal]. Consequently, the worker is forced to bear endless oppression and only when things reach the point of extremity, when all patience comes to an end, then there remains one way out—to flee and perhaps die of hunger and exposure. Such circumstances require special measures to guarantee the interests of the working class and engender a need for special legislation for the gold-mining industry.[31]

Help of this kind was slow in coming and never unstinting.

Even so, the decade of the 1890s indisputably witnessed a maturing of the Siberian gold-mining industry. This pertained to legislation, aspects of the industry itself, and the state's relationship to gold-mining labor. Modern business practice reached its full flowering in the Olekminsk region. Russia's 1897 establishment of the gold standard, long in preparation, was perhaps the most important factor. These developments set the stage for the rise of the industrial giant Lenzoto. During the 1890s imperial law for the first time specified the Civil Law Code as the basis for all legal transactions in Siberian gold mining. In 1892 a statute pointedly subjected the industry to general law codes on women's and children's labor. These were the first signs of the long death of Siberian legal exceptionalism. The mining legislation of 1895 addressed a series of abuses by, for example, ensuring the workers' right to complain about violations and forcing employers to abide by certain rules when firing miners. Other statutes dealt with questions of status by extending worker designation, which invoked certain protections, to wives employed around the mines and to clerical and other subordinate employees. One statute outlined the duties of "mining administrators," a newly important category in the region as personal ownership and administration waned. New regulations fined administrators for violations such as accepting unwitnessed work contracts.[32] These were all signposts of modern business.

After his 1891 tour of fifteen Olekminsk mining companies, Governor-General Goremykin sternly reprimanded government mining officials for allowing rampant violations of workers' welfare. In 1893 he even recommended changes in the work contracts. In these respects, the governor-general represented a widespread opinion that "management take the first step toward a humane attitude toward the [workers]" as the key to reducing tense worker-entrepreneur relations. Regardless, ameliorations never extended to work contracts. Flying in the face of the bitterest criticism, this omission meant that the most basic issues for working people, such as hours, pay, rewards for off-time work, housing, and provisions, escaped meaningful regulation. A witnessed work contract achieved validity merely by specifying anything at all about these matters. In fact, general tsarist labor legislation, now applicable in Siberia gold mining, demanded nothing more of work contracts. A special twist for Siberian gold miners was that the law still prevented them from quitting, although the employers at least had to conform to regulations in firing miners. One innocent-sounding new statute allowed mining companies to operate stores at mine sites, a first official ratification of company stores that soon led to total commercial monopolization in the Lena mining region. Shortcomings aside, the 1895 code lay the basis for applying general civil and industrial law to Siberian gold mining. Late tsarist legislators were finally deploying a universal concept of law.

The last legislative additions before the 1912 Lena strike appeared in 1906, a year of vast change in Russian governance on the heels of the 1905 Revolution. The 1906 code gave regional mining engineers sweeping on-site oversight (nadzor) over all mining regulations, including those concerning women's and children's labor, food, medical treatment, and transportation back to populated points. In the Vitim system, this last simply meant that the companies had to transport workers a few miles to Bodaibo, after which they negotiated the remaining vast distances themselves. A sign of professionalization was the1906 code's mention of the St. Petersburg Mining Institute (founded in 1866) and two recently created mining schools in Ekaterinburg and Ekaterinoslav for the training of mining engineers and other personnel.[33] Although the 1906 code, like that of 1895, suggested the tsarist regime's resolve to prevent the outright abuse of workers, it left the work contract untouched. In addition, the authority given to mining engineers, many of them sincerely dedicated, lacked the power of enforcement. They could only appeal about violations to Siberian governors and to ministers in St. Petersburg, which they often did. In the Lena taiga, this hardly insured company compliance.

Nonetheless, during the late 1880s and 1890s the Olekminsk region gold mines fit a nationwide pattern in witnessing real improvements in workers' living conditions.[34] The industry's overall productivity (see table 2.2), accompanied by intensified government scrutiny at the central and local levels, induced gold-mining companies to improve facilities for workers and their families. The demise of penal labor in the mid-1880s and regional officials' concerted efforts had an effect. For one example, at a time of very high industry profitability the Irkutsk governor pushed a program to found schools for the hundreds of children who had accompanied their families to the mines and who themselves often worked in various capacities. One description of the mining children pointed out that "[y]our twelve-year-old boy at the mines already smokes tobacco . . . swigs down a jigger of vodka in one gulp . . .

Table 2.2

LENA GOLD-MINING DATA

Year	No. of mines	Sand processed (in millions of puds[a])	No. of workers	Gold obtained (in puds[a])
1880	51	98.988	10,798	939
1882	62	90.173	10,712	759
1885	65	76.418	12,382	538
1887	75	76.421	11,256	451
1889	77	85.587	13,166	495
1890	79	92.414	6,464[b]	575
1892	92	101.299	7,684[b]	657
1894	97	129.300	7,873[b]	692
1895	101	117.818	7,418[b]	718

Source: Semevskii, *Rabochie na Sibirskikh zolotykh promyslakh*, 863, 875.
Note: Several large firms accounted for the vast majority of the activity in each category measured here.
[a]A pud equals 16.38 kg or about 36 lbs.
[b]An anomaly in counting methods during 1890–95 significantly underestimated the number of workers, which actually rose throughout the period, as suggested by the increased number of mines and the quantity of sand processed.

and neatly washes a tray of gold." The very first company-sponsored school opened in 1881 and by the 1890s hundreds of children attended free company schools, where they learned reading, writing, arithmetic, and religion. The Lena Gold-Mining Company (known as Lenzoto) opened its tuition-free school in 1891 and in 1896 added a boarding school. Lenzoto and other companies also opened subscription libraries, arranged readings for workers, and sponsored magic lantern displays and theatrical performances. Some companies put up Christmas trees and arranged for Easter festivities for the mining children.[35]

New possibilities for religious observance arose. In 1879 only one church functioned in the entire Olekminsk region, whereas by 1890 three churches and three chapels (*chasovni*) had opened. These religious institutions and the priests attached to them operated solely at industry expense, which by the end of the 1880s, totaled six thousand rubles a year for each priest in the system. Even so, the widespread practice of Sunday work depressed attendance at services. Observers felt that most miners had totally lost the habit of religious observance.[36] Of interest is that despite the churches' utter financial dependence on the companies, the local Orthodox priests were consistent, caustic critics of the industry's practices toward workers.

After the elimination of hard-labor prisoners in the mines by the early 1880s, political exile labor also decreased, so that by 1912 this category constituted less than 1 percent of Lena miners. By 1900 freely hired Siberian and European Russian peasants dominated the workforce. Commentators noted the better health and physical strength of the new type of mine worker. Some observers felt that to survive mining labor the workers had to have athletic physiques. Increasingly, the hiring agents gave preference to physically strong types. Additionally, as allowed by the 1895 code, whole families now commonly hired themselves out to the mines, so that the number of workers with wives and children at the mines increased significantly. This entailed exploitation of women's and children's labor but partially relieved sexual tensions. Many mining concerns constructed new barracks, dining halls, and meeting halls (*narodnye doma*), along with the new schools and churches. In general, increasing capital investments promoted more solid infrastructure and facilities.

These alterations in part reflected the profound effect of the new emphasis on subterranean mining. The former summer work period, reflecting the impossibility of surface work in the winter, now shifted to year-round work, a possibility because temperatures in the deep mines fluctuated very little during the year. It was cold but always above freezing. Maximum production now required a normalization of the hiring period, another contributory factor in the tendency of workers to bring their families to the mines.[37]

In other words, the maturing of the industry brought new hiring practices that reflected the emergence of a free labor market and resulted in year-round work with whole families present. Pressure from high Siberian officials and the application of general tsarist labor law to Siberian gold mining combined to improve the working and living environment. The preceding decades' intense demoralization of the workforce faded somewhat. Had the incremental improvements of the late 1880s and early 1890s continued thereafter and had they extended more firmly into actual work conditions (salary, hours, and general status), then real progress might have occurred. This, however, did not happen. The tsarist government traditionally exerted a paternal, if not gentle, watch over workers. During the 1860s and 1870s the state backpedaled in the matter of its control of worker-industry relations in the Lena gold industry. By the 1880s, with the introduction of the factory inspectorate laws, the government recommended a robust intervention in labor relations. Leaving aside the overall effectiveness of the intervention, the principle of renewed state responsibility was clear. Certainly, it is no accident that improvements occurred simultaneously in such distant mining regions as the Donets Basin and the Olekminsk region. A reasonable conclusion is that the laws played a role.

To the profound misfortune of Lena gold miners, other factors arose that in essence induced the government to release them once again into the hands of the entrepreneurs and managers. All assertions of the universality of the law aside, by the turn of the new century Siberian, or perhaps one should say Lena, exceptionalism renewed itself, with only minimal limitations. The principal new factor was Russia's gold standard. The 1897 introduction of the gold standard, so beneficial for Russia's economy, availed the Lena miners very little. Quite the contrary, the government's obsession with the precious metal intensified in tandem with its lessening of concern for the workers who produced it. The transient nature of the improvements may also reflect other factors. One observer lamented that "[t]he notable softening of practices is not based upon the humanism . . . of our industrialists and their agents. . . . Make no mistake . . . the hearts and souls of these people remain even now hard as flint. . . . The easing of relations [with the workers] simply reflects . . . [the managers'] concern for their safety in the face of imminent worker revolts and . . . the pressure from higher administration."[38]

LENZOTO AND THE WORKERS, 1882–1912

Lenzoto's rise from a smallish shares company to a giant monopoly with international ties is, like the history of Lena gold mining, a saga in its own right. The company's history is also the backdrop for the 1912 strike and shooting. The Lena Shares Company arose in 1861 as the first of a new type of company that gradually supplanted the earlier merchant-owned concerns. Until the 1890s its mines were along the Olekma River, the location of the Lena region's earliest sites. Even as other companies abandoned the Olekma for the richer Vitim River sites, the Lena Shares Company continued its mundane existence along the Olekma.

The first sign of activism came in 1882, when Baron Horace Ginzburg and the House of Meyer Trading Company, of which he was a member, purchased a controlling block of the company's shares. Among other interests, this company owned the giant Petersburg Metallurgical Plant. At this point, the sleepy Lena Shares Company became the Lena Gold-Mining Company. Lenzoto then poured new capital into developing the supposedly defunct Olekma River system. Whether farsighted or merely lucky, this maneuver produced a flood of gold from one site on the Nygra River, an Olekma branch. From

1892 to 1896 this site yielded 533 *puds* of gold (1 pud = 16.38 kg or about 36 lbs), a sixth of the entire Olekma system's production and several times the entire individual production of the Nerchinsk, Altai, Verkhneudinsk, or Amur regions.[39] Lenzoto's rich returns proved temporary, since after 1897 the Nygra River site yielded little. By 1899 Lenzoto's status in Lena mining was a distant second place to the larger Industrial Company, whose early move to the Vitim River resulted in a phenomenal decades-long average of 275 puds of gold annually.[40]

In 1896, using its profits and state bank loans, Lenzoto purchased the last sizable rival company in the Olekma system, just as the region's production finally collapsed. Lenzoto had monopolized nonincome-producing assets, a dilemma that required new measures to insure the company's survival. The Ginzburg and Meyer families decided to transform Lenzoto into an open stock company and sell shares. E. M. Meyer became the company's director and Baron Horace Ginzburg his assistant. After Meyer's death, Baron Horace took his place, and he was succeeded by his two sons. The company's 1895–96 capitalization stood at 9 million rubles. With these new financial resources, Lenzoto made a hasty, if belated, descent on the Vitim River system. In 1897 it purchased sites along the small Bodaibo River, with which area its fate became inextricably intertwined. By coincidence, that same year Russia went onto the gold standard.

During the early 1890s Lenzoto had improved living conditions for its workers. It also introduced other innovations: organizing theatrical productions and holiday festivals, setting up libraries, and arranging for public readings. On the negative side of the ledger, Lenzoto levied the highest fines in the Olekminsk region. One observer claimed that Lenzoto was quietly "striving . . . to educate the workers in the spirit of discipline necessary for the modern conditions of capitalist production."[41] This approach combined old style paternalism and new style free market spurs toward modern labor conditions. An aspect of the former, which sharply attenuated the latter, was local managers' exceptional power over workers in remote mining regions.

On its arrival on the Bodaibo River, Lenzoto immediately undertook steps reminiscent of its past tactics. It invested heavily in its Feodosievsk mine, a below-the surface-enterprise of considerable potential, and lavished funds on acquiring rivals in the Vitim system. In 1897 and 1898 the company received imperial sanction to sell additional shares worth 4.5 million rubles. Even so, the double financial burden of developing new deep mines and acquiring competitors almost sank the whole enterprise. Prior to fiscal year 1899–1900 the company had punctually repaid bank loans incurred since 1891. As of 1900 it fell behind. Furthermore, just to cover running costs and debts for operations in

1901, the company had to borrow another 1.75 million rubles from the State Bank. Technically speaking, by 1901 Lenzoto was bankrupt in that its outstanding debts heavily exceeded its ability to pay them. At this point, Lenzoto sold shares in the amount of 6.5 million rubles in order to continue operations. Nevertheless, Lenzoto's prospects were bleak since production lagged in its mines under direct exploitation. The State Bank considered foreclosing its debt, putting the company out of business, and selling Lenzoto resources to collect its loans. To avert this, prominent company investors launched a campaign to advertise "the unlimited wealth" promised by Lenzoto's future. The State Bank stepped in by placing N. N. Boianovskii, State Bank director, on Lenzoto's board. As of 1902 the State Bank granted Lenzoto a 5.1 million ruble line of credit. Boianovskii then arranged for the appointment of I. N. Belozerov, former Bodaibo Company director, as acting director of Lenzoto's mining operations. Boianovskii, whose acquaintanceship with Belozerov dated from the State Bank's recent acquisition of the Bodaibo Company, admired his business acumen and administrative skills.[42] As of 1902 Lenzoto had a new acting manager, a reshaped board of directors, and a virtually unlimited line of credit with the Imperial State Bank.

Despite losses of more than 4.1 million rubles between 1900 and 1902, Lenzoto survived or, more accurately, was allowed to survive its crisis. For technical reasons, the Feodosievsk mine's production had lagged under the pre-1902 acting director, Mining Engineer L. F. Grauman, an individual responsible for some of the benefits workers received during the 1890s. Within a year or so of Belozerov's arrival, the Feodosievsk mine finally yielded its riches, for which the new managing director got the credit. The balance books quickly moved from red to black. Lenzoto earned increasing profits and produced ever larger percentages of the Vitim system's gold production (see tables 2.3 and 2.4).

Simultaneously, Lenzoto also purchased or leased many other mines. It made its last acquisitions during the years 1910 and 1911, partially accounting for those two years' enormous outlays of more than 54 million rubles. Acquisitions aside, the company's huge expenditures, more than 240 million rubles between 1902 and 1911, also reflected the building costs of a small-gauge railroad between Bodaibo and the Feodosievsk site.[43] Lenzoto now accounted for well over 90 percent of Lena (Olekminsk) region gold production and over one-half of Siberia's, a third of the empire's, and 3 percent of worldwide gold production. This one company controlled no fewer than 423 mines (54 by lease) spread out over 38,600 *desiatinas* of land (1 des. = 2.7 acres). During 1911 it made its last big expenditure by obtaining concession rights from the North-East Siberian Company in connection with the

Table 2.3
LENZOTO'S PROFITS AND LOSSES, 1897–1912

Year	Profits (in rubles)	Losses (in rubles)	Profit as % of share capital
1897–98	651,368	0	5.9
1898–99	441,778	0	4.0
1899–1900	0	43,345	0
1900–1901	0	897,672	0
1901–1902	0	3,300,650	0
1902–1903	n.a.[a]	n.a.[a]	n.a.[a]
1903–1904	479,000	0	4.3
1904–1905	846,600	0	7.6
1905–1906	311,000	0	2.8
1906–1907	1,977,000	0	17.8
1907–1908	2,698,000	0	40.5
1908–1909	4,709,000	0	70.7
1909–10	6,812,000	0	61.4
1910–11	5,273,000	0	47.5
1911–12	0	415,171	0

Source: A. V. Piaskovskii, Lenskie sobytiia 1912 g. (Moscow, 1939), 14.
[a]No data available.

government's planned construction of a two-thousand-mile railroad connecting Irkutsk and the Trans-Siberian Amur line via Bodaibo. In reality, Lenzoto held sway over a roughly one-hundred-thousand-square mile territory since it owned or controlled all facilities throughout this vast expanse, including transportation, utilities, and commercial networks.[44] A mining company had become a small kingdom.

Lured by the promised cornucopia of wealth, famous people purchased Lenzoto stocks. In 1908, under pressure from the State Bank to seek private sources of credit, Alexander and Alfred Ginzburg, Horace's sons, created the Lena Goldfields Company, a British stock company, whose shares traded on the London and Paris exchanges. The new company purchased over 70 percent of Lenzoto's shares, an action that poured new funds into the enterprise. A stellar group of Russia's industrial-commercial firmament entered the company's Petersburg committee, including A. I. Putilov (director of the Russko-Aziatskii Bank), V. I. Timiriazev (a prominent Octobrist politician and former minister of trade and commerce), and A. I. Vishnegradskii (director of the International Bank). Investors included Count S. Iu. Witte; the empress-mother, Maria Fedorovna; and the current minister of trade and industry, S. I. Timashev. In 1912 the director was M. E. Meyer, and

Table 2.4

LENZOTO'S SHARE OF VITIM SYSTEM GOLD PRODUCTION

Year	Vitim system gold production (in puds[a])	Lenzoto's share[b] (in puds[a])
1897	591	93 (15.7)
1899	562	190 (33.8)
1905	521	236 (45.3)
1906	543	371 (68.3)
1908	663	497 (75.0)
1909	785	644 (82.0)
1910	1,088	783 (72.0)

Source: A. Nevskii, *Lenskie sobytiia i ikh prichiny* (St. Petersburg, 1912), 6.
[a]A pud equals 16.38 kg or about 36 lbs.
[b]Percentage of total gold production is given in parentheses.

the board of directors included State Bank director Boianovskii, the Ginzburgs, Timiriazev, and Putilov.[45] The close ties between Lenzoto and government personages, including the director of the Imperial State Bank, ensured privileges for the company. In 1909 the State Bank provided its last service by interceding with Nicholas II to issue an imperial decree (*vysochaishee povelenie*) that wrote off Lenzoto's debts through a fiscal maneuver.[46] Increasing profits, new investments from the London-based Lena Goldfields Company, and several helpful imperial decrees had put Lenzoto in a position to rid itself of all debt, purchase all significant competitors, acquire all local railroad and steamship concessions, and pay huge dividends to its investors. It was an entrepreneurial paradise.

Unnoted by commentators, a close connection existed between Russia's 1897 conversion to the gold standard and the state's intimate involvement in Lenzoto. As part of its autocratic prerogative the Russian government had always controlled precious metals. Peter the Great had launched gold mining in Russia as a state-owned industry. Even during the nineteenth century, when the government at last encouraged capitalist gold mining, state and cabinet (royal) ownership continued in some regions. Furthermore, by law all gold mined in Russia went directly into the state treasury. For roughly fifteen years prior to Minister of Finance Witte's 1897 gold standard conversion, the government's fiscal policy aimed at accumulating gold reserves sufficient to cover all currency. After 1897 the state further intensified its efforts to build the gold reserves to back the increased currency of an expanding economy. The 1901 recession, the 1904–1906 Russo-Japanese War, and the 1905–1907 Revolution spurred a frenzied resolve to maintain the threatened gold reserves. One historian remarked about "the bright glitter of Russia's colossal gold reserve" lighting the way, in the eyes of high officials, to ever higher levels of industrial development. Naturally, domestic gold production was a key element in this strategy. (In the early 1900s Russia's gold production was 15 percent of the world's total, whereas by 1912 it had fallen to 9 percent.) Furthermore, the imperial treasury channeled much of its huge gold reserves to the State Bank in order to shore up its status as the empire's issuer of banknotes. A 1912 industry publication commented on the "exceptional significance for the state of the gold industry [whose role was] to strengthen the [national] balance of payments without exporting valuables abroad."[47] Thus Petersburg ministers, the emperor himself, and the directors of the State Bank took a profound interest in Lenzoto, the company that, with their explicit aid, became Russia's prime gold producer.

Lenzoto Workers before 1902

The underside of the development of the Lena (Olekminsk) gold-mining region and Lenzoto's ascent to predominance was the question of the workers. Under Mining Engineer Grauman's management the firm had displayed humane impulses toward workers. Throughout the 1880s and 1890s Lenzoto's salaries were slightly above the regional average. For example, during 1891 Lenzoto paid washers, the highest-paid specialty, 1.25 rubles per day, whereas in 1890 the Bodaibo Company paid 1 ruble per day. Meanwhile, Lenzoto paid sorters, water-pourers, and rock-splitters at the same rate (60 kopecks a day) as the Bodaibo Company. Lenzoto paid nonmining specialties such as carpenters, turners, and smiths between 50 and 60 kopecks a day, incrementally higher than regional averages. When deep, as opposed to surface or near-surface, mining came to predominate by the late 1890s, increased demand for nonmining skilled workers rapidly advanced their pay to 1.5, 1.8, or even 2 rubles a day, at which point they became a kind of elite.[48]

In the mid-1880s wages for miners in the Lena region (189 rubles a year) lagged far behind those of coal and iron miners in the Donets region (252 rubles a year), which themselves were considered inadequate.[49] Of course, the Lena wages at that time reflected a short work year, that is, miners worked only during months when surface or near-surface mining was possible (May–September). Even so, Lena miners depended totally on these wages for survival; the mines were too distant and isolated for miners to obtain supplementary employment.

Whether in 1866, when the parent Lena Shares Company paid the lowest wages in the region (119 rubles a year), or during the early 1890s, when Lenzoto's annual salaries (roughly 221 rubles) slightly exceeded regional norms, questions always arose about the levels of pay. Lena miners faced extraordinarily high transportation costs and elevated living costs. Computations consistently suggested the pay's inadequacy. One detailed estimate from the late 1880s claimed that the *maximum* possible annual salary was 248 rubles (the *average* was much lower), whereas the more or less standard cost of purchasing food and other items needed for mining work, plus transportation costs, equaled 263 rubles.[50] That miners were often in debt at the end of the work year was no surprise. Some workers skimped, others engaged in the drudgery of ill-paid off-time prospecting, which ate up days off that were desperately needed for rest, and still others simply toted gold. Inadequate Lena wages, along with the new year-round work schedule, help explain why in later years workers often brought their families and hired them out to the companies for pittances.

Regardless, prior to Belozerov's 1902 arrival as managing director, Lenzoto created the impression of an aggressive, forward-looking, closely managed, and expansive company. It sought to create a modern workforce through discipline, yet was innovative in improving the living environment for workers and their families. In terms of hours, salaries, rewards for off-time work, fines, firing, and transport to and from the mines, Lenzoto did not deviate from the parameters set by law and regional custom. The Belozerov era witnessed changes for the worse in these and other respects.

The Early Belozerov Regime, 1902–1907

The inverse history of Lenzoto's final precipitate rise and the workers' fall directly reflected Belozerov's tenure as managing director. This peculiar history also indirectly reflected the company's growing intimacy with the State Bank, which had insisted on Belozerov's appointment and, simultaneously, granted larger and larger credits that required repayment. With this in mind, Belozerov, an effective but crude administrator, soon established the so-called Belozerov regime, which earned the intense hatred of Lena workers and, eventually, gargantuan profits. Thus between 1902 and 1912, ever more Lena workers (by 1911 all of them) fell under the control of an individual not overly burdened by scruples in the search for profits.

Belozerov was an almost mythological type of capitalist, a person who had risen up by dint of his own labor from humble rank and modest education and become ruthless in his drive to succeed. Starting as a clerk-accountant in the Irkutsk region mining industry, he worked his way up to the managing directorship of the Bodaibo Company and then of Lenzoto. The government even awarded him the title "manufacturing advisor" (*manufaktur sovetnik*). By 1912 he was a millionaire who owned stores, gold mines, a mansion in Petersburg, and a palatial dacha in the Crimea. He spent three-quarters of the year traveling from the Crimea to Nice, then to London and on to St. Petersburg. Finally, he would arrive at the mines, where, reputedly, his mood and character left much to be desired. One newspaper described him as follows: "This is a simple, poorly educated but energetic and self-assured 'administrator,' who in his thirty-five-year career has passed through every rank of mining management. The former clerk is now the head of the entire Lenzoto enterprise and earns 150,000 [rubles] a year." Among other alleged misdeeds, he had cut in half the pay for off-time prospecting established by his predecessor, Grauman.[51]

Senator Manukhin, who investigated Belozerov, observed that "if it suited his purposes, [he] did not scruple to ignore the demands of the law." The lofty senator added that he came from the "lowest workers' milieu" (*nizshei rabochei sredy*), perhaps signifying day laborers. A mining police official spoke of his "natural intelligence, sharpness, insolence, utter absence of moral qualities," and said he was the "progeny of the dregs of Irkutsk society, constantly playing the role of an Alphonse [Lothario]." When he arrived for his annual quarter-year at the mines, he was greeted with full pomp, replete with a "triumphal arch and banners flying." Workers called him the "god [or] the tsar of the taiga." As befit those lofty titles, he allegedly demanded seignorial rights over the prettiest women.[52]

Lenzoto seems to have brought Belozerov to the managing directorship precisely to display the characteristics everyone recalled, after the 1912 tragedy, as repellent. State Bank director Boianovskii had wanted someone at the helm of Lenzoto, the new bearer of huge debts to his bank, to run a tight ship, wring profit from the enterprise, retire the debts, and, it would seem, pour gold into the treasury and the State Bank's vaults. With his limited moral sense, Belozerov set out to do exactly this. Late 1903 communications from Lenzoto's Petersburg headquarters to the managing director are revealing. With reference to a special company fund for "rewards" (bribes) to police and state mining officials, the Petersburg directors wrote that "[we] certainly do not propose to deprive you of the possibility of rewarding persons who provide . . . the company with help according to the services rendered." When the Petersburg headquarters requested documentation, perhaps for accounting reasons, of monies dispersed in illegal "rewards," Lenzoto's on-site management answered that "a list of confidential sums was not received from the mining police because of the illegality of the . . . donations from gold-mining industrialists."[53]

A 1904 exchange of messages between Managing Director Belozerov and the firm's top administrators also bears on the nature of attitudes they mutually promoted. Severe 1904 strikes and the alleged deliberate drafting of much of Lenzoto's mining workforce into the military to fight in the 1904–1906 Russo-Japanese conflict had depleted the labor force. Baron Alfred Ginzburg wrote to Belozerov about hiring new workers: "We are flooded with applications from various places, especially from Poland and Odessa, . . . as well as from the Petersburg area, the Donets Basin, [and] the Trans-Caucasus." The baron recommended hiring two thousand workers, either agricultural types or "those already working in mining" and, according to an arrangement with the Ministry of Transportation, dispatching them by special trains. Ginzburg continued: "Using the cooperation of the ministry seems to us to be more than desirable. . . . When hiring for the mines is seen . . . as a good deed, it will be possible to use this circumstance to lower salaries. . . . Even the lower pay will seem like El Dorado to hungry people. In any case, we are informing the police of 30 percent lower salaries. . . . There is [no] risk of hiring too may people. If there are too many workers, this will make it easier to present [them] . . . with stricter demands. . . . [E]xcess workers in the taiga will also help lower pay, a goal that must be pursued by all means." When Belozerov worried about hiring workers from areas characterized by "constant strikes accompanied by . . . acts of violence" and at the same time confronting them with lower pay, Ginzburg reminded him that police involvement in the hiring process would "protect us from taking on strikers." Other messages from headquarters advised Belozerov "not to scruple at getting rid of undesirable elements." In his replies, Belozerov consistently advised "no concessions" to workers.[54] Mutual lack of conscience left little reason for disagreement between top management and the director.

Manukhin later commented that "during ten years of managing Lenzoto, Belozerov not only managed to maintain the full trust of the Ginzburg brothers and other influential members of the enterprise. [He also] managed to solidify [his] manner of running the mine's affairs so that he never confronted any interference of any kind, as long as he met expectations." When the Ginzburg brothers formed the Lena Goldfields Company in 1908, they officially committed themselves to making "no changes in the management of [the mines'] affairs, either in personnel at the mines or in management." Belozerov's influence with top Lenzoto management and with Petersburg ministers is indicated by his maneuverings to develop the Feodosievsk mine. Convinced that improving the mine's productivity required a heavy water flow channeled from another company's neighboring mines, Belozerov persuaded the Ministry of Finance to purchase the mines and lease them to Lenzoto. High company officials, government officials, and investors, usually the selfsame people, continued to shower him with awards and praise until the very end. During 1908, a general meeting of shareholders "unanimously voted to express to the acting manager of the mines [their] gratitude . . . for his brilliant handling of the mine's affairs." A mere week before the outbreak of the 1912 strike, the company organized a banquet in Belozerov's honor, to which it invited the minister of trade and industry. The minister could not come but sent a letter and a telegram conveying his heartfelt regrets and expressing praise for this veritable eagle of enterprise.[55] Of course, what set these rhetorical banners flying earned only obloquy when things went sour. The 1912 strike and shooting ended Lenzoto's profits and Belozerov's career.

Lenzoto originally hired and maintained Belozerov in his lofty position to attain the highest profits at all cost. The profits were then dispersed in the attainment of a monopolistic hold on the region and, eventually, on heavy dividends. After a number of years with no dividends, beginning in 1910 Lenzoto paid huge dividends. According to Boianovskii, the dividends paid in 1911 on the 1910 profits actually equaled 56 percent of profits or, according to another source, 4.23 million rubles. The director who replaced Belozerov after the 1912 massacre wrote the following: "they did not give a kopeck to reserve capital nor to capital for debt retirement; they gave not a kopeck to current turn-over capital. . . . All was sacrificed to the greed for dividends . . . leaving nothing on hand even for the operating budget." Indeed, already in 1911 Chief Mining Engineer K. N. Tul'chinskii had warned the trade and industry minister about an impending financial collapse due to the company's improvident policies.[56] Especially between 1908 and 1912, observers noted the incredibly shoddy nature of Lenzoto's mining operations and its awful conditions for workers. The Belozerov/Lenzoto arrangement concerned a race for profits and dividends, in no small measure through the maximum exploitation of workers.

In his investigation of the causes of the 1912 strike and shooting, Senator Manukhin reached the conclusion that Belozerov deliberately inculcated among company personnel an attitude that miners were expendable items. Anyone sympathetic to workers was a "useless bleeding heart" (nekudyshnyi). During one early strike, Belozerov reputedly told workers, "If you don't want to, don't work! There are plenty of hungry people around here [to hire]," and on another occasion, "I'll make you all work until there's nothing left of you but skin and bones."[57] Lenzoto employees' provocative rudeness became legendary. When issuing poor-quality food, clerks often quipped, "a miner is not a pig, he'll eat anything." Workers took revenge with nicknames for the worst offenders: Wolf's Fang (Vol'chii zub) for an employee of beastlike address; Filaret the Merciful (Filaret Milostivyi) for a snooper; Iron Apostle (Chugunnyi apostol) for an overseer with quick fists; and Godfather (Kum) for another infamous for his pathological advances to miners' wives. The workers called the justice of the peace E. M. Khitun the Golden Judge (Zolotoi sud'ia) because of his propensity for demanding payments in that tender for his decisions.[58]

These data should not be dismissed merely as run-of-the-mill workers' complaints about a vigorous pursuit of profit by a well-connected and successful mining endeavor. Two well-informed bureaucrats with impeccable government credentials, Irkutsk governor F. A. Bantysh and Senator Manukhin, had the following to say about Lenzoto as personified by Belozerov. "For many years [Lenzoto]," commented Bantysh just three months before the 1912 strike, "has extracted the life's substance from whole generations of people. Neither the local administrators nor the local government has so much as lifted a finger to put an end to this social horror, for which there is no name, no justification." Continuing in the same vein, Manukhin wrote after the shooting that "at the Lena mines . . . exists the very darkest side, without a doubt. . . . A certain atmosphere permeates all . . . interrelationships between the administration and the working people, a spirit of oppression and cold indifference to the fate of human beings, a spirit that locally has long carried the characterization of the 'Belozerov regime.'"[59] The dark side was the spirit of Belozerov, wined, dined, and lauded in Petersburg until the very last days of his misrule in the Lena kingdom. The 1912 events, although not foreordained, hardly appeared out of nowhere.

The Prestrike Belozerov Regime, 1908–1912

After 1907 the Belozerov regime developed in full force in the deep taiga. (See chap. 3 for a discussion of worker unrest during the stormy 1904–1907 era.) The goldfield workers were the lowly of the empire's proletariat—the hopelessly unemployed, peasants yearning to strike it rich, and dwindling cadres of political-exile workers toiling out their terms. The company that hired them had a monopoly on the mines and on transportation (riverine steamboats and local railroads). Lenzoto also monopolized commerce by gradually purchasing the big provisioning stores and pushing the few remaining independent establishments out of business. By 1910–11 Lenzoto tyrannized the people in local law enforcement, justice, and political administration as well. In the past, the industry had subsidized local government officials, creating obvious conflicts of interest. The ensuing Lenzoto monopoly exacerbated the problem in the most extreme fashion. A bizarre example arose at the 1911 "congress" of the Lena mining industry, which by law convened entrepreneurs, managers, inspectors, and engineering officials in order to work out common policies. The 1911 congress was, strictly speaking, a Lenzoto business meeting. Shortly thereafter Lenzoto declared the previously existing Council of the Lena Mining Companies "legally out of existence" and simply assumed its responsibilities.[60] Despite the illegality involved, Lenzoto financial records reveal continued wide-scale subsidies to police and state mining officials. Senator Manukhin's commission also noted Lenzoto's "illegal payments" to regional military personnel. In his November 1912 personal report to the emperor, Manukhin emphasized Lenzoto's "unlawful payments to the police, postal-telegraph officials, and even the armed forces." In 1911 Governor Bantysh wrote, "The Lena Company feeds, teaches, treats, punishes and ministers to thousands. . . . It even supports government employees. . . . An official can hardly act independently of Lenzoto when it holds him hostage for everything—heat, electricity and so on." Lenzoto minutely controlled every aspect of local life. Lenzoto was hardly unique in this regard. Iuzovka, also a "company town," shared many characteristics with Bodaibo and the Lena gold mines. But Lenzoto's untrammeled autocracy in the utterly remote East Siberian taiga constituted its unique essence as, in Aleksander Kerensky's phrase, a "capitalist utopia."[61]

Problems began for miners even before they signed Lenzoto's employment contract. In past years, workers had traveled to the mines for hiring, covering the last 125 miles from the Lena to Bodaibo by foot. By 1903 contracts were for one year. The company deliberately hired once a year, in September, so that workers, unable to leave because of distance and deteriorating weather, had to accept the contract offered. And once hired, workers were unable to leave and seek other employment. The workers' only alternative was to take to the taiga in search of illegal gold, hardly feasible for those with wives and children and, in any case, extraordinarily dangerous. Formerly, a dissatisfied worker could seek employment at another company, a widely practiced, although illegal, tactic now precluded by Lenzoto's monopoly status. In contrast, workers in the Donbass area often exercised the option of leaving to work elsewhere.[62]

The contract itself certainly put workers on notice (see app. 1). Workdays were eleven hours during winter and eleven and a half in summer. The company provided housing where available (in remote areas, workers constructed their own), guaranteed a weekly bath, and awarded free medical and hospital care. It offered, however, no pay for sick days. Lenzoto issued monthly sums of money and food, with a final payoff at the end of the one-year contract. The company retained the right to use workers without regard to specialty and to levy fines for numerous causes. Two points best illustrate the Lena trap. First, workers could bring family members only with Lenzoto's written permission, but then could not, on pain of dismissal, deny the company the right to employ their wives and adolescent children at low pay. Second, Lenzoto could fire without notice at any time of the year, whereas workers had no right to terminate the contract (despite existing tsarist laws that provided either party the right to terminate with two-weeks' notice).[63] Siberian exceptionalism had a long half-life.

WAGES   Salaries were an especially vexing question. Lenzoto normally computed wages according to each miner's daily productivity, a record of which overseers maintained in logbooks. Lenzoto routinely—and illegally—denied workers access to the logbooks. At year's end, miners had no recourse when they got lower salaries than expected. Observers commonly noted that mine workers, mostly peasants, kept in their heads detailed records of their productivity, hours, and fines. Lack of access to the pay logs rendered it impossible for them to point out the alleged distortions and falsifications that had been an ongoing source of worker unrest at Lenzoto and other mining concerns for many decades. By 1911–12 the average daily remuneration in rubles at Lenzoto was as follows: 1.35 for unskilled laborers; 1.50 for miners; and from 1.50 to 2.75 for various skilled laborers such as carpenters, turners, and blacksmiths. Daily estimates are rough since an enormous range of specialties existed, each with its own remuneration level and criteria. Actual earnings reflected days worked, productivity, and fines accrued. Miners' wives and adolescent daughters received less than 90 kopecks a day and children, also indentured by contract, received 40 kopecks. They all performed menial, unsanitary, and arduous tasks on the surface rather than in the mines. Legal restrictions on below-the-surface women's labor prevented the tendency, noted by Glickman and other researchers, for some industries to replace male workers with female ones as more docile and cheaper. During the early 1890s, when surface or near-surface mining still predominated, women constituted roughly 12 percent of the Olekminsk region workforce. Thereafter, as deep mining came to the fore, the total dropped to just below 3 percent, evidently sufficient, along with children's labor, to perform auxiliary surface tasks associated with deep mining.[64]

By the mid-1890s the lengthened work year had drastically altered the structure of annual salaries. Mining now continued the entire year. Average annual wages for the 1886–89 period were 189 rubles, whereas

Table 2.5

COMPARATIVE REGIONAL DAILY WAGES IN 1910

Employment classification	Industrial Company's wages (in rubles)	Lenzoto's wages (in rubles)	Renters' Company wages (in rubles)
Laborer			
in dry mine	1.80	1.50	1.80
in wet mine	2–2.50	1.90	2–2.50
Helper	1.60	1.35	1.50

Source: GARF, F 1186, op.1, d.81, l.14.

for 1894–95, because of the virtual tripling of workdays, they reached 542 rubles (Lenzoto's figures). The company claimed that in 1910–11 the average annual wage reached 617 rubles 10 kopecks, more than in the rest of Russia and even abroad. Just after the April 1912 shooting, Lenzoto explained its refusal to lift wages as part of a strike agreement because they were "already the highest in the empire." These high estimates, however, reflected average aggregates for skilled and unskilled workers. Because of the huge numerical imbalance between low and high wage earners, the real average was much lower. The company's claims also ignored women's and children's pitiable earnings. During the 1907–11 era, one of Belozerov's innovations can be seen in Lenzoto's wages, which were strikingly lower than its competitors (see table 2.5). State mining engineers estimated Lenzoto's average yearly wages as ranging from 450 rubles for unskilled labor (the overwhelming majority) to more than 700 rubles for several hundred highly skilled nonmining specialists. Most observers insisted that Lenzoto's overall average annual wage was about 550 rubles, barely higher than two decades earlier. For example, Lenzoto paid common miners or hewers only 10 kopecks more a day in 1912 (1.5 rubles a day) than it had paid in 1895 (1.4).[65]

Other aspects of the wage question clarify the problem. For example, Lenzoto paid helpers a wage of 1.35 rubles per day for a yearly average salary, computed at 311 workdays, of almost 420 rubles. Most miners were paid from 1.50 to 1.70 rubles, which yielded annual average salaries of 512 rubles.[66] Governor Bantysh suggested in 1911 that "with the most careful figures, counting only the barest necessities for workers to maintain their ability to work, the sum of [their] expenses would run 414 rubles 14 kopecks per person per year." Others figured minimum living expenses at closer to 450 rubles. Wives and children further complicated the issue since women's and children's wages, for those who worked, fell far below minimum individual subsistence levels. When one adds in other expenses such as transportation costs to and from the Lena system, living costs for nonworking wives and children (Lenzoto hired only a minority of such people), and any accidental needs or pay cuts (for illness or fines), the picture becomes grim.[67]

Furthermore, the company increasingly resorted to paying workers in illegal coupons (*talony*), redeemable only in company stores. From 1910 to 1912 coupon payments averaged well over 10 percent and sometimes reached 22 percent of monthly payments. Workers sold coupons at a 20 percent discount or used them for high-priced goods in company stores that gave no change for balances due. Lenzoto also withheld increasing proportions of workers' salaries without interest till the end of the year—by September 1911 almost half a million rubles. In open violation of a 1908 law, Lenzoto also held salary reserves past the end of the work year for workers who signed new contracts, a sort of renewal penalty. Only in 1911, after years of constant pressure from Governor Bantysh, did the company cease this last practice. In its own report, Lenzoto referenced its belated relinquishment of the withheld salaries to the "Irkutsk Mining Administration's enforcing decree of 22 December 1910." The report failed to mention the law's 1908 origins, about which Bantysh had informed them on numerous occasions. Despite cost-of-living raises of 5 percent a year between 1908 and 1912, Lenzoto's average yearly wages actually fell in this period by about twelve rubles. In Lenzoto's recently purchased mines, pay reductions tripled and quadrupled that amount, a factor in the outbreak and stubbornness of the 1912 strike. Manukhin also noted that Kirensk and Cheremkhov coal miners received up to double overtime pay, whereas Lenzoto offered only regular wages.[68]

Closely tied to the wage question were the cost, availability, and quality of food. Company stores stocked food of normal quality but charged prices more than twice as high as in Moscow for many essential items (see table 2.6). (Lenzoto charged low prices for meat and fish because protein was essential for the miners.) In effect, Lenzoto took back much of what it paid out, earning profits in the process (277,000 rubles in 1910). Lenzoto also issued foodstuffs as part of workers' monthly wages. Here questions of quality arose constantly, with workers claiming that cabbage and potatoes were frozen and meat and fish spoiled. They also claimed that they sometimes received horsemeat, violating regulations and Russian cultural standards. The company vehemently denied these charges but most outside observers confirmed them. Government inspectors claimed that the warehouses were well appointed with appropriate meat storage. When meat or fish had begun to spoil from too lengthy storage or had suffered in shipment, the company evidently issued it to workers as salary replacements. A

Table 2.6

COMPARISON OF FOOD COSTS IN LENA AND MOSCOW, 1912

Food item	Lena prices (in rubles)	Moscow prices (in rubles)
Bread, rye	2.20	1.29
Butter	19.20	18.00
Fish, fresh	9.60	14.04[a]
Fish, salted	7.40	10.08[a]
Flour[b]	4.40	1.80
Meat, fresh	6.60	8.18
Oil, cooking	12.00	5.15
Salt	2.20	0.40
Sugar	10.00	5.20

Sources: GARF, F. 1186, op. 1, d. 42, l. 19; *Pravda o lenskikh sobytiiakh,* 27; Lebedev, *Vospominaniia* (1957), 21; *Rossiia 1913 god. Statistiko-dokumental'nyi spravochnik* (St. Petersburg, 1995), 317–18.
Note: All prices are for 1 pud, which equals 16.38 kg or about 36 lbs.
[a]Price is an average of several types of fish available in Moscow markets.
[b]Probably wheat.

shortage of warehouse clerks forced workers to stand in lines outside even in winter. Company kitchens were small, unsanitary, and also had long lines.[69] Quality and quantity aside, workers lacked control over proportions of wages withheld until years' end, received in illegal company store coupons, or issued in high-priced low-quality foodstuffs. The fact was that in the Lena region an honest day's work did not guarantee an honest day's wage.

HEALTH, SCHOOLS, AND HOUSING   Health care was one area where Lenzoto had made recent improvements. Company officials lauded Lenzoto for its full complement of hospitals and clinics and medical personnel. According to the company, six doctors, one for each thousand workers, exceeded availability for most of the empire's inhabitants. In fact, only by 1911, after Governor Bantysh threatened legal action, had the company complied with existing regulations by expanding its cadre of doctors from one to six. Bantysh's official 1910 report claimed that the abominable medical facilities and care "cause dangerous dissatisfaction among workers, capable of leading to altogether undesirable consequences." This dire report finally induced the government to force Lenzoto to improve its health facilities. Even so, problems persisted. Two years later, Tul'chinskii found that in cases of serious job-related injuries during 1910 and 1911, company doctors routinely underestimated the extent of disabilities. For example, a certain

Ivan Shchadrin had an 80 percent disability according to the government doctor and 0 percent disability according to the company doctor. In his 1911 railroad survey, Boltunov reported that the gold industry "views health care only as a burden imposed at the insistence of District Engineer [Tul'chinskii]."[70]

Although Manukhin rated the medical facilities as adequate, he found many code violations.[71] His findings also contradicted Lenzoto's self-congratulatory remarks about its health care. For example, during 1910, with only one doctor in attendance, two-thirds of male workers experienced treatable illnesses, as did women at an even higher rate. Illness and trauma caused 94 deaths, a high mortality given the population's youth and the absence of large mining disasters. Although not exposed to mining hazards, women died at more than twice the rate of men. During 1911, of a population of 7,000, Lenzoto health facilities had treated 32,938 ambulatory patients for a total of 75,528 visits and had hospitalized 4,876 people for an average of ten days. Six percent of hospitalized patients and 22.5 percent of ambulatory patients had gastrointestinal disorders, suggesting that statistically every worker suffered such problems, directly connected with food quality, several times a year. The balance of patients suffered physical traumas (i.e., mining injuries), lung disorders (an occupational hazard), and infectious diseases. Comparisons with an earlier era, when the region's mining had taken place on the surface and during summer, are problematic. Still, statistics highlight increased mortality and illness by 1910–12. For instance, during 1889 more than 14,000 Lena workers experienced roughly 4,500 illnesses requiring hospitalization and 54 deaths, rates strikingly lower than in 1910–11. The health situation placed a burden on Lenzoto, to which it responded only belatedly and under extreme pressure. Senator Manukhin also seconded Tul'chinskii's complaint that medical personnel depended solely on Lenzoto and lacked regular government medical supervision.[72]

As regards educational facilities, as of 1910 Lenzoto operated five schools, usually with two teachers each, at various locales with a total of 223 students. In 1894 Lenzoto's single school had had 27 students. As Lenzoto purchased rival companies, the number of schools in its domain increased. Commentators claimed that most pupils were children of white-collar employees and that workers' children were often turned away for lack of space. The company hired far more mine workers' children for menial tasks at forty kopecks a day than it placed in schools.[73]

The barracks that domiciled most Lena workers, and their wives and children, provided no surcease from their travails. Nothing elucidated Lenzoto's post-1902 penchant for skirting or violating labor laws than the issue of living quarters. These rough wooden structures, without foundations and mostly originating from the 1890s, housed an abnormal mixture of unmarried and married workers with wives and children. The post-1900 arrival of many workers with their families accentuated the psychologically demoralizing and physically unhealthy situation. After his 1911 inspection Governor Bantysh wrote: "I was simply shocked by the workers' quarters. . . . Extracting millions in profit from the workers' labor, Lenzoto does not consider itself obliged to provide even bearable living quarters and completely ignores the regulations' elementary hygienic and sanitary standards." The structures' uncaulked hewn wooden walls allowed moisture to leak inside, so that inhabitants sleeping next to outside walls often awoke with their hair frozen to the boards. The bare cubicles were so overcrowded that people occupied the corridors. Married families got cubicles of roughly seven by fourteen feet, but such cubicles usually housed one or two unmarried workers as well for a total of five to seven people. Inspectors found that one set of 103 barracks, 88 of which were unfit for winter habitation, provided its roughly four thousand inhabitants with only 76 percent of the legally required living space.[74]

Lenzoto's own carefully framed 1912 defense claimed that the "enforcing decree . . . [on minimum living space] only came into being in 1909," a semantic that ignored the law's much earlier provenance. The law required 1.5 cubic *sazheni* (roughly 1.25 cubic yards) per person and 3 cubic sazheni (2.5 cubic yards) for families of two adults and up to two children under twelve. Lenzoto estimated that one group of fifteen hundred mining families had 0.97 sazheni per worker, less than ⅔ of the legal requirement and even worse than the government had reported. The company claimed that despite its "annual expenditure of considerable sums of money on the construction of new barracks and the repair of old ones, it had not yet succeeded in bringing the living space for the mining population into agreement with . . . the law." It was difficult, Lenzoto's management continued, for the company to "struggle effectively against a certain overcrowding in the barracks, especially as the number of hired workers increases."[75] Increases in the workforce, however, reflected the company's own expansion.

The company claimed to have spent 302,458 rubles between 1907 and 1911 to build or repair barracks.[76] This "considerable" sum equaled less than the company's food store profits for the same period (more than 350,000 ruble for 1908–11). Furthermore, 84 percent of the expenditures occurred at six new mines to construct barracks, without which the mines could not function. Only piecemeal improvements occurred at existing barracks. Mining inspectors observed that several new or renovated barracks were quite acceptable whereas all the rest were deplorable.[77]

Lenzoto claimed that barracks were in bad shape because "few carpenters were available," an assertion bordering on the surreal since the company could hire carpenters as it wished and, in any case, many workers had such skills. Lenzoto also claimed that its "constant attempts" to expand living space were frustrated by state mining inspectors' insistence that the company hire everyone who arrived in September. This last was positively malevolent since the company hired on site in September, in essence forcing workers to accept the work contract's onerous conditions. The alternative would have been to send the unemployed home by foot in the worsening weather.

The overcrowding adversely affected workers' daily lives. People cooked, smoked, argued, chatted, and tried to rest; children dashed about; there was an incessant clamor; clothes hung everywhere. The damp, smoky, odoriferous atmosphere weighed even on peasants used to close quarters. In one early 1912 inspection, inspectors found code violations with regard to inadequate ventilation and lack of separate space for washing and drying but observed that, despite the harsh conditions, the "workers maintain cleanliness" in their living quarters. During the summer some workers escaped the barracks by building lean-tos nearby, where they withdrew "to the dacha." (Donbass workers did the same.) The intermingling of unmarried males with married couples and adolescent girls led to quarrels and fights. This peaked on winter holidays, when workers, bent on relaxation, remained indoors. They drank, sang, and become amorous. In the words of a mining inspector, such holidays became "Babylonian orgies."[78]

Work Conditions in the Mines

Conditions in the mines also constituted a daunting problem. I. N. Gorbunov of Manukhin's investigatory commission reported that "over the entire works lies a stamp of incompleteness and primitiveness. Everything is . . . temporary, makeshift." The company had "not built a single substantial structure," and it carried out excavations "with the least possible expense and then moved on." Although Lenzoto had built a seventeen-mile railroad in the mining area and used electric elevators to haul out ore in some large mines, its basic mining technology was outmoded. For example, Lenzoto had not introduced cyanide processing of gold ore, an efficient technique used in the Urals by the turn of the century. In general, the mining sites were simply primitive. Support beams in the mine shafts were inadequate; ladders were rickety and unlit; and the mines had no resting or sanitary facilities. Most lacked mechanical ventilation, a problem because of the constant use of dynamite, fumes of which caused headaches and nausea, and also because of the off-shift use of heating devices to melt the permafrost. At the start of the workday, miners sometimes collapsed into unconsciousness from the accumulated gases and had to be dragged to the surface. Many shafts were "wet mines," in which dripping water flooded the floors and soaked the workers to the skin. Lenzoto provided no protective clothing, so that in winter, when miners exited for lunch or had to walk home several miles after work, they were cloaked in ice. The total lack of sanitation facilities at the mines created an indescribable miasma, far exceeding the insalubrious Donbass conditions. These factors help explain the abysmal health problems of Lena workers.

Because of the harsh work conditions, Lenzoto conceded a de facto ten-hour day in dry shafts, despite the contracted eleven hours, and in wet mines eight hours, work being unproductive thereafter. Regardless, long trips to and from mines and the company's refusal to count midday breaks as work hours meant that miners spent twelve to fourteen hours away from the barracks.[79] The use of guards and overseers in the mines had expanded to such a degree—one for every ten miners—that Governor Bantysh had blocked further such hiring, complaining that it only heightened tensions. Bantysh's 1910 report counted three policemen, eleven mounted guards, and sixty-nine on foot, not to mention numerous overseers. The company applied fines for serious offenses such as the "toting" of nuggets and insubordination, as well as for less serious ones, such as lateness. Workers complained that supervisors routinely levied fines indiscriminately, significantly lowering their already pitiful incomes. Chief Mining Engineer Tul'chinskii's 1910 report, a particularly scathing one as regards Lenzoto, indicates that during 1910 the company imposed fines of 2,875.35 rubles. If accurate, the company was imposing fines at a lower rate by this time than back in the 1890s, although the number of workers fined in 1910 was quite high. Still, given the wage problems and constant inflation, the 1910 level may have imposed a greater burden than the 1890 level. In comparison, during the last year of its existence (1911), the Industrial Company imposed minuscule fines (a total of 186 rubles).[80]

During the Belozerov regime, company employees routinely denigrated workers and sometimes inflicted physical abuse. Workers universally complained that employees sexually harassed and exploited womenfolk. Stories continued to circulate about Belozerov's "seignorial rights" over the women. Regardless, the company employed women and adolescents at quite low wages to carry out filthy, arduous tasks. Manukhin and other commentators noted the astounding nature of women's employment at Lenzoto. "The enforced labor of women is practiced nowhere else in Russia," commented the senator. Yet, as a condition of bringing their families with them, workers had to agree, on pain of dismissal, to allow wives and all adolescent children to work for Lenzoto at tasks and for pay of the company's choosing. Workers complained to the Manukhin Commission that the company routinely forced them to work on days of rest and holidays. Inspectors confirmed this and insisted that this allowed workers insufficient rest, given the arduous nature of the work. The threat of mining accidents further contributed to the grim atmosphere. During 1911, 869 mining accidents killed seven people, permanently disabled one, temporarily disabled twenty-four, and accounted for thousands of traumas. Lenzoto also continued the practice or firing workers during the winter, when travel was impossible and no work was to be found.[81]

Tul'chinskii continually warned of the "heavy . . . tense atmosphere" at the mines (1910 report). He denied accusations from the company and certain high government officials that he "paid no attention to Lenzoto's interests." He insisted instead that "the harsh conditions of work and life and Lenzoto's constant ignoring of all recommendations . . . reflect badly on mining in the region" (1912 report). In the final analysis, at fault were both the policies of the higher Lenzoto administration and Belozerov's exceptionally inhumane attitude. Page after page, mining inspectors' reports listed violations of laws, codes, the work contract, and basic human norms. After a lengthy visit during 1911, Lenzoto director Ginzburg had "promised on his part to take necessary steps to eliminate . . . violations." Perhaps Ginzburg's promise ran afoul of the superb profits that year; in any case his visit brought no improvements. As regards Belozerov, Tul'chinskii recognized "the necessity for discipline in mining work," but added the mining engineer indignantly, "ridicule of labor enters into the entire Belozerov system" (1909 report). Furthermore, he continued, Belozerov "dislikes any independent attitude and ignores . . . the district mining engineer." The acting director was "very short with all local officials . . . [but] seemed well informed about the mood in Petersburg."[82]

The Working Population

Like workers elsewhere in Russia, Lena miners were overwhelmingly peasants. Most were contracted laborers from various parts of the empire, although a small proportion (between 1 and 2 percent) were political exiles. As of 1911–12, 57 percent were from European Russia and 43 percent from Siberia and Central Asia; more than 80 percent were from areas of Siberia and European Russia most accessible to the Lena-Vitim system. The workforce reflected the extraordinarily onerous working conditions. Adolescent and older workers rarely labored in the mines, almost three out of four workers being between twenty-one and forty. Likewise, employment time in the mines was brief. As of 1911–12 fully three-quarters of Lenzoto miners were in their first, second, or third year of employment (by the fourth year most left). Women as such were not hired, although wives and daughters of miners were obliged to work at Lenzoto's wish. Lena workers were equally balanced between literate (41.7 percent) and illiterate (41.3 percent), with no information for the rest. Of 4,383 male mine workers surveyed, 73 percent were married and 27 percent single. By this time company policy encouraged the hiring of married workers as being more stable. Of the married workers, about half had families with them. Along with males, 1,615 women and 2,383 children resided in the barracks. In addition, the two hundred to three hundred families who had arrived without company permission lived in earthen huts in awful conditions. As of early 1912, Lenzoto employed 5,514 workers, including women and adolescents, a statistic that yields the additional data that well over 3,000 unemployed women and children depended on the meager earnings of male family members.[83]

The Lena workforce shared many characteristics with other industrial areas. The roughly 50 percent literacy rate for Lena workers in 1911–12 was somewhat lower than for Russia as a whole, where workers had achieved this rate by 1897. Although literacy statistics for Donbass miners and workers are not available, the information Theodore Friedgut adduces about the Donbass labor force suggests considerable similarities with that of the Lena minefields. For example, around the turn of the century, Donbass miners were 99.6 percent Russians and 98.3 percent peasants, the overwhelming majority were under forty years of age, and there was a sizable preponderance of males over females, all highly reminiscent of Lena workers. With caution, one may surmise that literacy rates were also similar. Friedgut's and McCaffray's data show that Donbass metallurgical workers were a cut above mining workers in skills, salaries, and living conditions.[84] A similar differentiation existed at Lenzoto between the miners and the skilled workers located mostly at the Nadezhdinsk workshops. On the one hand, the degree of desperation implied in taking on life and work in far eastern Siberian mines suggests depressed sociocultural characteristics. On the other, the sprinkling of political exiles on the Lena, presumably not present in the Donbass, might have created a countervailing tendency. Perhaps the two canceled one another out.

Although Lenzoto's early history suggests nothing remarkable in entrepreneurial intrepidity or worker relations, by the 1890s clever management and quite modern worker relations had turned things around. By the new century, heavy acquisitions led to indebtedness and the threat of bankruptcy. Government bailouts and new management, especially in the person of the new acting director, Belozerov, altered the tone of post-1902 Lenzoto operations, especially as regards workers. What resulted was the Belozerov regime, during which employment at Lenzoto was tantamount, in Boltunov's phrase, to "penal hard labor" (*katorzhnyi trud*), dangerous to health and life. The government's desire to acquire as much gold as possible for the state treasury in association with the gold standard was an operative factor, along with heavy investments by prominent personages. Local management wrung huge profits out of the company's undertakings. In return, top management and high officials worked hand in glove in the capital to sanction unethical and often illegal company practices and routinely subvert attempts to correct things. For instance, Tul'chinskii received a series of verbal and written reprimands from the trade and industry minister for alleged overzealousness in his complaints against Lenzoto. The Interior and the Trade and Industry ministers also complained about Bantysh's alleged overconcern with the company's workers. Even so august a personage as a provincial governor received the stamp of disapproval from above if he attempted to aid the workers. As for workers, by signing the contract they fell into a trap defined both by the physical impossibility of abandoning the mines and the inhumane terms of the contract. Moved by ethical motivations and outright fear, some officials attempted to intervene and repeatedly warned against potential "unpleasant consequences" of Lenzoto's practices. Tul'chinskii initiated his barrage of complaints about Lenzoto during 1909. In his 1910 report he averred that, in view of current conditions, "even in the nearest future one can expect highly undesirable complications in worker-Lenzoto relations." In their 1911 reports, both Governor Bantysh and Chief Engineer Tul'chinskii specifically warned about the likelihood of a serious strike if something were not done. The interventions and warnings of several years went unheeded. Indeed, even after the 1912 shooting the Council of Ministers' internal report emphasized that "it is possible . . . to state with absolute certainty that the 1912 [Lena] strike was completely unexpected." With blithe inaccuracy, the council's report insisted that "the very first reports" of Lenzoto misdeeds, which the Council of Ministers now conceded to be true, had come to the attention of the Ministry of Internal Affairs "only in 1911."[85]

The History of Worker Unrest in the Lena Region, 1842–1912

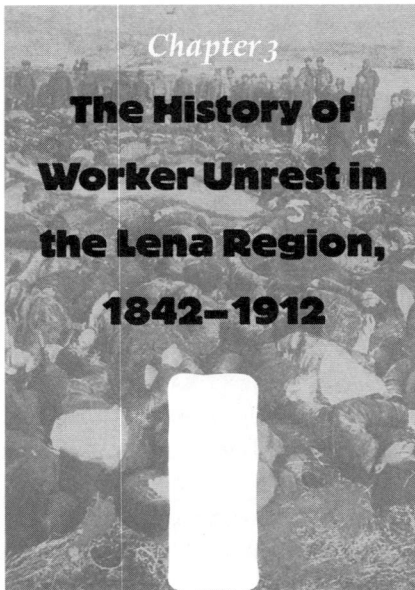

n his report about the April 1912 tragedy, Senator Manukhin wrote that the "Lena gold-mining workers' strike was not a new phenomenon and not accidental." The prehistory of the 1912 events supports both aspects of his contention. In its account of the 1904 strikes in the Lena mines, the Blagoveshchensk Church chronicle commented that workers' desire to improve their material conditions was not the whole story of the strikes:

> The cause of the strikes has to be sought at a deeper level, in those abnormal relations created between those who hire workers and the workers, especially in such remote places as the taiga. Workers arrive here from home, from distant Russia, often chased from the homeland by hunger and other hardships. Arriving here hungry and cold, they agree to all conditions. . . . They have no idea what recompense they will receive for their labor. And then, after a few months, it dawns on them that, without additional income, their wages don't even cover basic support. At this point certain misunderstandings arise [claimed the church chronicle with blessed understatement]. They purchase supplies at the company store, where some clerk, in the interests of the company, gives no choice of meat, hands out bread that is often half-baked, and so forth. From experience the workers know that it is useless to complain because here they simply tell you to quit if you don't like things. . . . And so begins the strike. . . . The strikes here usually have an economic character.[1]

The Blagoveshchensk priests, longtime witnesses of worker-management conflicts, captured the specifics of the workers' situation in the remote taiga. Acute economic hardship, the unimaginable remoteness of the mines, and the resulting utter worker helplessness, or put another way, workers' utter dependence on the very people who caused their travails, constituted the underlying characteristics of strikes in the Lena gold-mining region.

Until the 1890s, miners' protests were completely unorganized and sometimes stormy. In his 1898 study, Semevskii remarked that most worker resistance was "passive" in that it consisted of workers simply fleeing the mines. In essence, workers voted with their feet, as physically hazardous and fraught with criminal consequences as this mode of protest was. Beginning in the 1830s and 1840s Siberian mine workers, at the time mostly in Western Siberia, created quite a record of mutinies and strikes. Since most of that era's West Siberian enterprises were state owned and the laborers were possessional (tied to the enterprise) or were serving terms at exile, the government invariably responded forcibly, as the law required. For example, the government employed military force against the 1842 uprisings throughout the Eniseisk mining region to the west of the Lena system. After summary trials in military courts, the authorities, according to one commentator, "cruelly punished" those involved. Thereafter "a lengthy quiet prevailed" in the Siberian mines. This relative calm, punctuated by occasional protests, prevailed in West Siberian gold mines well into the 1900s. The disorders that occurred normally found their cause in personal conflicts between the miners and individual mining administrators or government officials. They usually took the form of short-lived rampages, some drunkenness, raids on liquor supplies, and occasional attacks on offending officials. On the whole, the scattered nature of the West Siberian mines precluded concerted action.[2]

The same cannot be said of gold mining in Eastern Siberia where mines were often concentrated in a particular district and where conditions were remarkably challenging. As a result, collective protests in the region increased steadily, if not at first alarmingly. Even so, during the 1870s and early 1880s "disorders" in Eastern Siberia and, in particular, in the Olekminsk region were not unlike those of Western Siberia. They were mostly spontaneous and brief, if sometimes violent. For example, during 1872 several workers at one Olekma mine refused to be transferred to another mine owned by the same company. The local police officer blamed the episode on the poor conditions in the first mine, which had not lived up to the owners' expectations in terms of profitability. That same year, when a Cossack detachment arrested a worker at the Sibiriakov, Bazarov, and Nemchinov Company mines, his companions forcibly freed him. In another incident, 120 miners at the Trapeznikov mines refused to report to work in protest of poor conditions. During 1873, at another Olekma mine, a group of drunken workers attacked the Cossack detachment in its living quarters and severely beat two Cossacks involved in the earlier arrest of a worker. In the fray one miner was killed. Such episodes continued from time to time over the next decades, even leading to the deaths of one or two detested mine owners and administrators. Citing the Trapeznikov sit-down strike, the Irkutsk chief of gendarmes complained during the 1870s about the miners' "impudent and willful manner. . . . After hearing that the governor-general [Sinel'nikov] . . . accepts complaints from everyone," continued the police chief, "the mine workers have become so spoiled they won't even obey the local police [or] fulfill their work quotas." Still, in his 1898 study of labor in Siberian mines, Semevskii noted the rare and isolated nature of such occurrences.

By the late 1880s observers noticed a new type of worker protest in the Lena mining region: the organized strike. In such episodes, instead of venting their frustrations in outbursts of violence, workers simply refused to work until the elimination of certain irritants or violations. McCaffray notes a similar gradual rise in organized strikes among Donbass coal miners during the 1880s and then a much steeper one during the 1890s.[3] In the Siberian gold mines, this phenomenon coincided with the disappearance from the mines of hard-labor prisoners and the gradual decline of political-exile workers. Replacements came in the form of workers, mostly from European Russia or Western Siberia, who had the same experiences, culture, and consciousness as those of the Donbass coal miners. In truth, by the 1900s workers from all parts of Siberia were also "strike-prone," as Ginzburg commented to Belozerov in reply to the latter's suggestion during 1904 that they hire only Siberian workers.[4]

According to Manukhin, the organized strikes, as opposed to past stormy protests, "did not violate order at the mines. The strikes often ended quickly when the mine owners yielded to the workers' more substantial demands." For example, in 1886 the entire work force at one Olekma mine struck for ten days to protest spoiled meat they had received. During 1895 workers at another mine struck because the administration wanted them to work at night at a surface site under electric lights, whereas the workers insisted that the dimness made it impossible to see the gold nuggets that brought a small reward. Semevskii counted a total of only forty-five significant episodes of worker protest throughout the entire Siberian gold-mining industry between 1870 and 1895. This was, he pointed out, hardly a grave threat to order or production before the turn of the century.[5]

Undoubtedly the ubiquitous early presence of Cossack detachments at or near mining sites and the draconian punishment sometimes inflicted on workers dampened worker enthusiasm for strong measures of their own. Furthermore, existing legislation, which the companies made known to workers, forbade concerted action on the part of workers. In other words, strikes were illegal and could carry highly undesirable consequences, although most did not. For example, 1874 mining legislation stated that "in cases where workers in privately owned gold mines openly disobey the administration in large groups, as well as in cases of uprisings or insurrections, the mining police can call in military force for help." Those detained, if they were not political exiles, could not be subjected to corporal punishment but instead must be turned over to the courts.[6] The restriction on corporal punishment for hired laborers aside, these and other such laws would have given pause to workers who wished to "disobey administrators" by refusing to go to work. In summarizing all pre-1895 worker protest, Semevskii noted the following chief causes: excessive work quotas, poor food, inadequate wine portions, insufficient pay, and "cruel treatment on the part of mine employees and owners." A less frequent but also notable cause concerned various inappropriate behaviors on the part of local mining and police officials.[7] In essence, these same problems underlay Olekminsk region labor unrest during the early 1900s as well.

The turn of the century witnessed worker tumult in all of European Russia, Siberia, and, of course, the Lena gold-mining region, which had already distinguished itself for a significant, although not extensive, strike movement in comparison to the rest of Siberia. In 1901 and again in 1904 a series of strikes broke out in Lena mines belonging to the Bodaibo Company, the Industrial Company, Lenzoto, and the Rat'kov-Rozhnov firm. These few companies comprised much of the Vitim mining system, until, of course, Lenzoto bought out all competitors or obtained leases to their mines. Contemporary commentators agreed that the 1901 and 1904 strikes were entirely economic. For example, on 2 January 1901 more than a thousand Lenzoto miners at one site refused to work and issued their written demands through their elected deputies, as specified by law. (Although strikes were still illegal, the law codes extended workers the right to elect deputies to speak for them.) The strikers demanded ⅔ of monthly salaries in money and ⅓ in provisions, the sale by private individuals of food in the mining areas, and the firing of several mine employees and a police officer. In addition, the workers' petition noted certain pay irregularities. In the presence of company officials and worker representatives, the chief mining engineer certified the complaints, after which the company made concessions, ending the seven-day strike uneventfully. Encouraged by these results, the very next day workers at a nearby Bodaibo Company mine struck with demands for increased pay and the firing of several rude employees. The company's management (the director was none other than Belozerov) offered token concessions, after which the workers threatened to quit en masse after a payoff. Quitting in this manner was allowed neither by tsarist law, which required two weeks' notice, nor by Lena region work contracts, which outright forbade quitting. Belozerov called in the Cossacks and prepared all pay books for a full settling. Their bluff called, the workers accepted the company's previous concessions and returned to work. During the first half of 1901, administrators' often substantive concessions quickly ended several other strikes.[8] After two years of relative quiet in the region, roughly the same scenarios repeated themselves in 1904. Between March and May of that year, several mines of Lenzoto, the Industrial Company, and Rat'kov-Rozhnov struck. This strike wave began at Lenzoto's Prokop'evsk mine, which in 1901 had belonged to the Bodaibo Company and which had struck then as well. Since Belozerov had by then moved to Lenzoto, the Prokop'evsk workers confronted the same manager. On 2 March 1904, 800 miners struck with demands about eliminating several mine guards and overseers and with complaints about inadequate provisions and poor quality tools. When the workers refused concessions, the company prepared for a full settling of accounts, in essence a release of the work force. Ultimately, most workers returned to work and the rest were fired. These latter workers were mobilized into the army and, allegedly through Belozerov's malevolent intervention, sent to the front to fight the Japanese. At Lenzoto's flagship Feodosievsk mine, 730 workers abandoned the workplace after the administration ignored several demands, including the firing of several mine employees. The state mining officials found the complaints unjustified and persuaded the miners to resume work with no concessions. At the same time, 650 Rat'kov-Rozhnov miners struck with substantive demands about pay, living conditions in the barracks, and rude officials. In this case, officials found the complaints justified. Most were acceded to and within three days the strike ended successfully for the workers.

On 12 April, more than 1,200 workers at the Industrial Company's Andreevsk mine struck over inadequate food, inaccurate work book accounts, and the rudeness (*gruboe obrashchenie*) of several overseers. At the strike's outbreak, the administrators quit issuing food, placing the miners, many with families, in an exceptionally difficult position. About a thousand workers set out for Bodaibo to obtain supplies but found their way blocked by a river crossing flooded by the spring thaw. Tensions mounted as sixty armed guards arrived at the mine site "to prevent disorders." The mining police chief attempted to disperse two large crowds of workers. When they united into one group and confronted the armed guards, the police chief ordered the firing of a volley over the heads of the workers. One worker was wounded and the rest dispersed to their barracks. The strikers accepted the concessions offered and, on 17 April, resumed work.

The 1904 strikes, especially at the Industrial Company's Andreevsk mines, were notably well organized under the leadership of experienced elected strike deputies (*vybornye*).[9] The Andreevsk strike also witnessed the most serious conflict between miners and armed guards of the entire period. In composite, the 1901 and 1904 strikes, especially the one at Andreevsk, eerily foreshadowed the tragedy of a decade later—rather like dress rehearsals minus the final act.

How state and company officials responded to these first concerted strike movements of the Lena region is illustrative. This is especially the case as regards Belozerov, who managed companies that experienced strikes during 1901 and 1904 and who, of course, managed Lenzoto in 1912. After both the 1901 and the 1904 events, high officials from the Irkutsk procurator's office arrived to investigate the underlying causes. The reports of these investigators, who could hardly be accused of a proworker bias, nonetheless convinced a series of state mining officials that the strikes were on the whole peaceable and entirely economic. Indeed, the state mining authorities often, but not always, found the miners' demands to have been justified. In several cases, the Irkutsk general procurator charged the companies with various violations, including illegally paying workers significant proportions of their wages "in goods from company stores . . . at quite high prices instead of in money." At an August 1901 conference dedicated especially to that year's strike movement, the Irkutsk governor concluded that "the disorders among workers occurred entirely for economic reasons, primarily because of conflicts about salary payoffs between workers and employees. The disorders usually ended quickly and work resumed, leaving hardly a trace on local life." At that point the Irkutsk district judge, on the basis of several weeks' personal direct observation of the mines, found the word "disorders" inapplicable since the workers' complaints had often been justified and their behavior acceptable. That same year the Irkutsk procurator sent a letter to the governor noting that the recent strikes at Lenzoto's mines "had not been characterized by any socialist propaganda." Consequently, he found it "undesirable" to bring criminal charges against any participants. Legally speaking, until 1905 all strikes were, to put the best face on the matter, extralegal, placing striking workers in legal jeopardy. Yet in this instance the very government officials responsible for enforcing law and order blamed the mine owners and administrators rather than the workers and refused to intervene other than on behalf of the miners. Meanwhile, rather than espousing repression to end strikes, the assistant procurator suggested "reorganizing the mining inspectorate and establishing better control over administration-worker relations in the mines."[10] This comment was fraught with implications for the future. Subsequently the Irkutsk mining inspectorate took seriously the procuracy's 1901 recommendations. Unfortunately, other government officials, not to mention company administrators, had different views of "administration-worker relations."

With regard to the 1904 strikes, the procurator concluded that measures taken by the state mining officials had brought the strikes to a conclusion "in a peaceful manner." The police chief additionally noted the complete absence of any indications of political agitation in association with the strikes. Manukhin later observed that the 1901–1904 strikes reflected virtually identical lists of familiar complaints. These included inadequate salaries, work contracts that violated existing laws, inaccurate issuing of pay, illegal payment with products and coupons rather than cash, the impossibility of filing individual complaints out of fear of being fired, and the rudeness of company administrators and employees. Complaints about the quality and quantity of food also arose, as specially noted by Manukhin.[11]

If Irkutsk mining and police officials consistently emphasized the workers' relatively peaceful deportment and the justness of their complaints, some police officers at the mining sites described the events differently. During December 1901 private entrepreneurs and government mining inspectors and engineers gathered for the fourth congress of Lena region gold-mining industrialists. Given what had occurred during the preceding year, the congress naturally paid close attention to the causes and nature of the recent strikes. Several individuals, including the Vitim mining inspector N. A. Ianche and the Olekminsk region police officer V. A. Aleksandrovich, recommended the permanent stationing of military forces in the area in order to deal with worker "disorders." Aleksandrovich felt that mine administrators and state officials had "yielded" to workers' strike demands only because, in the absence of armed forces, they were intimidated by the large crowds of angry miners. He also observed that the arrival of armed forces tended to halt worker protests. Aleksandrovich offered the opinion that the Vitim-Olekma systems had witnessed the most strikes in all of Siberia and that "most of the disorders had been stormy." The divergence between the opinions of these local police officers and the Irkutsk officials, who had concluded that the strikes were peaceful affairs brought on by genuine abuses, was acute and, even now, irreconcilable. Some local officials' testimony may have been corrupted by the individuals' financial subservience to the company. In any case, in the end, the congress rejected the arguments of the two local officials. A majority of the private entrepreneurs in attendance felt that a military force was "not especially necessary." Furthermore, the entrepreneurs noted that, given the economic recession of 1901, they could not "take upon themselves even a part of the expenses to support such a force."[12] Since subsidies for the armed forces contravened existing laws, this response, which ignored legal questions, indicates the endemically extralegal state of the region's gold-mining industry.

On a related matter, after 1901 the use of Cossack forces for strike control abruptly ended. Thereafter only conventional army units, when available, bore the responsibility for strike control. In all likelihood the workers' deep resentment of the Cossacks, as testified to by several violent episodes, induced the higher authorities to resort to other means. In a similar vein, the use of private armed guards for strike control, as occurred during the 1904 Andreevsk strike, also came to an end. This change took place in part because of the high cost of private guards and in part because several Irkutsk governors in a row pressured the companies to desist in their use. Like the Cossacks, private guards, insisted the governors, severely and unnecessarily irritated the miners. After 1904 private guards provided regular security at the mines but played no role in strike control. In late 1901 the Irkutsk authorities put in motion a plan to station 120 regular army troops at Bodaibo, directly adjacent to most Vitim mines. These troops augmented 130 soldiers of the Kirensk garrison, located roughly 747 miles away (a journey of many days).[13] Between 1901 and 1904, government authorities gradually normalized general security arrangements in the Olekminsk gold-mining region and did so at least partially in response to miners' reactions.

As for company mining administrators during the 1901 and 1904 strikes, evidence of skullduggery and bad faith exists. For example, a member of the procurator's office recalled how after the outbreak of the 1901 strikes the mining administrators and local police selected certain workers as negotiators. When these worker-negotiators spoke in defense of the workers, local officials immediately accused them of being "instigators and conspirators." They also routinely interpreted "the liveliness and outspokenness of [certain worker] deputies as signs of special unreliability."[14] In his 1904 report the procurator noted even more darkly that when state mining officials managed to end strikes peaceably "the mine administrators were quite dissatisfied." They always wanted, he recalled, "sterner measures." At the Industrial Company's Andreevsk mines (the site of the severest 1904 strike), continued the procurator, "the administrators had even prepared places in the hospital for the wounded and summoned the priest for the dying in hopes that workers would be shot." (The procurator was either an extreme cynic or had inside knowledge of the administrators' character.) The police chief recalled that, despite the absence of political agitation, local officials consistently displayed "a desire to give the strikes a political coloration."[15] Political strikes required repressive measures in tsarist practice.

Meanwhile, in his 30 May 1904 report to the Lenzoto Petersburg administration, Belozerov wrote: "In my opinion the cause of all the latest strikes . . . lies in what happened at the Industrial Co.'s Andreevsk mines, where, after this year's April strikes, the mining administrators satisfied all the workers' demands, including the firing of employees they found undesirable. . . . Such premeditated conciliationism [a phrase that would have astounded Industrial Company administrators who, according to police officials, were pushing for armed conflict] could not help but inspire worker pretensions at other mines. . . . A very dangerous situation thereby arises."

Belozerov went on to describe the "helplessness and powerlessness" of the mining officials and administrators against "the aggressive and provocative activities of the strikers in the absence of any sort of armed force."[16] Thus, in private communications with his Petersburg chiefs, Belozerov attributed "helplessness and powerlessness" to administrators and "aggression and provocation" to workers. Arguably, this stance, utterly at odds with Irkutsk officialdom's informed opinion and filled with mischievous potential, constituted the chief "dangerous situation" in the region, as 1912 would reveal.

Having negotiated the shoals of the 1901 and 1904 strikes, the workers, state mining officials, and administrators of the Lena gold-mining region engaged in no further serious disputes for several years. In his report to the emperor for the 1906–1907 period, the East Siberian governor-general wrote that "at a time of widespread strikes in European Russia, workers of the [Siberian] mining industry conducted themselves relatively calmly. . . . The few rare strikes . . . had economic causes and ended quickly."[17] Manukhin himself concluded that throughout 1905–1907 "workers of the Vitim-Olekma Mining Districts remained perfectly calm." This slightly overstates the case since during April 1905 miners of the Industrial Company struck for at least a week. According to Belozerov, the Industrial Company strikers demanded "workers' freedom": in his book, a virtually treasonous activity.[18] Whether this was a political strike on the model of the tidal wave sweeping the empire that year or whether certain administrators, as the Irkutsk procuracy claimed, saw "political coloration" in any organized worker protest is not clear.

In any case, during this same month (April 1905), Belozerov, the outspoken opponent of "premeditated conciliationism," offered his own workers a one-hour reduction in the workday to ward off a strike at Lenzoto. In his explanation to the company's Petersburg office, Belozerov dismissed the possibility of carrying out mining work with the "eight-hour workday," which, evidently, the workers were demanding. Instead, he recommended a ten-hour day. Other than this, no specific information is available about what Lenzoto miners were requesting or how they were going about making their desires known. It probably is significant, however, that just at this time government mining officials received a petition from a Lenzoto workers' deputy that referred to a recent decision of the minister of transportation to shorten the railroad workers' workday. The minister justified this action on the basis that "the twelve-hour day . . . was heavy for railroad workers," to which the Lenzoto miners' deputy responded that "we at the mines have much worse conditions." All this suggests prestrike pressures on the part of Lenzoto workers on the issue of work hours, to which Belozerov reacted with a quick concession. On 16 April, he reported to Petersburg that "shortening the workday to ten hours worked very successfully. . . . Work resumed [after the spring holidays] without a problem." Also of interest is that during April 1905, in the midst of what was a tense situation in the region's mines and at Lenzoto (as well as in all of Russia), a hectographed antigovernment proclamation turned up in the area of Lenzoto's mines. Although investigation disclosed that it originated from several clerks rather than from the workers, this marked the very first known intrusion of illegal political agitation into the Lena environment.[19] The perceived threat was evidently sufficiently severe that the flint-hard Belozerov quickly yielded with a substantive concession.

A mystery exists about how and under what circumstances Lenzoto had shortened the earlier fifteen-hour workday to eleven hours, now further shortened to ten hours. Presumably, the eleven-hour day occurred as a result of the improvements during the 1890s and because of the requirements of deep mining, which rendered longer work hours unproductive. Regardless, Belozerov's 9 April communication stated that "Lenzoto workers have no serious reasons for dissatisfaction as their situation is incomparably better than in other mines." Lenzoto workers probably would not have agreed. Still, Belozerov's remark reflected a Lenzoto management policy of carrying out some improvements in order to prevent worker protest. Later company actions revealed the merely tactical nature of this tendency.

Regardless, after 1907 the Lena mining area experienced a complete cessation of labor protest, as of course did the rest of Russia. The Belozerov regime, which blossomed unimpeded during the Stolypin era's repression and harsh economics, forced miners to accept their lot.

Table 3.1

STRIKES IN THE LENA GOLDFIELDS, 1900–1907

Year	No. of strikes	No. of participants
1900	3	1,497
1901	9	2,962
1902	1	478
1903	4	1,025
1904	6	3,965
1905	1	n.a.[a]
1906	2	258
1907	2	460
Total	28	10,645

Source: Dulov, "Zabastovochnoe dvizhenie na Lena," 32.
[a]No data available.

This included, by 1907, a renewed eleven-hour day. Shortly after his assignment to the Lenzoto mines in March 1909, Chief Mining Engineer Tul'chinskii reported to his mining administration superiors that "Lenzoto is practically ignoring obligatory regulations" in its treatment of workers.[20] Nothing really changed over the next few years. By 1912 Lena miners were the inheritors of a lengthy tradition of oppression, tensions, and as yet unmitigated justified complaints. Although workers' tenure at the mines by this era was relatively short (few chose to remain for more than three years), the long tradition of unsatisfactory worker-company relations stamped itself on workers' awareness, indeed on their very language. This ensured that when their patience broke, the resistance would be substantive.

FINAL PRESTRIKE ANALYSIS

The Blagoveshchensk parish priests pointed to "deeper causes" than material conditions for worker dissatisfaction, onerous as these conditions were. When the priests characterized the strikes as "economic," they meant to exclude politics as the origins of worker unrest. The real problem, the priests thought, lay in the workers' helplessness when they arrived at the Lena mines. This problem was not of recent provenance. At least since the 1870s observers of all kinds had criticized hiring, working, and living arrangements in the region's mines. In truth, the similarity of the descriptions over several decades all the way through 1912 is uncanny and, finally, convincing.

First and foremost, mine owners and administrators conducted themselves with utter impunity in relation to workers. Governors and governors-general toured the mines, labeled the conditions appalling, issued reprimands, and poured forth instructions and rules for improvements of every imaginable kind. Yet, few local police, mining inspectors, or other officials ever lost their positions. A common turn of phrase in evaluations was that, reprimands aside, this or that official "long stayed at his post." Nor, for that matter, did mining companies suffer the serious criminal and civil penalties threatened by the existing laws. In other word, Damocles' sword hung but never fell. The very rare cases when the wrath of a governor-general resulted in firings are instructive. The governor-general's 1886 inspection of the Olekminsk mines revealed numerous violations on the part of local mining police. These included cases of arbitrary arrests of workers against whom no charges were ever brought. This scandal resulted in the removal of the current mining inspector, who was then replaced by a certain Traskin. Unfortunately, Traskin turned out to be a taiga villain on a par with Belozerov and the gendarme captain Treshchenkov, two people implicated in the 1912 Lena tragedy.

In Semevskii's description, Traskin, "a person distinguished by habits from the era of serfdom," proceeded over the next few years to establish what might be called the "Traskin regime." He so intimidated the workers that when speaking to him they habitually "fell to their knees in front of him." His obesity prevented him from fulfilling his inspectoral and enforcement functions, which specifically required him to tour the inner reaches of all mines. Furthermore, he made no distinction between free hired workers and political exiles, although by law, corporal punishment applied only to the latter. Traskin ordered the lash for both. Especially revolting was his infliction of corporal punishment on exiled workers. For one such hapless individual he ordered 200 lashes with rods, tantamount to a death penalty. In another case, when ordering 100 lashes for a certain worker, Traskin asked the local feldsher whether this individual could withstand 100 blows, to which the medical assistant laconically replied "he can." Having thus exhausted his concept of his official duties in preventing abuses against workers, Traskin ordered the lashing. When Governor-General Goremykin made his 1891 tour, he issued Traskin a stern reprimand for his blatant derelictions of duty and outright illegalities. Goremykin did not, however, remove him from his post, although he fired the mining engineer, for whom expectations were evidently higher. Only in 1894 did Traskin change positions: he received a promotion to the position of Irkutsk police chief. Perhaps because bribes were not as prevalent in his new position, Traskin soon abandoned Siberian service entirely. Traskin, Belozerov, and others like them lend truth to one observer's

Table 3.2

FINES IMPOSED IN THE OLEKMINSK REGION

Site	Amount (in rubles)
Vitim and Olekma systems	
1885	10,679
1888	8,855
1889	9,854
Industrial Co. and Pribrezhno-Vitimsk mines	
1893–94	3,622
Lenzoto	
1893	4,357
1895	5,193

Sources: *Pamiatnaia knizhka Iakutskoi oblasti za 1891*, 111; Semevskii, *Rabochie na Sibirskikh zolotykh promyslakh*, 457.

comment that "the very word 'humaneness' seems foreign" to the East Siberian mines.[21]

While he was still in office as local police officer, Traskin publicly stated that "no fines are imposed" on workers in the Vitim system.[22] This was an outright lie (see table 3.2), and it highlights the most substantial problem confronting workers in their struggle for survival in the Lena mines. The simple fact was that in ways legal and illegal the mining companies owned the mines, the land, the facilities, utilities, transportation, and even the local government officials whose duty it was to regulate worker-entrepreneur relations. The companies also built or subsidized the building of churches and schools. More tellingly, they subsidized Cossack and, later, regular army forces maintained in the area. Even in 1912 such subsidies continued in full measure despite their illegality. The mining companies subsidized everyone in and around the mining areas. For example, during 1871 the Olekma system mining companies assigned to the mining police chief one ruble each for every worker in the system for a total of 6,000 rubles "to support the office and other expenses." In addition, they devoted another 6,000 rubles to support the Cossack unit, pay for the transport of arrestees, and so forth. The next year the companies provided no less than 30,970 rubles for the mining police chief, including 5,000 rubles to build him a new house, and for the Cossack unit. During 1880 and 1881, such sums came to 23,000 rubles and 24,000 rubles, respectively.

These amounts, primarily devoted to police functions, were further enhanced by 18,000 rubles a year for the direct support of the police officer in the Vitim system and 12,000 in the Olekma system.

Governor-General Goremykin's 1890 inspection found that as a consequence of these illegal subventions the police officers were fulfilling almost none of their duties in imposing restraints on the companies. Doubtless, living expenses were extraordinarily high in the region but the resulting situation led to obvious collusion on the part of the mining companies and those officially obligated to control them. Semevskii commented that "of course, the mining inspectors turn out to be loyal servants of the mining companies and do not defend the interests of the workers." At the same time, the individual companies were paying huge sums to government mining engineers. Lenzoto alone paid between 8,000 and 9,100 rubles a year to the Vitim system engineer during the late 1880s.[23] Senator Manukhin's 1912 report noted with bitterness the continued illegal support paid by Lenzoto to local government officials. This continued at a time when observance of legal requirements was rapidly becoming the norm in Russia. On a daily basis, workers had dealings with and depended on local officials who were simply another rank of company employee.

Irkutsk officials, who were not in Lenzoto's pay and who attempted to defend the workers' interests, were more than a thousand miles and several weeks' travel away. Their efforts to improve the situation also floundered on the blind eye Petersburg ministries turned on the abnormal situation. The same high government officials owned Lenzoto shares, served on Lenzoto's board of directors, and headed the state bank and various ministries. The stark necessity of maintaining the state gold reserves entered heavily into their calculations. Governors and governors-general, august personages in Siberia, paled in significance before the high society of Lenzoto, the Imperial State Bank, the imperial ministries, and the imperial family, let alone the highest state interest. The fate of the Lena workers was small change in these weighty equations.

Chapter 4
The Lena Goldfields
Strike and Shooting

On a wintry day in early April, far out in the Lena River basin to the northeast of Lake Baikal, a file of workers some three thousand strong marched determinedly out of the deforested hills along a road toward a company settlement on the Bodaibo River. Most walked several abreast on a road narrowed by the previous night's snowfall, as others trudged along a parallel railroad track a few yards away. Within the sparse township, a small figure in the distance waved his arms and shouted but his voice faded in the chill late afternoon air. As the miners proceeded past lengthy stables and stacks of firewood, a uniformed guard hurried forward to try to persuade them to turn off onto another road. As they rounded the stables, they came into full view of their goal, a substantial building some seven hundred feet away just the other side of a stream crossed by a wooden bridge. A company of soldiers stood in formation beyond the bridge. The workers in the lead faltered but others pushed forward from behind edging them forward.

A mining engineer familiar to the workers ran up to the growing crowd from the direction of the building. As the miners gathered around him, he begged them not to proceed. One worker handed him a petition, as hundreds of others pressed forward from the narrow road along the stables to join the mass of workers in the open area. Some leaned on a nearby fence or sat on stacks of firewood, lighting cigarettes, while the conversation continued. Just then the engineer, hearing the slip of rifle bolts, turned toward the soldiers and shouted, gesturing, for them to hold fire.

The first volley cracked the winter air and ripped mercilessly into the crowd. Bodies collapsed into the reddening snow. Workers hurled themselves to the ground. Another volley, then a third and a fourth cut into the prone bodies. When the shooting seemed to have stopped, many rose and began to walk away, but the soldiers now fired individually at their targets. After what seemed an eternity, silence prevailed, broken only by the cries of the wounded. Hundreds lay dead, dying, or injured. By morning the corpses had been removed but lurid traces on the snow still testified to the previous evening's nightmare. The tragedy of 4 April 1912 had entered the annals of late tsarist history.

IMMEDIATE CAUSES OF THE STRIKE

A simple dispute about food quality initiated the chain of events that culminated in the strike and the subsequent shooting of workers during the spring of 1912. On 25 February, the kitchen at the Andreevsk mine issued meat to workers, who immediately questioned its freshness. On the twenty-eighth a miner's wife showed some of it to a livestock expert of Tatar origin, who identified it as horsemeat, in specific, a stallion's sex organs. In essence, this added insult to injury because horsemeat was not normally consumed in Russia and was illegal as a food item to serve workers, with the character of the cut having further symbolic resonance. Indignant workers complained to local mining administrators, who allegedly told them to "eat the bad meat now and the quality would improve later," after which the miners called for a walkout and began contacting nearby mines. It is presumably at most an intriguing concidence that this was the same Andreevsk mine, at that time owned by the now-defunct Industrial Company, that had experienced the worst worker-management conflict of the 1901–1904 era. The personnel would have changed entirely and even the memory might have been lost, but the foreshadowing remains for observers to ponder. In any case, the Lena goldfields strike had begun.

The mere issuance of poor quality food hardly drove Lenzoto mine workers to the most stubborn and prolonged strike in the area's history, with such tragic results. Rather, the unacceptable meat was the proverbial back-breaking straw, an incident whose gravity hypertrophied against the backdrop of the entire recent context of life and work under the Belozerov regime. No recorded strikes at all had occurred in the Lena river basin since 1907 and none at Lenzoto mines since 1904. One can only imagine the accumulated tensions. Furthermore, participants in the negotiations quickly became aware that, amid the welter of workers' complaints and demands, the bedrock issue for them (and for Lenzoto) was salary. Lenzoto had created a system in which workers labored long and hard in abominable conditions for nothing at all. That is to say, when they left they had nothing to show for their efforts. This was worth striking for, as some informed observers had clearly foreseen.

In a 1912 internal report to stockholders, the company claimed that all meat issued to workers was "first quality" beef and that the provisioning system supplied meat identically to workers, service employees, and managerial personnel. The inherent unlikelihood of this statement, especially the assertion that managers and workers received the same meat, raises doubts about the company's veracity. Numerous worker depositions painted a different picture, in which the company often (not always, qualified the workers) issued them poor quality meat, sometimes black from age. More often than not, it was simply the picked-over remains after service personnel had taken the first choices. Fish, they said, was rotten, frozen, then half-thawed, and falling off the bone even before cooking. One Lenzoto employee, a member of the medical staff, had this to say about workers' provisioning. "Meat and fish were a luxury. Workers got fish only when administrative and white-collar personnel (*sluzhashchie*) found it undesirable. The employees would often say to workers that if they did not take the [spoiled] fish, they would not get meat." This individual had unpleasant things to say about the bread and cabbage issued to workers as well.[1]

Lenzoto's report went on to complain that the workers could not produce the horsemeat and instead had displayed a large rotten fish as proof of the company's bad provisioning. But numerous witnesses, both workers and employees, whose depositions had begun to be collected on 5 March, stated that Steppanida Zavelina, A. G. Bykov, and other Andreevsk mine workers got horsemeat. They showed it to Sh. M. Rakhimov, a livestock expert, who made the scandalous identification. During the court hearing about the case, Lenzoto officials did not contradict witnesses who identified the item as horsemeat. Instead, the company claimed, lamely, that someone "with bad intentions" had introduced horsemeat into the supplies. In all likelihood, the workers refrained from showing the meat to company officials out of fear of its being confiscated, which would have compromised their court case. Senator Manukhin's commission investigated the matter, questioned numerous witnesses, and accepted the account given by the workers. This version found substantiation in the court testimony of various company employees in the first instance and in depositions to the investigative commission in the second instance.

THE OUTBREAK

On February 29, Lenzoto acting director A. G. Teppan, a mining engineer by profession, and District Mining Inspector A. N. Galkin advised a workers' meeting to elect strike delegates and submit demands in writing.[2] That evening, Teppan wired company headquarters in Petersburg about the strike and summoned Acting Chief Mining Engineer P. Aleksandrov back from a trip. When the strike broke out, both Belozerov and Chief Mining Engineer Tul'chinskii were in Russia. The former, keeping his distance, remained there, whereas Tul'chinskii returned to face the music for an event he had feared, warned about, and striven to prevent. By his own account, Teppan appealed to the workers' good sense in asking them to return to work and submit written complaints through channels. (As early as 1904 the Blagoveshchensk priests had noted the utter uselessness of such "complaints.") In response to the workers' question, "What are we supposed to do with bad meat?" other sources have Teppan saying, "Eat the bad meat now, you'll get better later," and telling the workers, "If you don't go back to work at once, I'll fire you all." If accurate, these words would stamp him as a person of the Belozerov type. Indeed, what other type would be Belozerov's immediate subordinate? In any case, his telegram to Belozerov on February 29 confirms that he threatened to fire all strikers if they did not resume work within three days. "Workers should submit their causes of dissatisfaction in written form," stated the letter. "If they don't voluntarily return to work in three days [i.e., by 2 March], the consequence can be mass firing." This turned out, for the moment, to be an empty threat, but it reveals the stony face the top local administrators showed to workers. Beginning on 3 March, the more conciliatory Galkin, chief mining inspector, sent telegrams to his superior, Governor Bantysh, describing the strike as "economic" and "orderly." Workers held several fruitless meetings with officials, as tensions mounted, rumors flew, and Teppan continued to threaten the mass firing of all strikers. By 4 March, all the major mines and the Nadezhdinsk metalworking shops were on strike. This display of worker solidarity for the time being precluded the "mass firing" of strikers. Lenzoto could hardly fire its entire workforce. By midmonth even the "distant mines" had joined the strike, bringing Lenzoto production to a complete halt.[3]

From the outset company and state authorities urged workers to elect delegates for negotiations. Even before the 1905 legalization of strikes, tsarist law had provided for the election of worker delegates empowered to bring complaints and negotiate for workers. Between 1 and 3 March, separate meetings of the Andreevsk, Utesitsk, Aleksandrovsk, Feodosievsk, and Nadezhdinsk workers took place with the goal of choosing delegates, in this case as strike leaders. The Andreevsk workers elected Bykov (one of the first complainants), R. Zelionko, I. Romanov, and E. Mimogliadov; Aleksandrovsk miners chose Bondar',

Mal'kov, M. Lebedev, and E. Nosov; Nadezhdinsk workers—V. Via-zovoi, P. N. Batashev, D. Zhuravlev-Ivanov, and several others; the Vasil'evsk miners chose A. Sobolev, T. Solomin, and A. Gerasimenko; Feodosievsk workers chose A. G. Petukhov and A. Lesnoi; and the Ivanovsk miners elected Prokudin, Sorokin, Karpov, and so on. As one might expect, many of these individuals performed the functions of worker leaders for the next several months. Since it had long been the custom at the mines, and required by law, for workers to elect their ar-tel' or work party representatives, one can assume that they now often selected people already having leadership status.

Each mine's newly elected strike deputies then contacted their counterparts at neighboring concerns, so that even during the first days a structured strike leadership came into place. Lenzoto later viewed with suspicion the happenstance that at one of the early Andreevsk meetings, "some orator stepped forward with a sheet in his hand and began to read it to the workers." Although subject to various interpre-tations, this probably simply reflected the quick rise of strike leaders from among already respected elected worker representatives (vy-bornye).[4] Since new mines were joining the strike every day, the leaders delayed presenting general strike demands, drawing some criticism from Lenzoto administrators on this score. Some commentators noted the suddenness of the strike, so that even the workers and their leaders allegedly found it difficult to formulate a definitive list of demands on the spot.[5]

THE STRIKE LEADERSHIP AND EARLY NEGOTIATIONS

During early March meetings a coordinated strike leadership took more or less definitive shape. In doing so, at some point it transgressed what company and local government officials had expected or thought desirable when they advised the miners to elect delegates for negotia-tions. Each mine and workshop elected deputies. In addition, each bar-racks elected one or two elders to meet with the delegates and replace them if necessary. On 3 March, in secret session, the full corps of more than fifty strike delegates elected an eighteen-person strike commit-tee, which in turn selected a smaller central bureau that included E. Dumpe, G. Cherepakhin, P. Batashev, R. Zelionko and I. Popov (also known as Popov I). Workers elected some individuals into this central strike leadership who were not mine or workshop delegates. These in-cluded Nadezhdinsk worker Dumpe; Cherepakhin, an effective speaker living in the area illegally; and Popov I, a political exile employed as assistant railroad stationmaster. The first two were Social Democrats (SDs) and the last was a Socialist Revolutionary (SR). Furthermore, an informal advisory council, including, in various versions, Dumpe, Cherepakhin, I. Rozenberg (a Nadezhdinsk worker of anarchist persuasion who was also not an elected delegate), Popov I, and I. A. Budevits (a nonparty worker from Latvia), quietly laid down plans and set priorities.[6] The personnel of this advisory council and the strike committee "bureau" overlapped to such a degree as to suggest they were identical. So successful were the workers in concealing the exact names of the chief strike leaders, it is hard to identify them with certainty even now. Of alarm to company officials was that four of the overall strike leaders were political exiles and several had tenuous ties to the mines.

Politics aside, a very flexible system arose, stretching all the way from barracks elders up through mine delegates, the strike committee, and on to the bureau-advisory council. The system had the joint goals of providing firm leadership and concealing the identities of the main strike leaders from the authorities. As a result, officials and miners often spoke about a strike committee chairman, variously naming Dumpe, Batashev, Cherepakhin, Popov I, and Zelienko for the honor. In fact, even today it is by no means clear that such a position existed at that time. One eyewitness of an early meeting overheard Popov refer to Batashev as "our assistant chair" (*nash' tovarishch'- predsedatel'*) or alternatively, depending on intonation, as "our comrade, the chairperson" (*nash' tovarishch', predsedatel'*). Batashev at one point allegedly referred to "our central strike bureau" (*nashe tsentral'noe zabastovochnoe biuro*).[7] More than that cannot be said. Several strike committee members had party affiliations, as did some of the strike delegates. Also of note is that roughly two-thirds of identified strike leaders were political exiles. In view of the small number of exiles at the Lenzoto mines by this time (estimates ranged from twenty to about one hundred), this too caused concern from above.[8] The authorities soon got wind of what seemed to be a highly suspicious complex of circumstances. Numerous strike leaders were political exiles; some resided illegally in the area; and several showed up in the main leadership without having been elected as mine or workshop delegates. Perhaps not surprisingly, all this pointed at the possible "political" nature of the strike. Interesting questions arise about why workers chose leaders with known antigovernment backgrounds, sure to provoke the authorities (see chap. 5).

As the strike leadership took shape, it won the right to hold sessions at the People's Center (*Narodnyi dom*). This was a kind of cultural center and meeting hall located at the Nadezhdinsk mine, location of many Lenzoto facilities. Later in the month, People's Center manager V. K. Gorinov gave a deposition that described how on 3 March Batashev, Popov I, Dumpe, and several other strike leaders, accompanied by about three hundred workers, arrived and requested the premises for a meeting with the purpose of working out strike demands or, as they put it, "our questions." Gorinov at first refused to allow the center to be used "for a strike meeting." At one point in the discussion, he alarmed the workers by threatening to call the police. Some workers shouted, "We don't want the police!" As several leaders negotiated with Gorinov, Popov lectured the workers against any raised voices or disorderly behavior. "Gentlemen! stop yelling about the police. Anybody who is shouting must be a provocateur, we don't need any shouting," said Popov, after which he set up a patrol around the People's Center to maintain order. With the agreement of Teppan and the aid of Acting Mining Engineer Aleksandrov, an agreement was reached that allowed the workers to use the center for strike meetings. This may have been the only worker-management agreement of the entire conflict. Gorinov then described how a group of about ten strike leaders—he recalled Batashev, Popov, Dumpe, and others—sat at a table, upon which they spread papers, and discussed their affairs for about three hours. At that point the leaders told the crowd of workers to come back at 2 P.M. the next day for a general meeting. About fifteen or twenty people, evidently the entire strike committee, stayed with the top strike leaders until 10 P.M. to work out a text, which they then dispatched to Teppan. Although a potentially hostile witness, Gorinov characterized the entire affair as "quiet." "The crowd," he recalled, "conducted itself modestly."[9]

After examining the demands early on 4 March, Teppan answered that he could fulfill some of them but would have to refer others by telegram to the Petersburg management. An answer, he informed the strike leaders, could be expected in two days. The strike leaders at the People's Center the next morning received Teppan's message with some impatience. Batashev expressed annoyance that Teppan communicated with them only by written messages carried by "boys" (mal'chiki). He also wondered how it was that Teppan could approve some demands on his own authority but not others. In fact, this last does not seem unlikely. Meanwhile, more than five thousand people, virtually Lenzoto's entire workforce at the near mines plus many family members, arrived for the meeting scheduled for 2 P.M. outside the center. The crowd heard and approved the text "Our Demands," which requested the correction of numerous shortcomings in worker-company relations. These included better living conditions and food, higher pay, employment by specialty, abolition of fines, polite address, regulation of women's labor, improved medical care, and technical improvements in the mines. In addition, workers demanded the eight-hour day and the firing of certain abusive employees. Other points bound the company to feed miners during the strike, punish no one, and guarantee the status of all strike delegates.[10] The last point suggests prior strike experience among the workers or, more likely, their elected leaders. It refers to the tendency of Russian authorities, on the one hand, to advise workers to elect delegates for the orderly conduct of strikes, as required by law, and, on the other, to become suspicious of and even arrest the delegates when they tried to defend the workers' interests. In such cases, officials were known to accuse the worker leaders of being members of an "illegal secret organization," a pretext for arresting them and disrupting the given strike. During the 1901–1904 strikes the Irkutsk procuracy reported such outlooks among Lena company officials. In any case, the tactic of arresting the strike leaders ultimately played a central role in the 1912 strike and shooting.

To the workers' surprise, that very day the St. Petersburg management returned a negative reply to all demands, with only a token concession about lighting in the barracks. When the strike leaders at the People's Center got this message, they suspected that Teppan had simply fabricated the telegram since he had stipulated two days for an answer. The leaders and workers at the center agreed that Teppan was not trustworthy and voted overwhelmingly to continue the strike. By late 5 March further hard-line messages had arrived from Petersburg. Indeed, Teppan had not fabricated negative company responses. The company ordered Teppan to fire all strikers and turn off the pumps, flooding the mineshafts. Lenzoto officials in Bodaibo and Petersburg also admonished Governor Bantysh to send troops, on the basis that the workers constituted a threat to mining property. For his part, the governor firmly refused since his subordinates at the site, Aleksandrov and Galkin, both reported the strike's orderliness. On 5 March Bantysh sent an alarmed telegram to Aleksandrov and Galkin about the "possible terrible consequences" if Lenzoto "fired the 7,000 striking workers," that is, workers plus families. As responsible officer in the region, the governor was acutely aware that no shelter, food, work, nor means of travel existed in the still frozen Lena taiga. For the time being the worst did not occur. Instead, an uneasy stalemate arose.[11]

Threats not having worked, on 6 March the Petersburg Lenzoto directors offered further minor concessions. These, however, had a supercilious tone and ignored the principal problems of pay and hours. In a deposition several months later, Aleksandrov recalled how he urged the workers to accept these concessions. According to the People's Center manager, Gorinov, Aleksandrov also patiently explained that some of the workers' demands were "illegal." For instance, the eight-hour day existed nowhere in Russia. Batashev, the only leader who identified himself by name to Aleksandrov, countered that, if the demands were not met, the strike leadership would divest itself of responsibility for the workers' actions. Aleksandrov allegedly replied that "the mining police would maintain order." Aleksandrov's 24 June deposition about these matters coincides closely with that of Gorinov's on 14 March, suggesting the accuracy of both accounts.

In the end, the workers rejected what they saw as token offers and sent a telegram to Petersburg urging real concessions. In reply, Lenzoto curtly ordered that the miners return to work or risk "unfavorable consequences." Like the earlier small concessions, the threat did not work. On 9 March Lenzoto abruptly suspended negotiations, closed the People's Center, and took other punitive measures. That same day Galkin and Aleksandrov informed the Irkutsk and Petersburg authorities that the workers had formed a "strike committee" (*stachechnyi komitet*), a matter with some potential for repercussions. On 12 March, the strike leaders made a last attempt to negotiate higher wages, which drew a terse new rejection. No "additional pay, shorter work hours, or changes in hiring conditions," replied Lenzoto, could be expected. Thus ended quite inconclusively the first round of strike negotiations between the workers and Lenzoto. Workers' hopes now rested on the trusted chief mining engineer, Tul'chinskii, scheduled to return soon from leave.[12]

Meanwhile in distant Petersburg, decisions were reached and plans laid that would have far-reaching effects at the Lena mines. On 9 March, the very day when company-worker cooperation broke down, Minister of Trade and Industry Timashev wrote a crucial letter to the governor-general of Eastern Siberia, L. M. Kniazev. In this letter, the minister explained that he had been unable to act on the suggestion of Lenzoto director Alfred Ginzburg to send an objective observer to Bodaibo to ascertain whether the workers' cause was just or not. (Ginzburg, after visiting the mines the previous year, had promised that he would take steps to improve conditions there. Although nothing had come of this, it is possible that memories of what he had seen now caused pangs of conscience.) In any case, Timashev claimed that "he could not fulfill the request because the Irkutsk governor [Bantysh] insists that the strike is peaceful." Consequently, continued the minister, "there is no need to send a special person there," although, he noted with sublime hypocrisy, "an objective judgment would be useful." In his very next missive to Kniazev (date unclear, probably 11 March), Timashev explained that "I decided yesterday to request . . . the reinforcement of the military garrison at the mines . . . [because] the peaceful tendency [of the strike] is not reliable and can change at any moment." At the joint order of the two high officials, troops from the Kirensk garrison then headed for Bodaibo, where they arrived on the eighteenth. Only bad faith can explain the refusal to send an objective observer because of information that the strike was "peaceful" and then the prompt dispatch of soldiers instead because, as Timashev explained, "force may be necessary."[13] Unfortunately, an objective observer with the backing of the Lenzoto directorate was precisely what was needed, whereas additional troops were destined for mischief, as Bantysh pointed out to no avail.

CONFLICTING VERSIONS OF THE STRIKE

The foregoing account fits the widest range of evidence and opinion about the outbreak and early conduct of the strike. It therefore seems to be historically accurate. Nevertheless, it omits several noteworthy incidents and does not constitute the only version or "story" of the strike. With regard to omitted incidents, beginning on 29 February Teppan's telegrams to Petersburg emphasized the "taking out" (sniatie s raboty) of workers by strikers, a turn of phrase that implied illegal threats of violence by strikers against nonstrikers. Each mine's strike announcement prompted another message from Teppan to the effect that at that particular mine the workers had "wished to continue work but had been forced to strike" (nasil'stvenno sniaty) by emissaries from other mines or strike leaders.[14] Whether or not such incidents occurred or were serious enough to merit attention is unclear. Regardless, the telegrams themselves, with their messages about threatened violence, became artifacts of the developing strike. Additionally, during the first week or so of March, rumors spread among workers about the arrest or impending arrest of their elected strike delegates. Consequently, at one point about a hundred workers appeared at one of the mining site police stations and asked the policeman on duty if any delegates were being held there. Although told no, they expressed doubts, after which the officer allowed Batashev and Bykov, who led the group, to see the empty detainment room. On another occasion, on the basis of rumors that a passenger train contained "arrested delegates" being transferred to Bodaibo, a group of workers went to the train at the Aleksandrovsk station. Again, on being shown the cars with no arrestees, the workers left and the incident ended. Ultimately, Galkin, Aleksandrov, and, on the basis of their reports, Bantysh evaluated these incidents as "routine," "nonviolent," and "nonthreatening."[15]

However, on 8 March, Galkin and Aleksandrov, overreacting to the first reports of the train station incident, had wired Bantysh that the strike was assuming a "threatening character" and that insufficient means existed to suppress potential disorders. After further investigation, they backtracked and reemphasized the strike's peaceful, nonviolent aspect. The contemporary telegrams and reports of eyewitnesses such as Gorinov, Galkin, and Aleksandrov—the last of whom months later altered his story— repeatedly negated the existence of violence, of calls to violence, or for that matter, of antigovernment talk or slogans. As Gorinov, a company-oriented observer, put the matter on 14 March, fully two weeks into the strike: "During all this time, I have not heard a single antigovernment appeal or call to violence. The workers are peacefully inclined and seem to obey their delegates in everything."[16] Two days later, Galkin turned in a report in which he noted that a certain policeman by the name of Goriaev claimed to have heard "incendiary speeches" outside the People's Center. Galkin insisted that the speeches, many of which he had heard, had had no such character. "No violence," he asserted, "nor threats on the part of the workers" had occurred. At one gathering, four speakers read a list of economic demands and urged workers not to return to work until these demands were met. Further, they advised the workers to preserve order, not to get drunk, to be polite to company employees and police officers, and to disperse quietly and peacefully from meetings. The last speaker of the four ended the meeting by crying "Long live the strike!" to which the workers responded with a "Hurrah!" This slight violation of the injunction against raised voices hardly counted as "incendiary."[17] Regardless, company officials put a different spin on all these matters and thereby set in motion the creation of a second version of the strike.

THE STRIKE DEEPENS

From 9 March on, along with closing the People's Center, which thereby ended worker-company cooperation, Lenzoto began preparations for firing the entire workforce. The first step was to cut off food. The closing of company kitchens led to a series of complaints. On the twelfth Bantysh ordered Lenzoto to continue feeding workers. (No other sources of food were available in the region.) Fearing the consequences of the company's policies, Galkin and Aleksandrov reluctantly began to request additional troops of Bantysh since only a very small force was stationed at Bodaibo. Deprived of the option of starving the workers out, the company decided to evict them, beginning with certain individuals under suspicion as alleged strike instigators. On the fifteenth, Galkin and Aleksandrov warned the Irkutsk police chief that "mass evictions before navigation were impossible" and questioned the practicality of the whole plan. If troops from Kirensk arrived, asked Galkin, should the evictions be carried out "through repressive measures or in a way aimed at preserving the peace?" With eviction notices from Justice of the Peace Khitun, police and soldiers from the small Bodaibo garrison under the command of Captain Sanzharenko arrived at one of the Feodosievsk barracks on Palm Sunday (18 March). The miners shamed them into leaving in view of the religious holiday. They returned the next day, accompanied by Khitun and Galkin, only to find that the workers scheduled for eviction had hidden. Just then, indignant crowds from other barracks arrived, forcing Galkin to cancel the evictions. In an 8 April deposition, Captain P. A. Lepin, commander of the Bodaibo garrison, indignantly described the ignominious "step-by-step" retreat of the unit back to its barracks, followed closely by a crowd of two thousand workers. The mining officer Galkin, he recalled with annoyance, gave "no orders to stop the crowd . . . a shameful inaction that gave the crowd a sense of its own strength and the weakness of the armed forces." Only at the barracks did the crowd heed the command to halt. Afterward Captain Sanzharenko told Galkin that he regretted that the soldiers "had not had a chance to warm their hands." Meanwhile, in distant St. Petersburg the trade and industry minister suggested to a Lenzoto director that the "issuing of . . . 300 eviction notices was not tactful." Lack of tact, of course, was the eviction plan's least inadequacy.

Upon hearing of the day's events, Bantysh forbade evictions before the ice broke on the rivers. In truth, Lenzoto's plan of depriving workers of housing before navigation, like the earlier plan to cut off food, threatened their very lives. That very day, however, over Bantysh's objections and at the joint order of Minister of Trade and Industry Timashev and Governor-General Kniazev, the seventy-five soldiers from Kirensk arrived and were quartered in the People's Center, the former site of strike meetings. During the attempted eviction incident, some workers had fraternized with the Bodaibo garrison soldiers, with whom, presumably, they were already acquainted. In any case, after their arrival the unfamiliar Kirensk soldiers performed most duties at the mines.[18] Clearly, Lenzoto and certain high government authorities had graduated to a newly aggressive stance.

When by midmonth several strike delegates from the large mines toured the distant mines and brought them all out on strike as well, the authorities responded by issuing arrest warrants for all those involved. After sharp criticism from workers, who, as noted, were quite protective of their elected delegates, all arrestees were released, except for one or two illegal residents such as Ukraintsev. This suggested a certain surviving residual desire on the authorities' part not to provoke the workers outright. When, however, the specially appointed police chief N. V. Treshchenkov arrived, he evaluated such concessions as indicative of the authorities' "helplessness" in the face of the workers' superior numbers, a view he shared with the army officers. For those of such views, the only remedy was the newly arrived Kirensk troops.[19]

Faced with mounting pressures, the strike leaders devoted additional attention to discipline and organization. From the outset, the strike leadership and the workers themselves had enforced strict rules against alcohol. The leaders had also set up patrols of mining areas, dynamite warehouses, and heavy equipment in order to prevent depredations against company property. The central strike committee now adopted expanded rules that delineated the responsibilities of elders, established soviets of elders, and tied these organizations to the strike delegates and the central strike committee. The committee organized the collections of funds to support the strike organization. Strike discipline was exemplary, as noted by Lenzoto and state officials. In Galkin's view "the strike is well organized; discipline is firm." Justice Khitun described the strike organization's "solid planning" (*planomernost'*) and the strike leaders' "quite authoritative" status. Treshchenkov, who arrived on 22 March, noted the "workers' solidarity." For some observers, however, organization, discipline, and solidarity carried sinister implications, an interpretative twist with grave potential consequences.[20]

By 20 March, a complete stalemate prevailed. The entire labor force had struck, while Governor Bantysh, with waning support from above, blocked the company, which eschewed real concessions, from taking harsh action. The armed forces were almost useless in the face of worker nonviolence. Even so, Lenzoto did not give up its attempts to force the issue. On 19 and 20 March, the company defied Bantysh's earlier order by again cutting off food, which brought a new order from Bantysh to feed all striking workers. When Tul'chinskii arrived back on the scene, he ardently supported Bantysh on this issue. Meanwhile messages from Bantysh to the Petersburg director of police, S. Beletskii, and Minister of the Interior Makarov stated that "I categorically affirm that above and before all Lenzoto itself is to blame for the strike. A quick end to the strike depends entirely on its good will" (17 March) and "mutual agreement on the basis of negotiations is the only way to end the strike peacefully. Lenzoto must fulfill the requirements of the law" (20 March). A document in the Ministry of the Interior files dated 20 March contained Bantysh's concept of the concessions Lenzoto would have to make to end the strike. Among them were that fired workers would be paid off according to the law, daily tables would be kept of work hours and initialed by the workers, medical help would be provided without delay, and employees would treat workers politely.[21]

Rather than make these concessions, most of which reflected existing laws, Lenzoto attempted to cut off food supplies and evict workers.

The company added insult to injury by also ignoring the workers' repeated requests for a payoff of all back wages, which would, they felt, enable them to purchase food. Perhaps they had in mind the last existing private food store in Bodaibo, which could hardly have fed the entire working population. In the middle of this tense situation, the minister of trade and industry commented at a 21 March meeting that "Governor Bantysh has taken too much to heart the workers' interests and excessively exaggerates Lenzoto's guilt and does not scruple to say so in uncoded messages." That same day, the minister of the interior alleged to Governor Bantysh that this same minister of trade and industry was "trying to influence the Lenzoto management to adopt a more peaceful attitude toward the workers and raise their pay as much as possible." Whatever the case, just then, to the discomfiture of the company and its supporters, the Irkutsk Mining Administration found in favor of the workers and against Lenzoto in the current dispute. It accused Lenzoto of violating regulations and its own contracts. It listed violations in the areas of food, medical care, and mining work and insisted that, as the basis for ending the strike, Lenzoto redress the violations.[22] In other words, government mining authorities confirmed Bantysh's judgment about the company's misdeeds. Neither Bantysh nor the Irkutsk mining authorities, by the way, supported the miners' demands for higher pay, which does not suggest blind support for the strikers.

GOOD GENIUS, EVIL GENIUS

Two methods of solving the impasse now hung in uneasy balance: negotiation or confrontation. This balance found perfect personification in Chief Mining Engineer Tul'chinskii and Irkutsk assistant police chief N. V. Treshchenkov, the good and evil geniuses of the Lena tragedy, who had arrived at the mines together on 22 March 1912. The good genius, Tul'chinskii, had fought the company's abuses, forced it to hire more doctors, and joined with Bantysh to warn of a possible strike. As Tul'chinskii, with some melodrama, described his own efforts, "beginning in 1909, [I] have attempted to destroy the years-long arbitrariness and stubborn unwillingness of Lenzoto . . . to take into consideration existing legislation about the protection of the lives, health, and labor of the workers." His prior career had consisted of difficult assignments on the behalf of the State Mining Administration against mining companies involved in abuses of workers.[23] He had become Lenzoto's bete noire and earned reprimands from Petersburg ministers and mining officials. This had won him considerable authority among workers. Although the pressures of the 1912 strike revealed character flaws, he was humane. For example, on the eve of his arrival in Bodaibo

Tul'chinskii sent telegrams to Petersburg insisting that Lenzoto bear the cost of feeding the workers, the alternative being their starvation. One message stated that "if . . . Lenzoto is even partially to blame for the strike, there is no reason to absolve [it] of paying for feeding the workers."

The evil genius, Treshchenkov, was a policeman of unsavory reputation, who bragged about his exploits in having already suppressed "eight strikes." He claimed to have been involved in suppressing Ivanovo workers and of being in the ranks of those who fired upon the demonstration led by Father Gapon on 9 January 1905 (Bloody Sunday). Although many of his claims were pure braggadocio, he had indeed ordered the bombardment of a railway station in Nizhnii-Novgorod during 1905 disorders there and had investigated with success certain cases associated with the anarchists. His personal life, that of a déclassé nobleman and roué, was the subject of repeated scandals, for which he had been demoted in 1908.[24] On his arrival at the mines, he was quoted as saying, "I came to put down this strike or die trying," and "I've dealt with bigger things than this! I'll take care of this scum quick enough." His written messages suggest arrogance, coldness, and contempt for others.[25] That two such individuals, with their starkly opposing personalities, career paths, and assignments, should have arrived at the mines on the same day is perhaps the supreme irony of the entire affair. The savior of oppressed mining workers would now be pitted against the grand inquisitor in the titanic struggle between a company and its workers. This was a drama worthy of the Russian stage.

Tul'chinskii's Time

Events now moved rapidly. Tul'chinskii quickly wrangled a promise from Teppan to rehire everyone who came to work on 1 April and, for his part, offered workers his personal guarantee that Lenzoto would obey all laws and fulfill the 6 March concessions. Armed with these negotiating tools, Tul'chinskii took only two days to persuade a majority of the strike-weary delegates to resume work. Indeed, Lenzoto's negotiating position contained new concessions, not including, however, pay raises or the firing of offensive employees. Bantysh forwarded Lenzoto's new negotiating planks to the minister of the interior. They included the right for workers to sue in cases of company violations, the eight-hour day in wet mines, extra pay for extra hours, and the district mining engineer's right to enforce all laws. In truth, the concessions were not overly benevolent. For instance, the eight-hour day in wet mines already existed de facto, and overtime pay was by no means the main salary issue. The planks about legal redress and the rights of the chief mining engineer did, however, offer potential indirect benefits. Even so, matters did not go smoothly. A split among the workers' elected delegates, with a minority of thirteen still for the strike, sparked misgivings among miners. At the request of the majority, Tul'chinskii spent 26 March making the rounds of the mines, using the "magic of his words . . . to hypnotize" the workers. Nevertheless, the wary miners insisted that he provide them with written assurances of his promises and of Lenzoto's guilt in violating the work contract. Recalling the Irkutsk Mining Administration's recent determinations, Tul'chinskii agreed. After Justice Khitun and Assistant Procurator N. I. Preobrazhenskii informed him that only a court could decide Lenzoto's guilt, he withdrew that part of his commitment. Nevertheless, most strike leaders, including Dumpe and Batashev, still recognized a basis for ending the strike, to which, after sharp debate, the mines and workshops agreed. To uphold workers' pride, the appointed day was 29 March, rather than Teppan's 1 April. Prostrike agitation prior to the twenty-ninth, aided by Tul'chinskii's backtracking about assurances of Lenzoto's guilt, wrought a change of mood. Some workers accused those who wanted to end the strike of betrayal. In consequence, few miners reported to work on the twenty-ninth and, yielding to the adamant mood of most workers, the strike leaders proclaimed the strike still in effect.[26] In view of later developments, it is worthwhile emphasizing that as of the twenty-fourth the main strike leadership promoted an end to the strike.

Treshchenkov's Time

With Tul'chinskii's failure, Treshchenkov's time had come. Indeed, activities behind the scenes had already prepared the ground for antistrike measures. Beginning on 20 March, Teppan showered high officialdom with messages about the workers' allegedly abusive and violent behavior. Among other charges, he reported to the minister of trade and industry that miners were using threats to enforce the strike, a charge the Manukhin Commission later found baseless. A Lenzoto lawyer, A. Ivanov, also sent messages to the justice minister that emphasized alleged "incendiary speeches" and threats against workers who wished to return to work. The trade and industry minister appealed to the interior minister, who promptly told Bantysh that the "no longer peaceful" strike required strong steps, a notion that Bantysh again indignantly rejected. The courageous governor angrily informed his superior that he did not countenance force against orderly workers to abet the unlawful Lenzoto. Things now drifted away from Bantysh, as they would also slip from Tul'chinskii's hands. A 23 March telegram from Irkutsk police chief N. Poznanskii to his subordinate, Treshchenkov, informed him that "[y]ou will probably be named chief of police [at the mines]. For the time being act carefully and . . . do not take active measures. Quietly check on the activities of Mining Inspector Galkin [who had come under suspicion for insisting that the workers were peaceful]. . . . Telegraph as soon as possible about the *real reasons for the strike* demands, initiatives, conditions for ending [the strike], and possible excesses" (emphasis added). Indeed, on the twenty-fifth the minister of the interior made the appointment mentioned by Poznanskii, who on the twenty-seventh telegraphed Treshchenkov that "all mining police officers of the Vitim district are under your command. You must obey the orders of the governor." This last was a formality since Treshchenkov communicated directly with the Irkutsk chief of police and vice versa, thus in effect circumventing Bantysh.[27] Of note in Poznanskii's message was the phrase about the "real reasons for the strike." The dual versions of the strike continued to develop.

On the thirtieth Treshchenkov warned the striking workers of possible harsh consequences if they did not return to work at once. Messages posted at various places around the mines announced that new workers would soon be hired to replace all strikers. In fact, on 1 April about one hundred newly hired workers went into the mines. According to Tul'chinskii, Treshchenkov told workers' meetings that "no violence or disorders would be tolerated and that he would use the armed forces at his disposal to suppress any disorders if they occur." Tul'chinskii later emphasized, however, that at no time did Treshchenkov warn the workers against holding meetings or from moving from one mine to another, as was their right.[28] Messages between Treshchenkov and certain Irkutsk and Petersburg authorities were replete with images of worker violence and violent government countermeasures. Manukhin's investigatory commission later found it impossible to verify a single significant incident of actual worker violence, threatened violence, or even threatening language. Perhaps the violence resided entirely in the minds and hearts of certain authorities.

Beginning the very day of his appointment as local police chief, Treshchenkov issued a stream of messages that urged the arrest of the strike leaders, who, he insisted, were politically motivated and without whom the strike would collapse. One of his telegrams from 31 March asserted: "A split has taken place among the workers. If we arrest the committee now, a move the [local] judiciary fully supports, we can expect the strike to end." The objections of Galkin, Aleksandrov, and Tul'chinskii that the arrests might cause disorders led Bantysh to postpone the arrests while Tul'chinskii again negotiated with the miners. "Delay arrests until Tul'chinskii's negotiations are ended," insisted the governor. On 28 March, the governor ordered that "If [Tul'chinskii's] negotiations fail [and] you decide to arrest prominent [strike] leaders, do it quietly. I command you to preserve order." On the twenty-ninth, he issued a supplementary order to "arrest only those with criminal responsibility, maintain peace, and put down disorders, even with force."[29] The only "disorders" Bantysh contemplated were in potential response to the arrest of the workers' leaders, whereas Treshchenkov, Teppan, and certain other officials alleged mythical worker disorders as a reason for the arrests.

ARRESTING THE STRIKE COMMITTEE

By 29 March the negotiations had ended. Meanwhile, Treshchenkov dispatched a barrage of alarming telegrams directly to Poznanskii, who promptly forwarded this (mis)information to the Petersburg police authorities. Treshchenkov's messages constantly emphasized that strike leaders and prostrike workers "forcibly" prevented others from returning to work and that the arrest of the "committee" would end the entire affair. He portrayed workers as "fearful" of the "committee" that "threatened them with violence." This ignored the reality that the "committee," far from prolonging the strike by means of threats, was trying to end it. Certain of Treshchenkov's messages and his June 1912 report make clear that he was quite aware of these factors. This casts a very malevolent light on his descriptions of the strike committee as "violent." Regardless, under the influence of these alarming messages, on 30 March the Petersburg police authorities ordered the "immediate arrest of the strike committee." At Bantysh's vociferous insistence, early on 2 April the Irkutsk police chief Poznanskii sent a telegram that countenanced arrests only as a last resort, "if this would help peacefully end the conflict." Later that day, however, the police chief sent a second message to Treshchenkov ordering the arrests outright, thus sidestepping the governor's conditions. In sending the second message, Poznanskii responded to a direct order, dated 2 April 1912, from Beletskii, the Petersburg director of the Department of Police, "to liquidate the strike committee at once." Poznanskii's formal subordination was to the Irkutsk governor rather than to the Petersburg police director, just as Treshchenkov's was to the governor rather than to the Irkutsk police chief. Formalities aside, the Petersburg-Irkutsk-Bodaibo police authority nexus in effect bypassed the hapless governor, whose own messages had become fatally ambiguous ("arrest only if it will preserve order" and so forth). His hands finally untied by the direct order, Treshchenkov filed criminal charges against seventeen delegates and by 3 April had their arrest warrants in hand.[30]

Lena Goldfields Strike and Shooting

The timing of these events is crucial. On 1 April the Progressist newspaper *Russkoe slovo* (Russian Word), which represented the empire's largest industrialists and entrepreneurs, reported that Lenzoto "wanted to end the strike at once," in pursuit of which it was calling a special session of its executives the next day (2 April). The goal of the special session, asserted *Russkoe slovo* was to take "final measures to end the strike."[31] Late in the day of Lenzoto's special session (2 April), the Petersburg police director, after temporizing for days, issued the direct order by telegram to liquidate the strike committee forthwith. It would appear that, after the company's special session, Lenzoto's Petersburg director phoned either the Petersburg police director or, more likely, his superior, the interior minister. In any case, within hours the director of police sent the telegram. Perhaps mere coincidence, the timing more likely suggests that top government administrators received their marching orders from Lenzoto directors.

A documentary trail all the way from luxurious Petersburg chanceries down to the shabby Vitim-Bodaibo police offices reveals that the policy of arresting the strike committee had assumed talismanic significance as a formula for ending the strike. As the state inexorably tightened the grip of its repressive apparatus in preparation for a showdown, Lenzoto's last belated attempt to negotiate got lost in the shuffle. On 2 April the company accompanied its decision to bring about the arrest of the strike leaders with several new concessions. Although the new offer still did not address wages or hours, some observers felt that its measures were sufficient to preserve the workers' pride and serve as a basis for ending the strike. Unfortunately, the workers never found out about this new development. Negotiations had floundered on the twenty-ninth when Tul'chinskii refused to participate in any further fruitless discussions. Far from hearing about concessions, between 1 and 3 April the workers saw only harshly worded proclamations that Treshchenkov had posted around the mines with threats of retaliation for their alleged violent behavior. Tul'chinskii recalled that Justices of the Peace Khitun and Preobrazhenskii were busy preparing arrest warrants on 2 and 3 April. Having just received yet another reprimand from the minister of the interior for supposed inaction in ending the strike, Tul'chinskii did not feel it possible to interfere with direct orders from the Petersburg police authorities.[32] Thus drifted away the last infinitesimal possibility of avoiding the violent confrontation that some so abjectly feared and others so ardently desired.

The third of April was a terrible day, with a new uproar at the Aleksandrovsk mine about food. Treshchenkov received a telephone message that one thousand workers had surrounded the local police station. When he arrived there, he found workers angry about bad meat they had received. Furthermore, in the face of yet another temporary suspension of food distribution, they demanded food for their wives and children. When Treshchenkov told them to disperse to the barracks, they at first ignored him. According to Treshchenkov, they finally left at the advice of M. Lebedev, one of the strike leaders, a development that galled the police chief. On leaving, they allegedly threatened to storm the food stores if food was not issued. Treshchenkov then left Aleksandrovsk, met with Tul'chinskii at Feodosievsk, and informed him that they needed to return together to Aleksandrovsk to quiet the "very agitated" miners there. He added that he intended to go with troops.[33] On their arrival, with troops, Tul'chinskii tried to explain that the bad meat, which the workers showed him, had been issued by accident. Treshchenkov again ordered the miners into the barracks, which they ignored, outraging the police chief. Finally, Tul'chinskii managed to smooth over the affair, not without cost to his reputation among miners. He noticed a distinct fading of their usual trust in him.

Little did the miners know that he too had succumbed to intense pressure in finally acquiescing to arrests. For example, on 2 April Tul'chinskii sent Bantysh a telegram that, like Treshchenkov's messages, noted the split among workers and that recommended the "arrest of several [leaders] exercising a harmful influence." This wording indicates that the chief mining engineer had in mind only the minority of strike leaders still pushing for the strike's continuation. Treshchenkov made no such distinctions. After the Aleksandrovsk contretemps on 3 April, Tul'chinskii further advised Bantysh to contemplate sending Cossack units. With fear as his advisor, Tul'chinskii, the miners' chief on-the-spot defender, took step-by-step positions inimical of their interests.

Later, half in confession and half in self-justification, Tul'chinskii admitted to having been terrified that the workers would finally seek revenge for all the provocations heaped upon them and that, it must be admitted, he had striven to avoid. The chief mining engineer also regretted having gone to the Aleksandrovsk mine site with Treshchenkov in the company of troops. This had, on the one hand, aggravated the workers and contributed to their distrust and, on the other, hardened Treshchenkov's resolve to wreak vengeance. After the shooting, Bantysh blamed his own decision to contemplate the use of troops, albeit under restrictions, on his increasing dependence on Treshchenkov for information. On his arrival at the mines, Treshchenkov took personal responsibility for dispatching all messages. Naturally, their tone was quite different from those of his subordinate, Galkin, who had always emphasized the workers' peaceful intentions. Both Bantysh and Tul'chinskii also recalled feeling overwhelmed with orders and reprimands from higher authorities, who simply insisted that they take forcible action. These assertions find ample substantiation in the archival records of the Ministries of Justice and the Interior. For instance, on 29 March Tul'chinskii received a joint telegram from the director of the mining department and the minister of trade and industry that held him in insubordination to previous instructions about arresting the strike committee.[34] Alarming and incendiary messages from Teppan and Treshchenkov created a widening circle of people resolved to suppress the strike by force.

In the early dark hours of 4 April, the police finally set out to arrest the strike leaders. Treshchenkov, Khitun, and Preobrazhenskii went to the barracks of the nearby Nadezhdinsk mines, where several of the central leaders resided, while Justice Rein and Inspector Galkin went by train to the Andreevsk mine. Both groups went with troops. According to Treshchenkov, at first things seemed to go smoothly at the Nadezhdinsk barracks. Then, suddenly, Purgin, a worker in the secret employ of the police, began to scream in alarm because he mistook the armed police officers for workers coming to kill him (the wages of bad conscience). The alerted workers then managed to hide Batashev and Popov I, "the ones most needed," complained the police chief. Consequently, for some time thereafter they continued to provide strike leadership or, in Treshchenkov's words, "agitate the workers." Other strike committee members at the site, including Dumpe, Rozenberg, and Cherepakhin, were arrested. Dumpe recalled that just as he fell into a deep slumber after an enervating day, a hand rudely shook his shoulder and a loud voice announced his arrest. At the Andreevsk mine, a crowd of seven hundred workers threatened to stop the arrests there: "Let's go, let's go, they're arresting our leaders." Warned that the soldiers would shoot, they stopped. Ultimately, ten strike leaders from several mines were placed under arrest that night. Treshchenkov sent those in custody under heavy guard, with Galkin in command, by railroad to the Bodaibo jail, out of the miners' reach. The reports of several police provocateurs had led the authorities unerringly to the strike leaders, the balance of whom, along with numerous strike delegates, they rounded up on succeeding days.[35]

Workers' Reactions to the Arrests

At dawn, calls poured in from the mines reporting not the anticipated end of the strike but the miners' outrage. A huge crowd awoke Tul'chinskii, who lived near the Uspensk mines, to demand the delegates' release. The angry miners also accused him of identifying the strike leaders, a charge Tul'chinskii always vehemently denied and that was wide of the mark since police spies had named the leaders. From the porch of his house, the chief mining engineer addressed the hostile crowd. Somewhat disingenuously he denied that he had backed the arrests (he had in fact called for the arrests of prostrike leaders) and calmed the workers' agitation by promising to do what he could to release the delegates. The only partially mollified workers returned to the mines after vowing to go to Bodaibo themselves if necessary to free the leaders. Before heading for Nadezhdinsk, Tul'chinskii wired Bantysh that the arrests had exacerbated the situation.[36]

The balm of Tul'chinskii's words notwithstanding, workers from the Andreevsk, Aleksandrovsk, Vasilevsk, and other mines decided to pressure Lenzoto by delivering individual workers' complaints en masse. This decision originated from a situation several days earlier when workers from one of the mines had attempted to bring a group complaint against Lenzoto. Assistant Procurator Preobrazhenskii had told them that only individual complaints were legally appropriate. Workers from several mines now wrote and signed many hundreds of carefully worded complaints.[37] The march to deliver the legally valid petitions began sometime after midday and eventually collected more than three thousand workers from the middle-distance mines. Most had donned their Sunday clothes, replete with watches and chains. Over a snow-packed mountain road, the trek would take several hours. Mining Administrator G. M. Savinov watched the entire procession pass, joked with the miners, and later recalled their calm mood. They had carried nothing, he reported, that could be considered weapons. As the road approached their goal, Nadezhdinsk, it paralleled the railroad tracks. A train from Bodaibo overtook the line of marchers trudging along the nearby road. By eerie coincidence, on the train were the very troops that had earlier escorted the arrestees to Bodaibo. Witnesses recalled how miners and soldiers, unaware of how their fates were soon to become intertwined, eyed one another warily.

On the way to Nadezhdinsk by horse, Tul'chinskii met with a large crowd of irate Aleksandrovsk workers, who "posed rather provocative questions." The workers' grapevine had evidently broadcast suspicions of Tul'chinskii's alleged betrayal of the strike leaders. Meanwhile Treshchenkov, after being awakened by phone calls from Tul'chinskii and other administrators about the tumult at various mines, headed for Feodosievsk with troops commanded by Sanzharenko. Upon arriving, the police chief, as usual, ordered the crowd to disperse, to which the workers replied "Get out of here" and so forth (*Von! Doloi!*). Seeing the miners' truculent mood, Treshchenkov followed prudence's dictates in abandoning the site with the small unit of soldiers. He noted in his report, meaningfully, that Galkin had not yet returned from Bodaibo with, of course, the balance of the armed forces. Treshchenkov also noted that the workers had referred to the troops under Sanzharenko's command as "ours" (they were from the Bodaibo garrison). Worker orators on the spot also, he recalled, told the workers "don't worry, they won't shoot us." Many workers, erroneously as it turned out, firmly believed that the soldiers would not shoot.

Immediately upon arriving in Nadezhdinsk just after midday, Chief Engineer Tul'chinskii spoke briefly with the police chief and set out by sleigh for Feodosievsk to try, yet again, to mend the damage done by Treshchenkov. Treshchenkov himself later recalled that even then Tul'chinskii advised him to remove the armed forces from the Nadezhdinsk area because in their absence "the workers would harm no one." This, however, did not fit Treshchenkov's concept of how to deal with workers. In truth, by this time he had come to fear worker vengeance for his harsh words and actions. At the Feodosievsk mines, Tul'chinskii faced the "sullen" (his term) miners who now blamed him personally for betraying their strike leaders. Eyewitnesses recalled that strike leaders Cherepakhin, Zelionko, and I. Korneev interrupted him and called him "scum" and "scoundrel" (*svoloch'* and *podlets*). Even more problematically, the Feodosievsk miners threatened to descend en masse on Nadezhdinsk. By promising to attempt to free the strike leaders, the intrepid engineer managed to placate the two thousand Feodosievsk workers and, almost miraculously, persuaded them to do nothing until the next day. The exhausted Tul'chinskii arrived back in Nadezhdinsk at about 4 P.M. As he climbed out of the sleigh, someone told him that three thousand workers from the other mines had entered the opposite side of town.[38]

Even as the various strands of the strike's history came together late in the afternoon of 4 April outside the People's Center, Bantysh was sending another frenzied telegram. Addressed to the workers, it advised them to remain calm. This well-intentioned missive was profoundly misdirected. Earlier in the day, Petersburg police director Beletskii, an official directly subordinate to the minister of the interior, telegraphed the Irkutsk police about elements "who are threatening those wishing to go back to work. Have you liquidated the strike committee? And if not, why not?" In a reply addressed to the minister of the interior, Bantysh described the round up of strike committee members and hoped that "the arrests, along with Lenzoto's latest concessions, will break the strike."[39] Informed by telegrams from Tul'chinskii about the workers' indignation, Bantysh sent the message to the workers urging them to remain calm. The miners never received it, just as they never received notice of Lenzoto's "latest concessions." It was not, of course, so much the workers that needed calming but Treshchenkov and the other authorities at Nadezhdinsk, many of whom had done everything they could to provoke the workers. The consequences now confronted them in the form of three thousand workers headed directly for the People's Center.

THE VICTIMS

Tul'chinskii joined Treshchenkov, Preobrazhenskii, Khitun, Galkin, and Captains Lepin and Sanzharenko in front of the People's Center. They stood near the railroad tracks to the right flank of the deployment of about ninety soldiers under Lepin and Sanzharenko's command. As the marchers came through the center of the settlement, Treshchenkov strode forward on the railroad tracks and shouted uselessly at them to stop. Cursing loudly, he then sent Police Guard Kitov to warn them off to an alternative road, having decided on the spur of the moment to let them march toward Feodosievsk. "The devil with them," he shouted, "let them take the lower road [to Feodosievsk]!" Anything but that they should approach the People's Center. In fact the workers had had no intention of going to Feodosievsk. Moving forward on a narrow snow-enclosed path, they could not easily change directions and many stepped past the road branch that Treshchenkov now wished them to take. As the column neared, Tul'chinskii called out and hurried along the railroad tracks toward them. Becoming aware of the soldiers' formation and hearing the engineer's urgent tone, the crowd faltered. Popov II, the leader of the demonstration, handed Tul'chinskii a copy of the written petitions and agreed to turn off, a message that his coleader, A. N. Lesnoi, began to pass back to those out of sight beyond the stables. The open place near the bridge where the miners were gathering in large numbers contained a crossroad, with the alternative branch road. Preobrazhenskii started toward the workers to join Tul'chinskii, but was restrained by Khitun. Meanwhile, Treshchenkov had returned to the line of soldiers. The incident seemed to have ended when the soldiers fired the first volley. In one version, Tul'chinskii, hearing the sound of the rifle bolts closing, waved and shouted in an attempt to stop the first volley. In another, he fell to the ground after the first volley and then rose to his knees, waved his arms, and shouted "Wait!" just as the second wave of bullets hit the crowd. In any case, injured workers fell on top of Tul'chinskii, saving his life. When he attempted again to rise, some workers grabbed his legs and held him down. When the firing was over, he found himself under a layer of bodies and surrounded by the dead and wounded. After he extricated himself, a worker led him out of the crowd and calmly

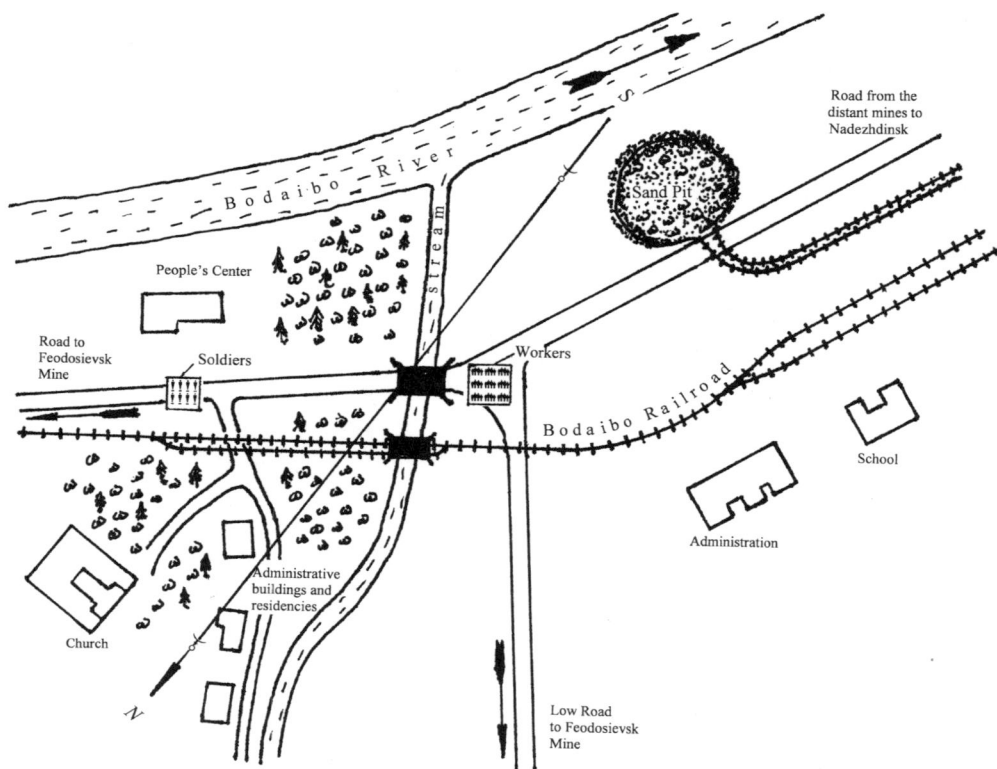

Map 3. Nadezhdensk, site of the Lena massacre. Source: S. S. Manukhin, *Vsepoddanneishii otchet chlena Gosudarstvennogo soveta, senatora tianogo sovetinka Maukhina* (Moscow, 1913), insert.

asked him to "tell them not to shoot any more." He stumbled, dazed and covered in blood, back to the People's Center, mumbling "Why did they shoot?" Miners still able to walk withdrew from the place.[40]

The historical record contains numerous versions of the number of miners killed and wounded. A telegram dated 5 April and signed "[a] former Lenzoto worker to the Minister of the Interior" claimed that there were "150 corpses and up to 250 wounded." Treshchenkov's telegram, also dated 5 April, claimed that 107 were killed and 80 wounded. Another set of data collected by the Manukhin Commission showed that on 8 and 9 April a total of 162 bodies were buried in fourteen mass graves. Another 7 people died and were buried between 10 and 18 April for a total of 169 deaths. The commission counted an additional 202 wounded people, for a total of 371 casualties. The chronicle of the Blagoveshchensk Church in Nadezhdinsk claimed that 119 were killed on the spot and 350 wounded, of whom 100 died during the following days, for a total of 219 deaths and 469 casualties. In a separate report, the pastor of the church, Father N. P. Vinokurov, stated that he had been told that 200 were killed and 300 wounded for a total of 500 casualties. The church compiled a list of 170 dead by name but noted that this included only people who received last rites and that the list was incomplete. Indeed it did not coincide with the numbers used in the church chronicle, which counted 219 dead. The Manukhin Commission's published report claimed that 372 people had been shot, of whom 170 died, figures agreed to by Treshchenkov in his 3 May report. The Manukhin Commission seems to have used the church's figure of 170 based on last rites rather than the figure of 169 arrived at by counting burials. Since the church itself considered the 170 figure incomplete, there seems no reason to accept its absolute accuracy. Whether it diverged from reality or to what degree is impossible to say.

The highest count came from an anonymous report handed in to the Manukhin Commission by a person on the medical staff of the company's clinic. This source claimed that 128 people had been killed on the spot and another 150 died later for a total of 278 deaths, and that 256 additional people had been wounded, for a total of 534 casualties. These totals are quite close to the number of mortalities and wounded (270 dead and 250 wounded) in the 1913 publication *Pravda o lenskikh sobytiiakh,* a volume published by leftist Duma deputies and journalists, including Nikitin and Kerensky. Perhaps the author of the unpublished anonymous report handed in to the Manukhin Commission also sent it to them. Some early Soviet-era researchers carried out counts based on surveys of all the clinics to which wounded and dead workers were carried. They concluded that about 170 were killed or expired shortly after the shooting and 370 received wounds, of whom about 60 died later, for a total of more than 230 deaths and 540 casualties.[41] In the days after the massacre the liberal and centrist Russian press reported similarly high totals. On 11 April the Constitutional-Democratic paper *Rech'* (Speech) repeated figures published in *Kievskaia mysl'* (Kiev Idea), according to which 250 had already died, more than 100 were "hopelessly" wounded, and dozens were dying daily from wounds. On 10 April *Birzhevye vedomosti* (Stock Market News) reported that 107 had been killed on the spot; 84 had died of wounds; and 191 still suffered from wounds, of whom 81 were ambulatory. These very precise figures, evidently representing an informed source, would have meant a total of almost 200 deaths as of 10 April and nearly 400 serious casualties. At midmonth the conservative *Tverskoe povolzh'e* (Tver on the Volga) published figures similar to those of *Birzhevye vedomosti*—107 killed and 84 subsequent deaths—but counted 210 additional wounded. On 19 April *Sibirskaia zhizn'* (Siberian Life) claimed that 250 had either been killed or died of wounds and that others were still dying daily.[42] Discrepancies may have reflected differences in counting methods. For instance, some totals for wounded counted people hospitalized, whereas others counted all wounded no matter how minor the injury.

The exact figures will likely never be determined. Bearing on this difficult matter is evidence that shortly after the shooting Treshchenkov chased away all remaining workers, including some from the Feodosievsk mines who were gathering up firewood to use as stretchers to carry away the injured. Treshchenkov himself recalled ordering away these workers because they were "hindering me from taking away the wounded." An eyewitness described the matter in quite different terms. When Treshchenkov saw the Feodosievsk workers putting together makeshift stretchers, he started screaming at them, using "military profanity" (*ploshchadnoi bran'iu*). "Get out of here or I'll shoot," he yelled. "I killed [the others] and I'll kill you." The workers took this threat seriously and left. In effect, Treshchenkov sequestered the area for several hours. Only later did he allow soldiers and workers remaining in the area to fashion stretchers from shovels and load the dead and wounded into sleds made of firewood, ten or so to a sled. No distinction was made between the dead, the dying, and the wounded. Afterward, the soldiers shoveled up bloody snow and other unmentionable remains from the slaughter, hauled it to a mining shaft, and dumped it in a vain attempt to hide the evidence of what had occurred.

During the transfer process to the clinics, marauding took place. The miners' watches, gold chains, money, and other valuables disappeared (the miners had dressed in their Sunday best to deliver the petitions). At the clinics, bodies of the living and dead lay in piles on the floors and in the corridors. During the long night, cries of the injured, moans of the dying, and the wailing of the wives and children caused a terrible pandemonium. Doctors, feldshers, and nurses were in such short supply that many wounded miners lay uncared for, until during the endless night wives and other workers finally bandaged those who still needed it.[43] Since many injured workers wound up at various clinics and hospitals, even in Bodaibo, and since Treshchenkov had been in charge of the area of the shooting for hours before transfers even began, any final figures would be speculative. The statistics on the burials (169) and on the last rites for the dead (170), at first glance persuasive in their close coincidence, unfortunately pertained only to the happenings at the two main clinics. They counted the same incomplete group and, as the priests of the Blagoveshchensk Church pointed out, almost certainly did not tell the whole story. Suffice it to say that the shooting led to extensive loss of life and severe injury to many.

The story of one youth, whose parents worked at the mines, elucidates what occurred. On 5 May, the sixteen-year-old I. M. Dmitriev, who had lived for three years with his parents at the Aleksandrovsk mines, accompanied the crowd headed for Nadezhdinsk "with some other boys . . . to look," in the universal fashion of the young. At Nadezhdinsk, the boys stayed to the side and sat on a fence as the workers gathered nearby at the crossroads, in the open place across from the People's Center. Dmitriev had heard no signal when the first bullets hit. Wounded in the arm, the youth fell from the fence to the ground, landing on his back. Near him lay a worker, "lying face down with a shattered skull. I was crawling over him [to get away] when two more bullets hit me in the back and I lost consciousness," continued Dmitriev. Later, he continued, "the Cossack Cheregov carried me away."[44] Other witnesses recalled members of the crowd sitting on the fence and smoking just prior to the first volley, not the pose of people with force on their minds. Workers planning or even anticipating a violent confrontation would hardly have allowed children to accompany them.

Justice M. F. Rein had been on the train with the soldiers on the way back from Bodaibo when it passed the marching miners shortly before the final confrontation. He recalled how Captain Lepin, the commander of the unit, had muttered, "We won't get by without shooting." Rein also described how between the volleys Captain Sanzharenko had stalked back and forth behind the soldiers shouting threats if they did not shoot straight. Meanwhile, Treshchenkov, according to his own report, stood well back from the line of soldiers as they did their work.[45] Both Tul'chinskii's and Treshchenkov's later reports made clear the latter's determination not to allow the workers to approach the People's Center. In his private report to the emperor, Senator Manukhin speculated about what would have happened if the workers had actually reached the People's Center that afternoon: "I assume, nothing [would have happened]," was his laconic answer. Indeed, the workers were decked out in their Sunday best with watches and fobs and carried carefully formulated petitions in their pockets that requested the release of the strike leaders.[46] The workers' aggressive intent was all in the minds of certain authorities. The imagined aggression begat a real one.

These bare facts leave much to be explained. Although mining personnel had telephoned Treshchenkov that the workers were coming to deliver petitions, in his report he claimed not to have known that this was their intent. In truth, he and other officials had behaved so harshly to the miners that their approach aroused the worst fears. Even Tul'chinskii later characterized himself as finally having "given in to the general panic." Treshchenkov repeatedly expressed the determination to prevent the 3,000 miners from uniting with the 2,000 at Feodosievsk. He summoned the troops out of the People's Center by shouting, "Hurry up, lads, that bunch wants to take away your weapons," which must have alarmed the soldiers, who numbered barely over 90 (Manukhin claimed that 102 people fired weapons). Treshchenkov then passed general command of the soldiers to Sanzharenko and Lepin. Both officers testified that, when Treshchenkov realized that his various efforts had not deterred the workers, he ordered the senior officer Lepin to use arms, shouting, "Stop the crowd, stop them!" In answer to the criminal charges brought against him, in a July interrogation Treshchenkov rejected these allegations. "I categorically deny that in passing command of the unit to Staff Captain Lepin," he insisted, "I authorized him to disperse the crowd with arms."[47] What other point, however, could there have been in passing control of the unit to the chief military officer? The buck passing back and forth between the military and police captains, however, is beside the point. Testimony strongly suggests that both were spoiling for an armed confrontation with the workers.

The police chief's ultimate motivations remain opaque. He seems to have been prone to violence and had perhaps tired of bandying words with workers whom he held in contempt. For their part, the miners were violating no norms by delivering written petitions, of which they carried many hundreds, hardly the act of a group bent on violence. Nor, as Tul'chinskii later emphasized, had they been forbidden to meet or demonstrate. Given recent experience, even the soldiers' formation signified little more than a cause for moderate concern. After all, until then military units had repeatedly backed down. Numerous rumors had spread that the soldiers would not fire on workers. In his report, Treshchenkov recalled hearing, in the seconds after the first volley, how workers shouted "the soldiers are firing blanks." Some accounts claim that the first volley was in the air, causing workers to fall to the ground, with the real volleys starting only when they got up. Most accounts support the version that the first and all subsequent volleys were deadly. A professional photographer, V. P. Koreshkov, a political exile employed by Lenzoto as a carriage driver, took numerous photographs during the day of the massacre. Among them were snapshots of the procession of workers headed for Nadezhdinsk, of the shooting itself, and of the dead bodies afterward. Some of these photographs survived and appear in Soviet-era studies, as well as in this book. Informed about the photographs, the Ministry of the Interior quickly ordered the preservation of the negatives as evidence. Unfortunately, Treshchenkov had already summoned Koreshkov and confiscated and destroyed the negatives of the shooting, which might have shed light on the postures of the miners.[48]

Supported by some soldiers' testimony and several Lenzoto eyewitnesses, Treshchenkov later claimed that the crowd threatened Tul'chinskii and continued to surge forward with sticks, stones, and bricks in hand. After the first volley, the miners allegedly arose from the ground, shouted "Hurrah!" and again charged forward. (This would have been a worker's version of hara-kiri. In a spirit of self-immolation, without weapons, dressed in their Sunday best with watches and fobs, and often running in the opposite direction, the workers attacked the soldiers.) In the immediate aftermath of the massacre, Tul'chinskii at first agreed that the workers had carried threatening objects. Two days later, he dramatically recanted in a telegram in which he confessed that, in a terrible psychological state, he had only made the claim "under the influence" of Treshchenkov. The police captain, he claimed, had insisted that everyone coordinate stories and send identical telegrams. After his recantation, Tul'chinskii always firmly insisted that he "had seen no forward movement of the crowd" and no weaponlike objects. He also insisted that at the People's Center that entire evening he had repeated to everyone: "Why did they [the soldiers] do that? Why did they do that? If they had just waited another minute or two, the workers would have turned off." Most eyewitnesses supported the accounts of the workers and of Tul'chinskii's later testimony. Workers had no weapons and simply tried to flee. A local priest, Father Aleksandr Chernykh, paralyzed by a stroke after watching the scene, agreed. From his sickbed he testified that "they slaughtered the workers like cattle, that's why I collapsed." According to Father Vinokurov, pastor of the Blagoveshchensk Church, during last rites the mortally wounded recounted their peaceful intentions and surprise at the shooting. "The dying do not lie," intoned the priest.[49]

Information about the type of wounds inflicted on the dead and injured further supports this version. Of the injured whose wounds were determinable, 69 had back wounds, 62 side wounds, and only 10 had front entry wounds. Examined another way, 117 were lying down and 37 standing when shot. These statistics drew from Justice Rein the biting comment that the miners had "attacked the soldiers with their backs." Many had face and head wounds so massive that their wives and children could identify them only by their clothes. Officials declined to examine the bodies of the dead before they were buried. In mid-May Rein requested the disinterment of the dead because no death certificates had been issued before their burial. The Irkutsk procurator's office delayed fulfilling the request on the basis that the "soil permafrost prevents the rapid decay of the bodies" and "the findings may be dangerous and undesirable as a cause for agitation . . . that may upset the workers." In early July the Irkutsk procurator, with less than perfect sincerity, canceled the plan entirely as "irrelevant" since "no evidence exists that the crowd attacked the soldiers [and] the case is being closed." Thus ended all possibility of determining the stances of the workers killed, presumably mostly those in the forward ranks. The procurator's office seems to have guessed the likely results. Senator Manukhin determined that there had been a total expenditure of 789 shells. These caused somewhere between 450 and 550 casualties, quite a number of whom had multiple injuries. Some bullets caused more than one injury. The summarized data suggest quite deadly, close-range, continued firing against individuals neither charging nor even mostly facing forward. Captain Lepin characterized the distance as "150 steps." The failure to employ a warning volley either of blanks or over the heads of the miners violated military procedure for crowd control, as did the individual firing after the volleys.

The testimony of Galkin is pertinent: "The entire time of the strike the mood of the workers was very peaceful . . . [whereas] the attitude of Treshchenkov, as well as of the officers, was always provocative." As for the workers, various witnesses pointed out that they had under their control several warehouses with dynamite. Many had military experience and skills in the use of dynamite. Some workers later claimed that had they wished to use force, they could have done so with great effect. With reference to their former military training, workers also noted that, had they had violent intentions on 4 April, they would neither have approached the line of soldiers in an unwieldy column nor gathered milling about directly in front of them.[50]

The testimony of Treshchenkov, some of the officers and soldiers, and several other Lenzoto employees—joined briefly by Tul'chinskii—about the workers carrying weaponlike objects merits further discussion. On 25 June the local police turned in to the Manukhin Commission a long list of objects supposedly found and confiscated at the site of the shooting. The objects, the police charged, "might have been" in the hands of the workers. Among these were wood, unspecified fragments, boards, metal rods and wire, and five red bricks. Three days later Justice Preobrazhenskii turned in a deposition with a small correction. There may have been sticks and coal, but "there were no bricks in the area. I did not see sticks and coal in the hands of the workers." Nevertheless, after the first volley, insisted Preobrazhenskii, "they rose up, shouted 'Hurrah,' and threw themselves forward." And what of Treshchenkov's testimony? He claimed that the workers carried "coal, sticks, bricks, and even metal objects" and, after the first volley, they rose up and so on, and so on. But, he explained lamely, "I personally did not see these objects in the hands of the workers since I am short-sighted but confirm that they were found [afterward] on the ground along the road, on top of the snow, [lying] loosely, not frozen."[51]

Contrast this with the evidence of Mine Administrator Savinov, whom the marching workers passed going in the opposite direction on the road between Nadezhdinsk and Aleksandrovsk shortly before the confrontation. They carried nothing, he claimed, were in a good mood, and even joked with him that "we've cleared the road for you," that is, from the heavy snow of the previous night.[52] Likewise, no one on the train that passed the workers on the way to Nadezhdinsk testified to seeing weapons. In fact, the heavy snow that restricted the workers to walking five to six abreast as they passed through the Nadezhdinsk area also signified that, if, as Savinov testified, they had carried no weapons with them, they could not have found them in Nadezhdinsk itself. Everything was covered with a thick layer of fresh snow. No one testified to seeing the workers leave the narrow roadway to forage in the fresh snow nor do existing photographs reveal any such actions. Yet this would have been necessary to locate weapons in the final minutes before the alleged charge. Some of the wood in the area after the massacre had been brought from the nearby firewood ricks to be used as stretchers. Other items may have been "introduced" there during the several hours when the area was closed off. Treshchenkov and the soldiers under his command had the opportunity and motive to falsify the record. Some items may have been uncovered from beneath the snow during the clean-up operation. Although many soldiers testified to actually seeing these "weapons" in the hands of miners, the unwillingness of Preobrazhenskii or Treshchenkov to personally confirm this seems decisive. In light of Tul'chinskii's testimony about Treshchenkov's postshooting efforts to coordinate stories, the soldiers had almost certainly been ordered to say what they said.

What about the story of the miners rising up after the first volley, shouting "Hurrah," and charging forward? Quite a constellation of people, including Treshchenkov, the two army captains and a number of soldiers, Justices Preobrazhenskii and Khitun, and several other Lenzoto employees, repeated this version. Many others, it should be noted, directly contradicted this inherently implausible story. The counterwitnesses included Tul'chinskii, Galkin, the priests of the Blagoveshchensk Church, numerous other Lenzoto employees, and several independent bystanders from Bodaibo, plus workers interviewed later by the Manukhin Commission. Manukhin paid close attention to the matter, collected massive eyewitness testimony, and reached a definitive conclusion. It did not happen. Numerous witnesses, including police guards standing nearby, drew attention to a single individual, a worker standing at the forward edge of the crowd when the shooting started. Badly wounded by the first volley, he stood up, ripped off his coat, and dashed forward from the crowd, waving his arms and shouting "in a terrible voice": "So, finish me off." Subsequent volleys killed him. In the heat of the moment, was this enough to convince Treshchenkov and the soldiers that the entire crowd of hundreds of workers rose up in unison, shouted hurrah, and dashed forward? Senator Manukhin did not think so. He included this episode in his recommendation for Treshchenkov's indictment.[53]

One last matter deserves consideration. In his private report to the emperor, Senator Manukhin recounted a curious incident during the shooting. "Five persons," he claimed without elaboration, "coming from the rear were shot." This referred to a version of an episode mentioned by Treshchenkov and other witnesses. Treshchenkov commented that from five to ten Feodosievsk workers, supposedly a "vanguard" of the two thousand Feodosievsk workers "on the way to [sic] Nadezhdinsk, were also shot at by the soldiers." An unsigned report turned in to the Manukhin Commission also refers to this incident. "When the police captain saw several workers come around the corner of the barracks to see what the shooting was all about," claimed the report, "he gestured there and another three workers were wounded."[54] Treshchenkov's comment about these workers as the "vanguard" of the Feodosievsk crowd was the purest fantasy. No such mass Feodosievsk descent had occurred that day, as Treshchenkov very well knew. The story had the design of concealing the fact that he had brought about the shooting of entirely innocent bystanders. Several soldiers commented, without explanation, that during the shooting, "the left flank of the soldiers broke up."[55] In order to shoot at the handful of workers coming around the building, these soldiers had to turn from the direction they were facing, breaking the lines. The whole affair smacks of a kind of "police riot." The authorities and their armed underlings, captured by blood lust, wantonly attacked anyone in their line of vision and even somewhat out of it. Manukhin probably introduced the episode into his evaluation without comment for this very reason. Malign intentions and execrable leadership caused the massacre.

THE AFTERMATH

The hopes of the government and Lenzoto notwithstanding, neither the arrests nor the shooting ended the strike. Displaying strong discipline, the workers quickly elected a new strike committee with

Petukhov as head, sent off a barrage of telegrams to the socialist factions in the Duma and other institutions, and continued their demands. Lenzoto yielded nothing. The unrepentant Treshchenkov, spurred on by police officials in Irkutsk and Petersburg, retained his accustomed stance toward the miners. On 5 April he issued a proclamation that warned workers against "forceful attacks on stores, arson, . . . the movement of crowds to other mines, . . . and listening to leaders who urge criminal activities. If necessary," continued the police captain, "send deputies who are not agitators for discussions." Perhaps bad conscience and fright elicited this message since the sources contain no sign of worker violence.

Treshchenkov then launched a wave of arrests in the days and weeks after the tragic events of 4 April. On 8 April Irkutsk police chief Poznanskii requested information about those arrested "in order to initiate criminal proceedings." Treshchenkov complied by sending the meager available data about arrestees. On the ninth Treshchenkov reported more arrests but informed Irkutsk that he was constrained by the capacity of the Bodaibo jail, which was built for 40 but already had 173 prisoners. On the seventeenth the local police arrested and interrogated Lebedev, who in the meantime had sent signed telegrams to the State Duma and other institutions in Russia. On the twenty-first criminal proceedings were begun against Batashev, who had avoided early arrest by leaving the area but who had returned and been arrested with many others. In late April and early May, I. D. Romanov, I. V. Prokhin, and A. N. Lesnoi were arrested for agitation. On 27 April, Treshchenkov fretted about the difficulty of arresting Popov (evidently Popov I), who, although "under guard" in the hospital, was making a slow recovery from wounds. A separate listing of people arrested for being "worker delegates" included names of twenty-three people who were elected deputies at various mines but who did not figure in the central affairs of the strike. This suggests the indiscriminate nature of Treshchenkov's actions after the shooting. Ceaselessly roaming the barracks, mines, and environs, he screamed, threatened, and arrested, until the cells of the Bodaibo jailhouse overflowed with hapless detainees.[56] Was the police captain exorcising demons from the mines or from his conscience?

Meanwhile, until their arrests P. Batashev and M. Lebedev, wounded in the shooting, managed to send a series of telegrams to various important destinations. Immediately after the shooting, Lebedev directed one message to five high-level government institutions— the Council of Ministers, the Ministries of Trade and Industry and Justice, and members of the State Duma P. N. Miliukov and E. P. Gegechkori. This communication laid blame for the shooting on

Treshchenkov, Preobrazhenskii, and Khitun, who "used arms, not being convinced of our peaceful intentions."

Lebedev's telegram informed its readers that Tul'chinskii, present in the crowd when the shooting occurred, "miraculously emerged unharmed from beneath the bodies." Batashev's telegram addressed the State Duma and other prominent personages—M. Rodzianko, N. A. Maklakov, Miliukov, F. I. Rodichev, and T. O. Belousov—similarly informing them of the chain of events. Whatever the effect of those messages (a rancorous debate occurred in the Duma), a subsequent Lebedev telegram to Governor Bantysh had distinct results. This message informed the embattled governor that "the early investigation [of the shooting is being] carried out by persons involved in shooting. Negatives of photographs have been seized. Police Captain Treshchenkov [is] going to the barracks to enforce work by means of threats." On 14 April Bantysh requested the removal of Khitun and Preobrazhenskii from the investigatory staff, to which Governor-General Kniazev agreed, somewhat belatedly, on 5 May.[57]

In his memoirs, Cherepakhin claimed to have been elected to head the strike committee in the immediate aftermath of the shooting, Batashev having temporarily left the area. If so this situation did not last long as he too was soon in jail. Various sources agree that Petukhov, a prominent Feodosievsk mine leader, chaired the postshooting strike committee. This group consisted of him, P. I. Podzakhodnikov, also of the Feodosievsk mine, I. I. Trifonov and S. K. Gorshechnikov of Andreevsk, S. V. Shabalov and E. G. Nosov of Aleksandrovsk, E. D. Pinaev of Prokop'evsk, and A. S. Golovizin of Ivanovsk.[58] It survived in the underground until Treshchenkov's rage subsided. During June and July 1912, after Treshchenkov's removal from the scene, the strike committee, still using the neutral designation "deputies," negotiated the last stages of the strike with full and respectful attention from government and company officials. At one point during June the strike leaders negotiated a temporary startup of work in order to show the members of the Manukhin Commission the workings of the mining process.

Neither the workers nor Lenzoto wavered in their determination to demand, on the workers' part, significant improvements in pay, hours, and other conditions or, on the company's part, to deny these. The full impasse continued. Kerensky, Nikitin, and other moderate socialist advocates from the Duma soon arrived to investigate. The result of their efforts was the 1913 publication of pertinent documents under the title "The Truth about the Lena Events." Meanwhile, the government chose Sen. S. Manukhin, former minister of justice, to head an investigative commission, which arrived on the scene on 1 June.[59] The miners went back to work briefly in order to familiarize the Manukhin Commission with mining operations and then resumed the strike. When full navigation resumed during July and August, the entire workforce of 8,909 workers, wives, and children abandoned the mines and, traveling in seven large groups, departed the area.[60]

The postmassacre strike leadership faced daunting problems in the form of continued arrests, incessant searches, unceasing provocative behavior on the part of Treshchenkov and his associates, threatened criminal charges against numerous elected strike leaders, and the refusal of the company to bend on any of the major issues. Regardless, it continued to function with surprising authority among workers and officials until the mass exodus from the mines. Not a single disorderly episode made its way into any company, police, or other records of the postshooting period, any more than before the shooting. This was the case despite the continued efforts of some officials to create an impression of worker violence.[61]

Lenzoto's profitability suffered badly. Well into the fall, after the hiring of new workers, local rumors constantly forecast the outbreak of new strikes, although no such thing occurred.[62] In later years, Lenzoto began to rely in some measure on Chinese and Korean laborers because of their supposed quiescence in the face of harsh conditions. Beginning several years after the revolution, lengthy negotiations between the Soviet and British governments attempted unsuccessfully to find a formula for compensation of British investments and for the establishment of a British mining concession.[63] The area became part of the Soviet Union's gold-mining industry, as it is for Russia today.

Tul'chinskii emerged as a hero, retained his position, published his memoirs in the early 1920s, and died in the early 1930s. In 1938 the Soviet secret police posthumously calumniated him as a tsarist police agent. Lenzoto and the tsarist police lauded Treshchenkov, but information soon surfaced that the SRs planned to assassinate him. Following on Manukhin's recommendation that he be indicted for his actions during the strike and massacre, the Irkutsk procurator brought criminal charges against Treshchenkov. The charges, however, were soon dropped. Instead, the government arranged his move to Petersburg, where he lived under an assumed name with a monthly pension. Later, two versions of his death emerged: he perished in battle during the First World War or he survived to be shot by the Soviet government in 1920. During the fall of 1912 Lenzoto quietly released both Belozerov and Teppan from employment. Simultaneously, the Irkutsk authorities indicted Teppan for possession of contraband, presumably gold, with what results is not known.[64] In the 1920s a Soviet court convicted Teppan of complicity in the massacre. Presumably, he was shot, although the record does not specify his ultimate fate. Belozerov lived abroad until his death. Most of the worker leaders lapsed into obscurity. Several perished in Siberia during the civil war. Cherepakhin, Batashev, Petukhov, and Lebedev survived the revolution and civil war. During 1917 Petukhov chaired the Kuznetsk workers' soviet. The surviving leaders eventually became communists, held middling positions in and around the soviets, and enjoyed a modest fame.

Lenzoto managing director I. N. Belozerov. This and all subsequent images are reprinted from *Lenskii rasstrel. Al'bom,* comp. T. Takonulo (Moscow, 1932).

Member of the Imperial State Council and Lenzoto administrator V. I. Timiriazev.

Lena Goldfield Company director Alfred Ginzburg.

Work proceeds under the observation of guards.

Workers' summer living quarters.

Andreevsk Mine.

Workers meeting at a mine.

Members of the Strike Bureau, Strike Committee, and the Barracks' elders.

Police captain N. V. Treshchenkov.

Workers' March to Nadezhdenski mine, the site of the shooting.

Detail from an artistic representation of the Lena shooting.

Photograph of bodies after the shooting.

Photograph of bodies after the shooting.

Demonstration at the mass grave of the Lena workers.

Wives and children of the massacred workers.

The Committee of Workers' Deputies.

Workers discuss the governor's suggestion to return to work after the shooting.

Workers leaving the Aleksandrovsk mine.

Workers embark on barges.

Politics, the Strike Committee, and Competing Discourses

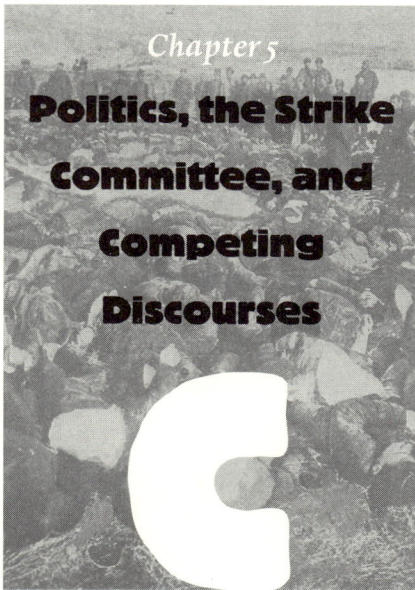

ontemporary observers strove mightily to crack the puzzle of the Lena goldfields strike. Was it political or economic, spontaneous or planned, and, if the last, by whom and how? Police Captain Treshchenkov belatedly portrayed the strike as of "purely Social-Democratic inspiration." Soviet historiography later asserted outright Bolshevik leadership. During the 1920s, the Soviet writer Zhukov cautioned against "bolshevizing" the Lena strike but then "menshevized" it by attributing its leadership primarily to Mensheviks. Acting Lenzoto Director Teppan insisted on the political nature of the strike but characterized the leadership simply as "socialist." Many state and company officials followed Teppan's lead in asserting the political, rather than merely economic, nature of the strike, without tying it to any particular party. An alternative interpretation eschewed political analysis entirely. Manukhin, joined later by early Soviet historians Sh. Levin and V. Vladimirova, in effect discounted politics by evaluating the strike as sheerly economic in origins and execution. A third approach approximated the actuality, in my interpretation, by blending politics and economics. The Irkutsk police chief Vasil'ev and procurator E. Nimander fixed the events firmly within the context of a generalized multiparty socialist culture within the workers' movement. In Vasil'ev's commentary, this generic socialist culture had arisen in Russia during the 1890s and early 1900s. In the Vasil'ev-Nimander interpretation, the purely economic Lena goldfields strike arose out of and reflected an acutely politicized socioeconomic context.[1]

Whatever motivations inspired these various evaluations, during the events themselves the question of political involvement, as well as the related potential characterization of the strike as "political," took on vast living significance. This was so because determinations about these matters, even if wide of the mark, played a role in measures taken in relationship to the strike and its leaders. For example, the authorities ultimately arrested the strike leadership, used armed force against a worker demonstration, and later, brought criminal charges against people accused of complicity in promoting and leading the strike and thereby violating statutes associated with political activities. The authorities thus "politicized" the strike by acting on the assumption that it had political goals and leadership. It is precisely at this juncture that competing discourses come most clearly into play.

Examining all available evidence, including that used by the government itself, is necessary to establish an accurate picture of the degree of socialist involvement. This pertains to direct, indirect, organized, unorganized, or any other type of socialist influence or activity in the calling and leading of the strike. The matter is complicated by the fact that the Lena mine workers, with economic motivations, indisputably chose as strike leaders a number of individuals with political and even party backgrounds. Indeed, in the Russian Empire of 1912 any group of eight thousand working people in any conceivable realm of production at any location would have contained a significant number of individuals who had contacts with radical political movements. In all likelihood, they and other workers would also have participated in the well-organized strikes and demonstrations that were common coin in turn-of-the-century Russia. In Eastern Siberia, where numerous political exiles or former such exiles eked out their livelihoods as best they could, including in and around the gold mines, the presence of members of "parties" was further insured. That on this occasion miners chose as strike leaders socialists and anarchists, whose numbers were quite limited in terms of the overall size of the workforce, is itself a commentary on worker oppositionist culture of the post-1905 era.

SOCIALISM ON THE LENA DURING THE EARLY TWENTIETH CENTURY

Early twentieth-century (1900–1906) Lena area strikes had been entirely economic. The police observed no notable agitation or involvement of political organizations or members. If political propaganda occurred, it was limited enough in scope that it left little trace. For instance, the Irkutsk procurator decided against bringing criminal charges against any strikers during 1901 because the technically illegal strikes had "not contained any traces of socialist propaganda." In his 1906–1907 report, the governor-general informed the emperor that "the [recent] strikes in several [Eastern Siberian mining] regions were exclusively economic and ended rather quickly."[2] Still, throughout this period elected strike delegates, sometimes characterized by authorities as "experienced," clearly helped introduce a new degree of organization into the strikes, presumably on the basis of expertise gained from previous contact with the radical movements then sweeping Russia. For example, an identified leader of the 1904 Andreevsk strike was a certain P. D. Palladiev, a former factory worker in his native Smolensk who had then labored on the construction of the Trans-Siberian railroad line in Manchuria before coming to the gold mines. He and others with analogous previous histories were elected as strike delegates (*vybornye*) during the 1901–1904 strikes. The authorities noted the presence of such individuals and attributed to them the increased level of "organization" and "discipline," to which might be added "well-constructed strike demands."[3] Thus from the beginning of the century Lena area strikes trod a fine line between, on the one hand, the economic nature of their goals and, on the other, experienced leadership. The leadership, despite the stated economic goals of this or that strike, might, under certain circumstances, be interpreted as having political motivations. For the moment, however, the authorities chose not to press the point.

In fact, rudimentary attempts at organized political agitation did occur. During the spring of 1902, a not particularly stormy period at the mines, the Vitim district engineer R. Levitskii reported that "among the workers several experienced orators have turned up who had participated in disorders in Russia or who had been trained by . . . political exiles." The engineer further alleged that two political exiles, clerical employees of Lenzoto, had for two years carried out "underground illegal agitation" and had "left among the workers and employees many pupils and whose lessons had not disappeared." That this last may have been true is suggested by the fact that during the spring of 1905, a period of almost complete quiet at the mines, the very first hectographed political leaflets appeared in the region. Their demands included the eight-hour day, the end of the Russo-Japanese war, and the overthrow of the autocracy. After an investigation, the police arrested three Lenzoto clerks, confiscated a hectograph machine located at the distant Krutoi mine, and, whether accurately or not, concluded that "no workers were involved." In later commenting on this episode, Senator Manukhin made no political identification of the arrestees, although a Soviet-era author identified one of them, A. A. Zalogin, as an Irkutsk Social Democrat (SD).[4] Perhaps this 1905 episode reflected the efforts of the two earlier exiles, whose "pupils and . . . lessons had not disappeared."

Shortly before the 1905 Revolution (and thus overlapping with the above-noted circle), P. M. Anan'ev, a long-time revolutionary of peasant origins and a member of the Socialist-Revolutionary (SR) Party, arrived in Bodaibo, where he lived for three years. Even in places far less remote than Bodaibo political exiles formed a cohesive subculture of close ties and relationships. Thus Anan'ev would have been fully apprised of the activities of other exiles. They all knew or became acquainted with one another and normally pooled their efforts. For example, a 1912 interparty (SD-SR) commission in Irkutsk investigated charges of provocation against a certain socialist. According to the author of a brief biography about Anan'ev published in the journal *Katorga i ssylka* in 1923, during his three-year stay in the area Anan'ev carried out direct propaganda in the mines and "sent quite a number of political exiles to live temporarily in the mines as workers." (One might call this a modified Lavrov approach to propaganda.)[5] He reputedly acted as a revolutionary coordinator and facilitator in Bodaibo, where he organized workers, set up readings courses for clerical employees, established circles for the exiles, and even managed to contact the garrison soldiers in the mining town. Before leaving for Irkutsk, where he worked for the SR Party, Anan'ev, in the words of his biographer, helped create "the ground for the explosion that occurred there . . . in 1912."[6] Perhaps so, but connections are tenuous between the earlier efforts of various SDs and SRs and the events of 1912. Most workers, employees, and political exiles did not remain long in the area. The people who emerged as leaders of the 1912 strike had only the haziest connection to the earlier activist groups. The collective experience of Lena area activism serves primarily to establish that at any given time revolutionaries and workers with previous involvement in strikes and demonstrations were on the spot and could step forward as the need arose.

Nonetheless not all ties with the past should be discounted. Propaganda and organizational activities connected with local political exiles and aimed in good part at mining workers can be loosely traced from the first years of the century and stretching through 1908 (and presumably beyond). Since political exiles had varied, staggered, and therefore overlapping terms and some came from elsewhere to work during their exile terms or stayed on to work after their expiration, lore about past people, groups, and activities inevitably filtered down. The thread of this story is picked up again by early 1910, perhaps eighteen months after Anan'ev's departure from the immediate area. The brief lapse of time would have ensured that some of the current exiles would have known Anan'ev or at least known about his activities, just as Anan'ev and his fellow conspirators would have known of the 1902 and 1905 circles.

Bodaibo Activism

Police reports and memoirs of participants indicate the existence by March 1910 of a communal apartment (*obshchestvennaia kvartira*) in Bodaibo where political exiles lived, had meals, gathered, and even maintained a mutual-help fund and library. According to a report turned in by a member who also was secretly spying for the police, the members formed a commission (Z. Ozolin, A. G. Gabalov, and A. K. Skrynnikov) to aid impoverished political exiles. For this purpose the commission collected 2 percent of employed exiles' monthly salaries, plus other contributions. Among the financial contributors to the endeavor were Police Inspector Galkin, Justice of the Peace Ivanov, Police Officer M. P. Dunaev, and the lumber magnate and trustee of the local hospital Butylkin. The establishment consisted of four rooms and a kitchen located on the bottom floor of a two-story stone building located near the Bodaibo hospital and police station. According to various reports and recollections, from twenty to thirty legal and illegal political exiles could always be found at the apartment. Why police officials, among others, contributed to the support of political exiles, some in the area illegally, is not clear. Perhaps the plight of the exiles had impressed them at firsthand. One report claimed that Galkin was sympathetic because his son was a political exile elsewhere in Siberia.[7] The existence of a centralized location, conveniently near the police station, also offered the police a way of keeping an eye on the activities and whereabouts of exiles.

Just before and after the Lena shooting, some police officials attempted to use Galkin's alleged support of the exile's cause to discredit him. His consistent evaluation of the strike as "peaceful" and "economic" definitely annoyed higher authorities. The memoirs of M. Lebedev, one of the people who frequented the premises of the communal apartment, indicate instead that the members were at pains to avoid even the appearance of political activities. As one observer warned, "if Inspector Galkin gets wind of [any political work], he will immediately shut down everything . . . communal apartment, the library, and the mutual-help fund." On one occasion, when Galkin found out that one of the group's associates was an escaped political exile living in Bodaibo under an assumed name, he immediately had him arrested and sent back to his assigned place of exile. In other cases, the police turned a blind eye to people who had no documentation whatsoever.[8] These factors support the idea that the police sponsored the communal apartment at least in part as a control measure. In any case, Galkin does not seem to have displayed undue softness to political exiles.

Sometime during 1910 an underground revolutionary circle, perhaps carrying on from similar earlier groups, began functioning with the direct involvement of some of the communal apartment dwellers. Police reports evaluated this phenomenon in terms of increased pressures by 1910 among the political exiles to expand the scope of agitation and organization among the nearby mining population. If accurate, this development in Bodaibo replicated national tendencies at that time. The group first met at the apartment of a certain L. G. Golubkov, an agronomist by profession locally employed as a teacher, allegedly a Bolshevik who had been involved in the publication of a party newspaper in Moscow. This underground group consisted of SDs, SRs, anarchists, and other "convinced oppositionists." The broad scope, according to the unidentified police spy, reflected the need to pool efforts since "otherwise a split would occur and everything would fall through." Ozolin, the upright member of the mutual-aid fund and clerk for Justice Ivanov, gave substantial help as an expert forger of passports and documents. The group set up an editorial commission of three, including Golubkov, Ozolin, and Marchinkovskii. According to the police spy, the editorial commission issued propaganda of economic tendency and distributed it at the mines. The recollections of Batashev (a Menshevik-oriented SD), Lebedev (a nonparty SD sympathizer who was living in the area illegally and who had received forged papers through Ozolin), and Cherepakhin all mention the circle. According to them, other members included Dumpe (a Menshevik-inclined SD), Rozenberg (an anarchist), and G. G. Sushkin. A certain N. I. Nagikh, reputedly an SD and former Second Duma deputy recently released from hard labor, at first proved unwilling to risk rearrest and declined to participate. Later, he played a limited role. A number of these individuals worked in Lenzoto mines and several were 1912 strike leaders (Batashev, Lebedev, Cherepakhin, Dumpe, and Rozenberg).

Although none of the memoirists mention it, several police reports claim that during 1911 some members of the group formed an underground labor union responsible for issuing leaflets with economic agitation that were distributed at the mines that year. According to one report, the labor union members included Ozolin, Sushkin, Golubkov, and various delegates to individual mines.[9] This tendency of activity seems to fit the general picture provided by the spy and the memoirists, although none of these individuals characterized the group as a "labor union." Possibly, people who later wrote their memoirs as members of the Communist Party strove to disassociate themselves somewhat from what was solidly economic, union-oriented rather than political work. This may also help explain why these same memoirists mostly "recalled" SD members, whereas the police spy's contemporary account emphasized SD, SR, and anarchist membership.

According to the memoirists, during 1911 the underground group attempted to move its activities closer to the mines. The members held meetings at the Peoples' Center and sponsored a library nearby. Several members entered the amateur theater group and laid plans for plays, which, for one reason or another, the vigilant Galkin always canceled. All told, the group counted about fifteen to twenty workers from the various mines. As far as the limited available information reveals, the union accomplished very little, except for the issuing of several leaflets, before the outbreak of the 1912 strike.[10]

Political Exiles and Parties

Local "revolutionary" activities prior to the Lena strike evidently therefore consisted of a communal apartment in Bodaibo under police observation, an underground group with a small editorial commission that allegedly issued leaflets, and a shadowy labor union either identical with or somehow associated with the underground group. Materials from police archives for the Irkutsk region during 1912 hardly enhance this less than expansive picture. Police Colonel Vasil'ev claimed that during the year or so before the strike's outbreak the police "had no agents in Bodaibo," since the single secret agent had moved to Kirensk. In terms of general surveillance, primary attention went to the SD and SR parties, which together accounted for most of the several thousand political exiles scattered throughout the vast region. About the SDs, routine surveillance indicated that various individuals in Kirensk and nearby localities received mail from abroad and SD newspapers such as *Pravda* (Truth), *Rabochaia gazeta* (Workers' Paper), and *Irkutskoe slovo* (Irkutsk Word). On 4 February 1912, a certain A. K. Vinogradov, an otherwise obscure individual, sent a letter from Bodaibo to the Petersburg address of V. M. Batashev, former SD Second Duma deputy and reputedly brother of the prominent strike leader P. N. Batashev. (In view of their different patronymic initials, "N" and "M," their degree of kinship, if any, must have been that of cousins.) The perlustrated letter addressed routine party matters, mentioned the party newspaper, *Zvezda* (Star), and commented on Plekhanov's and Lenin's views on certain matters. Nothing in it remotely concerned local affairs. On 14 April, ten days after the shooting, a raid on an underground SD headquarters in Nizhnii-Novgorod turned up the Bodaibo address of L. G. Golubkov and M. V. Skvortsov, individuals associated with the local group of political exiles. Neither, however, played any personal role in the Lena strike. A few weeks later, Treshchenkov, presumably informed of the Nizhnii-Novgorod discoveries, arrested Skvortsov as a political exile without documentation for local residency. The balance of the reports pertained to postshooting strikes, mostly in Irkutsk, as part of the general empirewide Lena protest movement. Reports noted the existence of SD circles in Irkutsk among bakers, railroad workers, typographical workers, and commercial clerks. Prominent SDs such as N. Rozhkov and several others involved with the newspaper *Irkutskoe slovo* helped organize Lena protest strikes in their city.[11]

The more detailed surveillance of the SRs followed roughly the same lines. Various SRs at political exile in Kirensk, Vitim, and Bodaibo received party newspapers such as *Znamia truda* (Banner of Labor), *Za Narod* (For the People), *Zemlia i volia* (Land and Freedom), and *Sibirskie otkliki* (Siberian Echoes). The last, a local legal SR equivalent of the SD *Irkutskoe slovo*, appeared with the involvement of the SRs I. Goldberg, Kazimir Gintoft, P. Ozernykh, and M. Kleinmeikhel. On 23 February the police initiated criminal action against an SR resident of Bodaibo, a certain N. L. Ivanov-Martynov, for a long list of political crimes dating back to 1907. During April Ivanov-Martynov received suspicious letters from Paris that were intercepted by the police. In late May, an Irkutsk SR by the name of S. I. Kravchinskii was arrested for attempting to organize illegal Lena protest demonstrations and strikes among government clerks. The police attributed to Gintoft the distribution of copies of a pertinent back issue of the SR newspaper *Zemlia i volia* in connection with the Lena strike and shooting. That same month, several Irkutsk SRs and the SD Rozhkov took part in a joint commission to investigate charges that a certain Sushchenskii had engaged in provocation. The Irkutsk SRs Vinogradov, Emel'ianov, and Mitroev were arrested for organizing a ring for robberies (expropriations). An SR-related police case in Vitim resulted in the arrest of one A. N. Alekseevskii. On 25 May E. Breshko-Breshkovskaia, an exile in Kirensk, received a letter from Vasilii Kalashnikov, an SR resident of Kharbin, who wrote that he "worried about the Lena; I always expect [bad news] and read the newspapers with beating heart. Unfortunately, there has been no list of the killed and I am alarmed about several of my acquaintances."[12]

Locally, the police seem to have considered the SRs a greater headache than the SDs. In truth, however, their activities were quite similar. The police reports firmly establish that SDs and SRs, including numerous exiles, lived in Irkutsk, Kirensk, Vitim, and Bodaibo They corresponded with party comrades in other places, including abroad. They received party newspapers, including illegal ones. They carried out some organizational work and other revolutionary work. Not surprisingly, they responded to the Lena strike and shooting in similar ways. What regional police surveillance did not turn up, as the Irkutsk police chief and procurator soon admitted, was anything at all about underground activities in Bodaibo that suggested the organized involvement of political parties in the onset or leadership of the Lena goldfields strike.

This may have merely reflected inadequate surveillance. At the time of the strike's onset the authorities had no agents in Bodaibo with whom to keep track of the exiles' putative underground activities. In considering these matters later, Senator Manukhin also noted that "for all of Irkutsk Province with over 3,000 political exiles, there is not one guard. I misspoke," continued Manukhin; "there are six guards assigned to Little Grandmother Breshko-Breshkovskaia." In order to pay for their upkeep, political exiles enjoyed the routine privilege of seeking employment wherever they could find it regionally. Consequently, at any given time roughly half the exiles were absent from their places of exile.[13] The relatively sparse police presence completed a picture of less-than-exacting police control of exiles. For the most part, the political exiles could have done what they wished with little chance of discovery.

Indeed, the mining engineer Aleksandrov, who initially had insisted on the strike's spontaneity and its thoroughgoing economic basis, several months later proffered a new version. "Undoubtedly, the strike was arranged beforehand according to a plan put together for at least two years [prior to the event]." As proof, Aleksandrov alleged that during July 1911 a prominent newspaper (he "thought" *Utro Rossii* [Morning in Russia]) had carried a spurious announcement of a strike of "8,000 workers" at the Lena mines and that many regional newspapers picked up the report. Furthermore, confided the engineer, this number of "8,000 strikers" had figured again in the first reports of the actual strike. Lastly, under interrogation one worker claimed, according to Aleksandrov, that "we were ordered to strike on 26 June [1911] but it did not work out, but now it worked out." Perhaps Aleksandrov had in mind a report handed in to the procurator's office by a certain K. V. Preobrazhenskii, resident of Vitim since 1891. Preobrazhenskii (not the assistant procurator of that name) claimed that a group of Vitim political exiles, obscure individuals whom he listed, directly organized the strike.[14] Bearing all the characteristics of a simple denunciation, this report worked its way into some internal police reports. Since no hint exists of actual ties between those denounced and the Lena strike, the matter deserves no further attention.

All such allegations about alleged responsibility for the strike lack credibility and suggest, on the contrary, the spontaneous nature of the strike. The region's footloose and fancy-free political exiles do not seem to have played a role, except for those already familiar individuals who actually worked in and around the mines. After all, what would have prevented involved individuals years or decades later from revealing a plan for a strike, had one existed? In the Soviet Union, this would have been an advantageous thing to do. In fact, it is surprising that no one chose to embroider reality by retroactively inventing such a plan. Indeed, some memoirists later fantasized a certain "Bolshevik" role in the prestrike exile association and within the strike leadership once it was under way. Not even these individuals, however, ever mentioned a "plan." As far as evidence reveals, the strike's outbreak caught by surprise local company administrators, police officials, and the political exiles, natural leaders of the local workers' movement. If any plan existed, its perpetrators enjoyed total success in hiding all traces down to this day.

THE STRIKE AND ITS LEADERS

Immediately after the strike's outbreak, alternative versions of its nature arose. The early and continued observations of Galkin, Aleksandrov, Tul'chinskii, and Bantysh, respectively, police inspector, mining engineer, chief mining engineer, and governor, indicated to them that the affair was economic and peaceful. The other version, that the strike was political, received initial sponsorship from local Lenzoto officials and then gradually from certain local, regional, and national government figures. In this interpretation, political exiles led, if not provoked, the work stoppage, which from the very outset was tainted by violence and threats of violence. Consequently, local company officials and police authorities at once attempted to ascertain the names of the strike leaders and sought information with which to characterize the nature of the leadership. To a certain degree, this was perfectly reasonable. Company and police officials had observed established modes of procedure in advising the workers to elect strike delegates. Ideally, such delegates would present written strike demands, negotiate with officials, and keep the strike within peaceful and organized boundaries. The officials who negotiated with them naturally evinced curiosity about their individual and group identities. Documents from local government officials, especially early in the strike, often referred collectively to the "workers' delegates," the "strike delegates," or simply the "delegates," signifying the people chosen by the workers to represent the various mines.[15]

Lenzoto had a different view. From the outset, company officials began to use less neutral terms for the strike leaders and the strike. As early as 29 February, Managing Director Teppan's messages to company headquarters referred to mines being "taken out" on strike. This turn of phrase robbed the strike of its voluntary nature by implying that some agency "impelled" miners to strike. On 3 March he stated that "everything suggests that the strike will be a prolonged one." To this glum but accurate assessment, he added, "one can [also] expect a strike of the railroads and telegraph," an imaginary, indeed paranoid, scenario that suggested images from the Russian Revolution in 1905. On following days, Teppan further sharpened his language. For example, a 4 March telegram referred to "strike instigators" (*zachinshchikov-zabastovshchikov*) who "exercised control" of the movement. The acting director also emphasized the "well-organized" nature of the strike and its "threatening character." On the eighth the acting manager added another dash of alarm by characterizing the workers' demands as "purely socialist," that is, he continued, they included "the eight-hour day."[16]

Thus during the very first days Teppan painted a vivid verbal picture, whose terms dominated the language and outlooks of top company officials and their ministerial acquaintances for the entire duration of the conflict. As regards Lenzoto officialdom in Petersburg, this too was understandable since for them Teppan served as prime source of information about the events. Top government ministers, however, should have relied on their own sources, who were painting a quite different picture. That they relied instead entirely on hardly disinterested company sources is one of the chief characteristics of the entire affair.

In any case, throughout the first two weeks of the strike, company and state officials carried out negotiations with the strike delegates, thus in effect conceding the delegates' legality and appropriateness. When, however, the first round of negotiations ended on 12 March, the authorities adopted a new stance toward the strike and its leadership, not just in terms of comments but in action. On the fourteenth Galkin conducted a detailed interrogation of Gorinov, director of the People's Center, where strike meetings had been conducted until the company closed its doors to workers. Gorinov's testimony revealed the names of several main strike leaders, whom he had already known by name or had come to know during meetings and negotiations. Gorinov designated Batashev as chair of the "strike committee" (a fateful turn of phrase) and named Popov I, Viazovoi, A. Bezpal'chenko, Dumpe, and "Kopach" (Digger; later identified as a nickname for Korneev) as members. From Gorinov, various mining engineers, and several snitches among the workers, Justice Khitun compiled a list that accurately named much of the strike leadership, that is, the strike committee and the bureau. Besides those named above, the list included Zelionko, Budevits, Rozenberg, Bykov, Romanov, Sobolev, Solomin, and Gerasimenko. By 20 March the authorities were able to specify a seventeen-person "central strike committee," missing only Cherepakhin and Lebedev. They also accurately identified the individual mine "committees," that is, the delegates elected at each mine.[17]

Some of this information was hardly fresh. For example, in a 4 March telegram Teppan had referred to the "assistant station master" (Popov I) as the "head of the strike movement." Until almost mid-month, however, identifications received casual treatment. No prior evidence exists in the police records of a concerted effort to compile a list of any kind. Between 12 and 20 March, such an effort occurred with good success. In the eyes of the authorities, matters now had to do with a "strike committee" that consisted in part of political exiles and some of whom lived in the area without documents. On 16 March directives went out to arrest all political exiles residing illegally in the area. When Ukraintsev and Karpov were detained for agitating at one of the distant mines, Karpov was soon released, whereas Ukraintsev, who had no papers, remained in custody despite workers' efforts to release him.[18] It is interesting to note that as yet the authorities were unwilling to disrupt the strike delegate collective, whatever they called it, even when members were political exiles, as long as they had residence permits.

Even so, the failed early negotiations, along with the dawning realization about the makeup of the strike leadership, led to a hardening of company and state resolve. Messages now regularly designated the strike delegates as the "strike committee." The authorities began to collect bits and pieces of evidence aimed at demonstrating the existence of a strike committee. Gorinov's remark that he had overheard Popov I characterize Batashev as the "chairperson" or "assistant chairperson" of the strike committee counted as proof, as did Batashev's alleged comment to Teppan about a "central strike bureau of delegates." Testimony surfaced that the Andreevsk miners referred to their strike deputies as the "committee." Various scraps of paper were collected after workers' meetings, some of which allegedly referred to the "strike committee," the "central strike committee," or even the "central strike bureau." One of the mine managers reported that on 8 March two deputies told him that they belonged to the "central strike committee." Evidence of this kind entered a special report compiled by local officials entitled "On the Strike Committee." Its purpose was to serve as justification for antistrike measures and as evidence in criminal charges brought against arrested strike leaders.

The police remained unaware of the existence of a central bureau or advisory group that including Dumpe, Rozenberg, and Popov I. In fact, direct knowledge of this shadowy group comes entirely from memoirs published later. Senator Manukhin's detailed report fails to mention any such phenomenon, although Procurator Nimander's July 1912 report uses the term "central strike bureau." Perhaps he simply meant "committee." After the publication of various memoirs, the Soviet historian Vladimirova was able to speak of both a "central strike bureau" that consisted of Batashev, Popov I, Dumpe, Cherepakhin, and Zelionko and a separate secret advisory bureau of Dumpe, Cherepakhin, Rozenberg and Budevits. Regardless, during 1912 the officials focused attention entirely on the "seventeen-person strike committee."[19] Conceivably, the "bureau" and the "advisory council" were figments of later imagination, although the existence of such groups was entirely plausible under the circumstances.

Setting aside the insoluble bureau question, much was at stake in the matter of whether or not the strike leaders were mere elected deputies or a full-blown "strike committee." Certain tsarist legislation bears on the matter. Beginning in 1858 tsarist criminal codes drew attention to organizers, leaders, and members of "secret organizations, no matter by what name, having an aim harmful to the peacefulness or wholeness of the state or in violation of any existing laws." Such people were subject to prosecution, imprisonment, exile to Siberia, or capital punishment. Even if such organizations did not have obviously criminal goals, if they in any way threatened existing national, regional, or local institutions, the people involved were still subject to all the above measures including the death penalty. Government officials could and did sometimes use such sweeping statutes to punish almost anything they found obnoxious or undesirable. Since at least 1845 tsarist laws had also specifically proscribed all strikes. The 1885 factory law codes, which in many ways enhanced the protection of workers, nevertheless penalized "strikes of workers of any plant, factory, or manufacturing enterprise." The 1902 criminal code (article 1358) further tightened the language by specifying the criminal nature of any work stoppage having the goal of "raising pay . . . [or] altering any work conditions." The law also forbade strike participants (*uchastniki stachki*) from destroying or damaging the property of entrepreneurs and employees or "forc[ing] other workers to stop work by means of violence or threats."[20]

In December 1905 a new law appeared that rescinded parts of article 1358 (1902 Code) by forbidding strikes *only* in state-owned enterprises or those with special "state or social significance." In effect, this legalized strikes in most privately owned concerns.[21] However, the 1857 laws against "secret organizations" remained in effect, as did statutes of article 1358 against property damage or inducing others to stop work by "violence" or "threats." In a 7 March 1912 written warning to Lena workers against disorders, Mining Engineer Aleksandrov specified still existing sections of article 1358. Similarly, one of Treshchenkov's messages referred to the criminal code statute against "criminal secret organizations."[22] When company officials and the police ceased visualizing the strike leaders as elected delegates and began instead to view them as a "strike committee," with, furthermore, the membership of political exiles, some of whom were illegal residents , they were in effect accusing them of being in violation of laws against "secret organizations." This also throws a special light on the cases when officials emphasized the "taking out of mines" by force, or alleged that strike leaders made threats against other workers, or spoke of threats against company or state property. In all such cases, by plausible interpretations of existing laws, they drew a bead on illegal behavior on the part of strikers and strike leaders. They also raised the possibility of repressive measures against them. Whether the individual charges or allegations had substance, even in the minds of those using them, is another matter. In this regard, government officials such as Inspector Galkin, Chief Engineer Tul'chinskii, Governor Bantysh, and the head of the postshooting investigatory commission, Senator Manukhin, consistently used the term *vybornye* for the strike leaders. They also dismissed allegations about the strikers' "violent" or "threatening" behavior as minor and routine.

Even as the authorities compiled the list of strike leaders, they also put together lists of local political exiles, an altogether more complicated matter. One such list dated 23 March counted fifteen people sent to the area for state crimes, most of whom worked for Lenzoto or in Bodaibo. An expanded version of this list with the names of 25 people appeared shortly thereafter. Treshchenkov later claimed that 43 political exiles lived in the area at the time of the strike and shooting, whereas other accounts mentioned even larger figures (80 to 120). The problem confronting the authorities in compiling accurate lists deepened because some exiles were actually assigned to Bodaibo for the term of their sentences, whereas others employed in or near Bodaibo had penal assignments to Kirensk, Vitim, or even farther afield, all variants of which were perfectly legal. Manukhin figured that fully 37 Vitim and Kirensk exiles lived and worked legally in the Bodaibo area.[23] Other exiles worked in the area with forged papers or simply lived in the underground without documents (the illegal residents noted above). Yet others were exiles whose terms had expired but who remained in or came to the area to work. Given the sparse surveillance and the tendency of police for conspiratorial reasons to ignore some known illegal residents, one can imagine how the different numbers arose. It is also clear that the 80 to 120 range actually described the likely number of people at political exile residing in and around the mines.

Regardless, two lists, which the police generated to help shed light on the strike leadership, named a total of 28 exiles living in Bodaibo. These included the following individuals who were members of the exile association–underground union: M. V. Makhlin, N. L. Ivanov-Martynov, L. Golubkov, I. Nagikh, I. Rozenberg, and G. Sushkin. None of the rest appear in any other sources whatsoever, much less in those pertaining to the strike and shooting. One may conclude that no fewer than 22 political exiles from the lists of those officially living in the area simply played no role in any known underground or strike activities. Nor could Ivanov-Martynov, an SR whom the police had arrested earlier in the year, have had a role in the strike. This leaves only Makhlin, Golubkov, Nagikh, Rozenberg, and Sushkin, all of whom figure in the data about the association of political exiles. Indeed, they were legally residing political exiles, as a consequence of which their appearance on lists of people of this status reveals nothing about the strike. Only Rozenberg was also a member of the strike leadership. According to some versions, he was also a member of the central strike committee, although he was not an elected delegate of the Nadezhdinsk workshop where he was employed. According to other versions, he was also a member of the secret advisory bureau. In any case, the police eventually arrested him as one of the strike leaders, which he was.

Meanwhile, the names of illegally residing exiles—Batashev, Cherepakhin, Ukraintsev, Zelionko, and Lebedev—and several political exiles employed legally in the area—Dumpe, Popov I, Sobolev, and others—did not appear on these lists. That Ukraintsev did not figure on this list is odd since he had already been arrested as an illegal resident. Regardless, some of them—Dumpe, Lebedev, Batashev, and Cherepakhin—had been members of the prestrike exile association. Presumably, several of them—Dumpe, Popov I, and Sobolev—had exile assignments elsewhere but had come to the area to work in order to support themselves, as allowed by law. Still others—Lebedev, Batashev, Zelionko, and Cherepakhin—appeared on no official lists of exiles because they resided in the area illegally. Only one thing can be stated with certainty. Although a number of political exiles of one or another status played roles in the strike leadership, the official police lists of locally residing political exiles singularly failed to zero in on the strike leadership. It is also clear that a sizable majority of local political exiles of whatever status did not involve themselves in the strike or in any other traceable organized activities. The political exiles involved in the strike leadership, with the single exception of Rozenberg, either lived in the area illegally or worked in the area legally but away from their assigned place of political exile. A likely explanation is that such individuals felt themselves relatively freer of police observation than officially residing local exiles. People of the former category were therefore more likely to involve themselves in activism.

The authorities also paid some attention to political parties in their attempts to characterize the strike. Early on, some company and police officials mentioned Social Democracy or socialism as potential factors. Within a week of the strike's outbreak Teppan had already characterized the strike demands as "socialist" in nature in that they contained the plank for the eight-hour day. Treshchenkov later claimed that he had considered the strike to be "Social Democratic" in inspiration but, he continued somewhat lamely, had not emphasized it at the time because "no agents' reports supported this." Indeed, no local agents existed, and regional police reports turned up nothing about any sort of party ties with the strike. As the investigation of causes, circumstances, and consequences of the strike intensified after the shooting, the government looked closely at the SD and SR parties and the anarchists as well. Indeed, as individuals, members of those groups took part in the strike in various capacities. If anything, the results of this investigation were even less conclusive for the authorities than their examination of lists of political exiles.

For example, the Manukhin Commission put together one partial list of strike leaders titled "Evidence about Members of the Strike Committee of the Bodaibo Strike, April 1912." The "evidence" was as follows:

> I. A. Budevits— in 1908 Eniseisk police heard that he was involved in revolutionary agitation in Kansk.
> E. Iu. Dumpe—peasant of twenty-six years, in 1908 condemned in Riga for belonging to group calling for forcible change of government. Exiled in 1910.
> E. Ia. Mimogliadov—from Kherson peasantry. Exiled to Eniseisk in 1908. Involved in criminal activity in Achinsk district. Concealed himself.
> I. S. Rozenberg—finished mining institute in Riga. Arrested in Chita in 1906. Exiled at hard labor for four years. Came to Iakutsk province in 1909.
> A. A. Sobolev—in 3rd Siberian Battalion in Vilno in 1907. Arrested for distributing SR leaflets among young soldiers. Exiled.
> M. F. Ukraintsev—in 59th Recruit Liubling Regiment. Distributed agitational leaflets. Exiled in 1906.

Perhaps more surprising than those laconic reports were what followed: "The Police Department has no information about Zelionko, Korneev, Bezpal'chenko, Sborenko, Solomin, Zhuravl'ev-Ivanov, Viazovoi, the Cossacks Popov and Gerasimenko, the petty bourgeois (*meshchan'e*) P. N. Batashev and Marchinkovskii, and the peasant Romanov." Yet these were well-known strike leaders either at the center or at individual mines, and most were known as exiles. "Other sources," continued the report mysteriously, "reveal that Zelionko, Popov, and

Batashev had also been exiled for antigovernment activity."[24] Even weeks after the shooting, officials with the responsibility for investigating these matters could not elicit from available police records the political pasts of three such prominent strike leaders and political exiles as Batashev, Popov I and Zelionko, let alone the rest. Local officialdom eventually developed better data about the political pasts of the strike leaders.[25] But at the height of the events surrounding the strike and shooting, Bodaibo and Irkutsk officials had failed to attain significant information about most of the individuals involved in the strike leadership, including indications about party ties, with Sobolev as a single exception. Official accusations about "political involvement" were little more than guesses.

The police also relied heavily in their evaluations on three leaflets allegedly found by Treshchenkov during a 14 April search, ten days after the shooting. According to their content, they appeared during the strike but before the shooting. Two had the signature "Union of Mine Workers" (presumably the union founded in 1911) and a third contained the rather unrevealing signature "general brotherhood" (*obshchaia druzhina*). All three addressed the workers about the strike in progress. One leaflet "To Bodaibo Workers from Workers" accused Lenzoto of abuses and "forc[ing] its slaves to labor for the benefit of the rich." Another criticized Tul'chinskii, probably dating it to late March or early April when his authority among workers fell, and asserted that "we must insist on the fulfillment of a payoff [of salaries owed to workers] and of [strike] demands. Down with traitors to the workers' cause!" The authorities concluded that the miners' union and its two leaflets reflected SD efforts and the "general brotherhood" and its leaflet SR activities.[26] However, the documents in the hands of the police contained not a shred of evidence to support this assertion. Both the original political exile association, to which the signature "general brotherhood" probably referred, and the mining union were multiparty. Underground efforts in a place like Bodaibo and the mines by definition crossed party lines. Party organizations did not exist or, if they did, they left no trace and certainly none that the police found in 1912.

In one report, the local authorities concluded that "the entire Bodaibo strike was prepared and led by political exiles who lived there, in many cases without permission." As sole proof, they offered the existence of the "communal apartment . . . of exiles" and the mining union. The report also named several members of the mining union, Ozolin, Golubkov, Sushkin, Makhlin, Skrynnikov, Nagikh, and others, not one of whom played any ascertainable role in the actual strike. These named individuals may well have issued the leaflets that appeared during the strike. After all, the mining union–political exile association had issued several leaflets during the previous year and might have decided to intervene at this point. Yet even were this the case, it would hardly constitute proof that these individuals planned and led the strike. Evidently aware of this flaw in their logic, the compilers of the report added that "other members [of the mining union] are not known." Presumably these unknown members were the ones who led the strike. If so, however, why would the police spy, who was otherwise telling all, have concealed this crucial information? Quite telling in this regard is Procurator Nimander's concession that none of the people identified as members of the union played any role in the strike. Furthermore, in an early 1913 reprisal of the case Nimander further noted that the leaflets in question (which appeared *after* the strike's outbreak) urged workers not to "hostility to the class of entrepreneurs or owners in general" but only to Lenzoto for concrete economic reasons.[27] The complete absence down to this day of any evidence of a strike plan, plus the initial denial by local police and company officials of any pre-strike agitation whatsoever, suggests the unsubstantiated nature of claims about a planned, organized strike with political leadership in the normal understanding of those terms. As evidence of any criminal culpability, all this rang hollow in the ears of Nimander and Manukhin.

In his searching report about the causes of the strike, the Irkutsk procurator Nimander noted the testimony of the Nadezhdinsk electrician Purgin, an individual who provided the police with information during the strike. Purgin spoke of meetings beginning in December 1911 between Batashev, Rozenberg, Podzakhodnikov, Dumpe, Zelionko, Budevits, Zhuravov-Ivanov, and Popov. At these meetings, the participants allegedly discussed the "need to prepare for and carry out an economic strike" in order to raise pay, bring about the eight-hour day, and have certain rude employees fired. Zelionko, according to Purgin, then went to work at the Andreevsk mine, where, of course, the strike started. Other witnesses reported that during the strike these and other strike leaders, namely, Lebedev, Bykov, Romanov, and Viazovoi, often met together to work out plans. That these and several other individuals were the strike's leaders is beyond question. Purgin's midstrike description of meetings beginning in December 1911 of just these people with just these goals, the very ones articulated by the strike once it was under way, is a bit pat, although not implausible. This would shed light on how a group of people, some of whom were not even mine workers (Batashev, Lebedev, and Popov I) and one who had not been elected by his mine or workshop as a delegate (Rozenberg), came together so quickly to lead the strike once it broke out. These individuals, probably associated with the political exile group, already knew one another and quickly won authority as natural leaders once the strike was under way. But none of this demonstrates an advance plan for the strike. Furthermore, the alleged prestrike discussions had to do with the desirability of an economic strike to improve conditions that obviously needed improving. By 1912 such discussions occurred from one end of the Russian Empire to the other, as the ensuing nationwide strike movement revealed. At the local level, the leaflets issued during 1911 by the exile association–labor union raised these very questions. Procurator Nimander reached no invidious conclusions about these data. To the contrary, he decided that no evidence of political involvement or criminality existed.[28] After all, economic strikes in private industry were entirely legal.

Party Affiliations

Still, armed with their determination that the strike was "political," potentially violent, and in violation of certain laws, company and state officials lay down plans to repress it. By midmonth, additional troops had arrived from Kirensk and were stationed in the People's Center, so recently the site of workers' meetings. Especially after the arrival on the scene of Treshchenkov, a stream of messages traveled up the chain of command to Irkutsk and on to St. Petersburg that made the case for repressive action. Treshchenkov's telegram of 26 March serves as a good example: "Strike led by strike committee under command of Zelionko [sic]. Agitators support strike. Constant violent taking out from work. . . . Want to arrest strike committee, striking exiles, agitators, about seventeen persons, even if need . . . force to do this. Evidence seen that strike organized by exiles." Governor Bantysh specifically warned on 28 March that the arrest of strike leaders—he used the term *vybornye* (deputies)—might worsen the situation. "This may serve as a reason," declared the governor, "for furthering the work stoppages." Still, Treshchenkov, joined by numerous company and state officials all the way to the capital, became convinced that the way to end the strike was to arrest the "instigators," the political exiles, who, they believed, had planned, organized, led, and forcibly maintained the strike. As Beletskii, the director of police in Petersburg, telegraphed to the head of the Irkutsk gendarmes just hours before the shooting, "Lenzoto administration thinks that almost all workers ready to return to work. It is necessary to get rid of instigators who threaten the workers. Have you liquidated the strike committee and if not, why not?"[29] Thus are malign fantasies constructed and, in a sense, brought to life. In point of fact, ten members of the strike committee had already been arrested. The Irkutsk gendarme chief Poznanskii could reply to his chief in Petersburg that "Treshchenkov has arrested Dumpe, Rozenberg, Budevits,

Marchinkovskii, Zhuravl'ev-Ivanov, Viazovoi, Mimogliadov, Sobolev, Solomin, [and] Bezpal'chenko."[30]

Far from ending the strike, this act led to serious new worker protests, the march on the Nadezhdinsk mines, and by the evening of 4 April, the shooting of hundreds of workers armed with nothing but watches and petitions. As some observers had predicted, the mere arrest of strike leaders lacked the power to end the strike. The strike organization had a structure that allowed the quick replacement of any arrested members by already agreed-upon delegates and elders from the various mines, which is what occurred. Furthermore, most of the arrested leaders, including Dumpe and Rozenberg, as well as Batashev, who temporarily escaped arrest, had been advising the workers to end the strike by accepting the concessions offered. Tul'chinskii had urged Treshchenkov to restrict arrests to several individuals who were urging workers to continue the strike. The chief mining engineer specified Zelionko. It seems that this individual had several times confounded his efforts to persuade the miners to return to work by making quite cutting speeches. After the arrests, Treshchenkov reported with chagrin that Popov I, Batashev, and others "who were most needed" had escaped arrest. Indeed Popov, Batashev, Zelionko, and Cherepakhin were still at large, as was Lebedev. But at least two of these individuals (Batashev and Lebedev) had in recent days urged ending the strike, and two others, the incendiary Zelionko and Cherepakhin, are alleged to have opposed the march on 4 April.[31] Treshchenkov routinely painted his picture of events with a crude brush. Since the arrest policy reflected the fantastical notion that the strike committee was prolonging the strike "by threats," the arrests failed utterly in their objective. Instead they hardened workers' resolve to continue the strike and prompted determined efforts to release their elected leaders.

As of 4 April, Treshchenkov had obtained arrest warrants for only twelve of the known members of the strike committee. Governor Bantysh's insistence that he restrict arrests to those "with criminal pasts" had evidently induced him to omit some people from the list and, of course, Popov I and Batashev, who were on the list, escaped. Some sources suggest that on 3 April, Batashev had secretly left the area on a strike-related mission, supposedly to inform the leftist factions in the State Duma about the impasse the strike had reached. Popov I was seriously wounded in the shooting and lay in the hospital after 4 April. In his memoirs published in 1957, Lebedev claimed that during the day of 4 April he and several other strike leaders who had gathered at the Feodosievsk mines tried to prevent the march on the Nadezhdinsk mines. Andreevsk leaders Popov 2, Pinaev, Brovarov, and Lesnoi, all, according to Lebedev, members of the SR or anarchist parties, decided on their own initiative to promote the march. Several other mines then joined in. Lebedev, at the time not an SD, also later claimed that Zelionko, Cherepakhin, and several others were Bolsheviks, with whom he aligned himself, and that they had attempted to discourage the march.

In truth, contemporary sources reveal nothing about whether these individuals were Bolsheviks or whether they attempted to prevent the fatal march. Furthermore, Lebedev's version does not square well with the previous radicalism of Zelionko and Cherepakhin. If after weeks of strident strike promotion these individuals suddenly experienced an April 4 epiphany of moderation, just in time to warn the workers off from the impending slaughter, then Lebedev should at least have said a word or two about how this happened. In lieu of such, his blame of SRs and anarchists for the march that resulted in the shooting must be taken with a grain of salt, as should his attribution to alleged Bolsheviks, plus himself, of attempts to prevent the march. According to recollections of Cherepakhin, he and other strike leaders "barely restrained" the Feodosievsk workers from marching, whereas the Andreevsk leaders, the very people Lebedev blamed for promoting the April 4 march, "did not manage to restrain the workers from the march." This version throws a different light on the matter by suggesting that the Andreevsk leaders also cautioned the workers but to no avail. In fact, Lebedev and Popov I accompanied the marchers and were wounded. Their presence reveals nothing about how they felt about the demonstration just as the absence of Zelionko and Cherepakhin reveals nothing except that they were miles away at Feodosievsk when the shooting took place. The actual demonstration leaders were Andreevsk delegates Popov II and Lesnoi. Despite some leaders' misgivings, the miners broadly supported the idea of delivering mass petitions for the release of arrested strike deputies.[32]

Some memoirists and Soviet-era commentators intruded later priorities into their accounts. They misleadingly divided the strike leadership into party groups and explained various actions and decisions on that basis. Some memoirists further attempted to align themselves retroactively with the Bolsheviks, a group to which they had not belonged and which as such had not existed in the area. They also blamed, variously and inconsistently, "Mensheviks and SRs" for wanting to end the strike, "SRs and anarchists" for promoting the 4 April March, and so forth. The "Bolsheviks," listed with ever shifting permutations as Zelionko, Ukraintsev, Cherepakhin, Podzakhodnikov, and sometimes Lebedev, Batashev, and even Petukhov, of course, always adhered to the correct line. All this aside, contemporary sources of all kinds observe sepulchral silence about party orientations. A thorough examination of all reliable sources suggests the appropriateness, if not the certainty, of viewing Batashev and Dumpe as SDs and Lebedev as close to the SDs; Popov I and II, Sobolev, and Petukhov as SRs; and Rozenberg and Lesnoi as anarchists. The Bolshevism of Zelionko, Cherepakhin, Ukraintsev and so forth was metaphysical, as would be their categorization as SDs. The memoirs and many Soviet-era accounts count Dumpe, Rozenberg and, sometimes, Popov I as moderates, whereas they describe Batashev, Lesnoi and, sometimes, Popov I as radicals. In Manukhin's account, Batashev was among the moderates. In such an interpretational morass, party labels emerge as useless in determining stances. No agreement exists about who was moderate and who radical. Party attributions are speculative and often contradictory. The early Soviet-era author Zhukov warned against bolshevizing the strike, and Vladimirova's authoritative account eschews mention of party roles, a clear hint in Soviet-era historiographical discourse.[33]

Several memoirists and Soviet-era sources claim that, of the main strike leaders during the last (postshooting) phase of the strike, Petukhov, Pinaev, and Gorshechnikov were SRs and Podzakhodnikov a Bolshevik. Since these Soviet-era attributions were neutral, that is, accompanied no allegations of SR misdeeds, perhaps they are accurate. If it is also true that the people who promoted and led the fatal 4 April march were Popov II, Pinaev, Brovarov (all SRs), and Lesnoi (an anarchist), than support arises for a certain interpretation of the "politics" of the strike leadership as it evolved over time. In this line of analysis, the strike found its early leaders in a group of experienced exiles of mixed party orientation, that is SDs, SRs, and anarchists, with a certain prominent role for moderate SDs. This evaluation at least roughly fits Zhukov's remarks about a leading Menshevik role. Such individuals would have been interested in urging workers toward assertiveness about their economic plight. This would have placed the early strike leaders in the mainstream of Social Democratic and moderate Socialist Revolutionary practice during the 1908–12 era. That is, they promoted joint (multiparty) economic activism over overt sectarian politics. Procurator Nimander noted that much current SD practice had an economic focus and Police Chief N. Vasil'ev emphasized prevalent SD and SR labor union activism. All of this also coincides handily with the police spy Purgin's allegations about meetings beginning in late 1911 of a group of exiles, including most of the eventual strike leaders. The meetings, according to Purgin's testimony, focused on economic activism. This version also coincides well with data about the growing caution of many strike committee members about continuing the strike and about marching to Nadezhdinsk on 4 April. These were not incendiary types.

After Treshchenkov arrested more and more of the original leaders, leadership by default gradually passed to mine-level, second-rank deputies, mostly of SR and anarchist orientation. If they were less cautious about a massive demonstration, this may have reflected lack of experience as much as party orientation. After all, a similarly constituted group led the strike movement through all the trials and tribulations of the postshooting period. All evidence testifies to the peacefulness, staunchness, and ultimate effectiveness of the last strike committee. Without further violence, the committee brought the affair to a close when the entire existing workforce abandoned the Lenzoto mines during June and July. This was a startling and by no means easily achieved denouement. One might conclude that, after the perceived failure of the original experienced socialist leadership (mostly illegally residing exiles, skilled workers in the Nadezhdinsk workshops, and the stationmaster), the workers turned to individuals closer and better known to them. These were actual miners, mine-level delegates, who also happened to be next in line for promotion into the central strike leadership. The foregoing propositions, although perfectly plausible and probably accurate, are still replete with ifs. In any case, party membership per se played no direct role in the strike.

A SOCIALIST CULTURE ON THE LENA AND IN RUSSIA

Indeed, what occurred out along the upper reaches of the Lena River was far more interesting than the customary historical questions of party identification and attribution. Several thousand gold miners, hardly the cream of the crop of the empire's new proletariat, had consistently chosen most of their strike leaders from a small group of political exiles. By nature of their status as exiles, these individuals had become members of one or another underground party or, at the very least, become involved somewhere in overtly oppositionist activities such as mutinies, strikes, and distribution of leaflets. The sources remain opaque about how it came to pass that the miners selected the people they did. One might surmise that the exiles, who had formed an underground association and a small union responsible for several leaflets during 1911, were already known to many workers or were otherwise able to assert their natural authority as the strike began.

The strike broke out because of accumulated frustrations and offenses. The first mines to strike, such as Andreevsk, were recent Lenzoto acquisitions from the Industrial Company, whose workforces were especially sensitive to the harsher practices of the new owners and managers, that is, the Belozerov regime. Regardless, all the mines joined in quickly enough, elected their delegates at the specific urging of police and company officials, and presented demands that similarly focused on pay, hours, food, and treatment. Some observers quickly noted that the otherwise similar early strike demands varied in one respect. Some requested immunity from arrest of "elected deputies," whereas others did not. For two or three days in late February and early March, the main strike leaders delayed submitting general strike demands. When they did so, the centralized strike demands contained the plank about protecting elected deputies. For hostile observers, this marked the rise to preeminence in the strike leadership of "political elements" since immunity of strike delegates, along with slogans such as the "eight-hour day," reflected current socialist practice.

In a sense, the authorities were doubtless correct. Constant barracks, mine-level, and general meetings characterized the entire period. The Feodosievsk mine manager reported that a nearby workers' meeting place came to be called the "Tauride Palace" (*Tavricheskii dvorets,* the home of the State Duma) in honor of its incessant sessions and debates. Experienced speakers, those who could offer analysis on the basis of past experience and who could outline a strike program with prospects for success, naturally received preference. Whether this preference reflected miners' direct knowledge or approbation of party membership is unknowable and perhaps irrelevant. Many witnesses recalled that anytime a speaker referred in any way to party matters or anything even remotely political, the workers shouted him down. The experienced leaders themselves widely discouraged anything political or even disorderly. As a condition of the strike's success, the mine workers' strike discourses deliberately excluded politics and anything at all about parties. Still, as one woman worker stated under interrogation, the miners had attempted to "select leaders who were *gramotnye* [well informed]," after which she described Popov I and Batashev as the "big orators."[34] The word *gramotnyi* can mean "literate" but the woman interrogatee clearly had in mind the other sense, that is, informed and knowledgeable, in other words, people who knew what was happening and what to do about it.

At precisely this juncture, many strains of late tsarist history intertwine in a compelling way to shed light on what occurred during the gold mine strike, the shooting, and the aftermath. Since the latter part of the last century Russia had witnessed the growth of an increasingly open oppositionist movement, including several socialist parties, the anarchists, and the liberals. This movement, plus the entire 1905–1907 era with its strikes, near revolution, and the granting of a semiconstitution, had broadcast certain messages to the broadest laboring population. Russian laborers had received confirmation that they possessed widely, if not universally, recognized economic and human rights. Earlier inarticulate expressions of dissatisfaction, sometimes tinged with violence, such as those in the Siberian mines of an earlier era, clearly indicate that even then people perfectly well understood violations of human standards. More recently, in Russia and in the East Siberian mines workers had shown a considerable degree of awareness both of their rights and of how to further their achievement in orderly, structured ways. The history of organized Lena area strikes as of 1901 supports this assertion.

The new awareness included general knowledge of the kinds of parties and movements that were attempting to speak for workers and laborers in general and specific knowledge of people with such orientation and experience at the local level. Choosing these very individuals as leaders, as occurred in the Lena goldfields strike, carried risks. The presence of such individuals in the strike leadership could serve as justification for calling the strike "political" and disrupting it by arrests and other repressions. This is not speculation. After Ukraintsev was arrested on 16 April for living in the area without documents, he wrote a letter to Batashev that fell into police hands. In this letter, Ukraintsev both urged continuation of the strike and regretted that "now they will have a reason to accuse political exiles [of involvement in the strike leadership], of which I now turn out to be proof."[35] Whether the authorities perceived a strike as sheerly economic or more sinisterly political had grave consequences. As Governor Bantysh pointed out in his agonized postshooting reprisal, "breaking a strike" was only one measure to be contemplated in managing economic strikes. In cases of political strikes, "breaking" the strike by arrests and other harsh measures was the prime method. The governor clearly felt that this strike had demanded other management procedures, to wit, substantive concessions on the basis of Lenzoto's goodwill. Strongly suggestive of the likelihood that he attempted to make this position known to Russian society before the shooting were reports in *Birzhevye vedomosti* and other newspapers during March that certain "informed commentators feel that Lenzoto is mistaken in not engaging in negotiations with workers about substantive demands." Alas, neither the requisite goodwill nor high-level support for such negotiations had existed, the governor's increasingly desperate maneuverings notwithstanding. Bantysh now referred to the enormous "civil courage" needed to buck Lenzoto and its allies. When higher and lower authorities short-circuited Bantysh and simply decreed the strike political, the die was cast.[36]

In a sense the hostile authorities were correct in calling the strike political, despite its unwaveringly economic demands. After all, the strike leadership contained numerous political exiles, including several who were not even employed in the mines and were living in the area illegally. Clearly, this was a cause for suspicion. But then, the presence of exiles played an enormous role in keeping the strike well organized, peaceful, and within the bounds of legality and acceptable norms of behavior. Witness Popov I, whose "nonworker political exile" status figured in numerous suspicious police commentaries, warning workers not even to raise their voices during meetings. Likewise, the clearly expressed strike demands, in great part reflecting the exiles' prior experience, placed the authorities on the spot. So did the impeccable comportment of the strike leaders and the thousands of strikers during the lengthy strike, too well documented to be in doubt. Finally, the hostile authorities had to fabricate "violent" or "threatening" actions to justify summoning troops, arresting the leaders, and firing on a demonstration. The experience, not to say expertise, derived from the political pasts of many strike leaders, which placed the strike leadership within the potential category of illegal "secret organization," was the very factor that kept the strike itself within the bounds of the economic and the peaceful.

This fact, clear to all objective observers, was what induced Governor Bantysh, Chief Mining Engineer Tul'chinskii, Inspector Galkin, and Senator Manukhin to ignore the political element among the strike leaders while insisting on the peaceful, economic nature of the strike. They hardly felt that workers should be blamed for choosing leaders capable of running an economic strike. Meanwhile, the hostile authorities searched for pretexts for declaring the strike political and violent and ending it as soon as possible by whatever means. They located a pretext in the political pasts of many strike leaders. The intense irony was that the successful organization and discipline of the strike constituted for some the very proof of its criminal nature.

Politics and even socialism in the broad sense of the word were precisely to the point. Without the collective experiences of the oppositionist and socialist movements, as expressed in the outlooks and advice of the political exiles, the strike would hardly have attained the degree of cohesiveness and organization that it in fact displayed. Negotiating the intricate shoals of what was or was not legal, what would or would not provoke harsh responses would have been beyond the capabilities of everyday miners, no matter how peacefully intentioned. For example, by placing the plank of immunity for the elected strike leaders in the official strike demands, which then received wide local publicity and became known higher up as well, the strike leadership made it awkward for the police to carry out the arrests. This tactic alone probably delayed the arrests for as much as two weeks. The previous experiences in question, however, transgressed individual party lines and, to some degree, even socialism itself. Many people in Russia who became involved with radical agitation and leadership of various strikes and other oppositionist activities, whether economic or political, were formally nonparty, although they tended to coordinate their activities with and operate under the aegis of the socialist parties. Locally and nationally the various parties formed the focal points of the oppositionist movement but were not identical with it.

Colonel Vasil'ev, head of the Irkutsk police, pondered this question at length and arrived at a fairly accurate understanding of what had occurred. His report, filed on 24 July 1912, stated that the Irkutsk Provincial Gendarmes "had the prime goal of proving . . . that the strike at the Lena mines arose under the influence of activities of local revolutionary elements and had a political coloration." The police collected voluminous evidence about the strike, the strike leadership, agitation, strike demands, leaflets, and so forth. Vasil'ev concluded that the files of the police lacked "sufficient data that would testify to direct ties between . . . the revolutionaries and the Lena affair. This report cannot be considered proof of supposed advanced planning for the strike at the Lena mines on the part of revolutionary elements." Having properly discounted any sort of planning or direct connection with socialists, Vasil'ev nevertheless asserted a "political coloration" for the strike. "In the final analysis," he wrote, "the leaflets of the mining union and general brotherhood are proof of the political character of the Lena gold mine strike." To these he added certain alleged actions such as the searches of a train and jailhouse for supposedly arrested strike delegates.[37]

The most telling part of Vasil'ev's analysis appeared in the section he called "General Essay on Activities of Revolutionary Parties," in which he attempted to characterize the role of socialist parties in the workers' movement. He first wrote of the "twenty-year struggle of the SDs for the eight-hour day and the economic and political cause of the proletariat." He then described the "established goal of the Party of SRs to protect the spiritual and physical strength of the working class . . . for the coming struggle for socialism." Both parties, continued Vasil'ev, participated in the labor union movement's efforts to raise pay and limit work hours. Since 1910 "a rapid growth of the labor union movement [has occurred], with the close attention of the underground parties, both the SDs and the SRs, who have undertaken to control the labor unions in order to use them for party goals and for the training of cadres for the struggle against the government. . . . The activities of these parties is directed in the broadest fashion toward the working masses." The Irkutsk procurator Nimander similarly noted the "general socialist character" of the strike demands rather than their connection to any particular party program.

Even so, these officials insisted on the overall political nature of the strike. After first raising the issue of potential SD influences on the Lena strike, Vasil'ev then rejected this narrow interpretation in favor of a broader one pertaining to all socialism. Procurator Nimander too placed a possible SD role in semantical first place but then joined Vasil'ev in favoring a broader socialist approach. If strike leaders were SDs, inquired Nimander, how was it that they "managed to conceal their SD views from others?" This strongly suggests that none of the police spies among the workers (Purgin, and possibly Marchinkovskii) or other interrogated workers revealed any special SD connections. Both officials seemed to respond to and abjure an existing discourse that posited a primary SD involvement in the strike. Indeed some of the messages that ricocheted back and forth between Bodaibo, Irkutsk, and Petersburg officials raised this very issue. For example, after the shooting Treshchenkov signed on to the SD theory, although, it must be said, his messages evince an extraordinarily low level of political sophistication. Some national press reports at first discussed the strike in terms of social democracy. This was especially the case when some newspapers misidentified P. N. Batashev as V. M. Batashev who had been an SD Second Duma deputy. This drew a terse comment from the Ministry of the Interior on 14 April that "P. N. and Vasilii Batashev are two different people, the latter ha[ving] no connection with the strike." Eventually, almost all newspapers of whatever alignment came to see the strike as purely economic without overt political overtones or involvement. Likewise, Lena area officials also ceased evaluating the events in terms of any one party. Even the Council of Ministers in Petersburg in its January 1913 special report on the Lena strike and shooting raised and dismissed the idea of SD involvement and noted that "no indication of real political involvement" existed.[38] The entire matter suggests the extent to which public discourse, by default, connected the workers' movements with the SD Party. When this tie proved amorphous in the Lena case, public opinion simply turned away from political explanations of the strike. Internal police analysis displayed a clearer awareness of socialism in general as a better approach to explaining the realities in Russia and in the Lena strike.

Senator Manukhin concluded that since the Lena strike was essentially economic, only Lenzoto and Treshchenkov bore any sort of guilt. At one point he approved the arrests of several strike leaders with past political convictions but in his final report recommended criminal indictment only of Treshchenkov. Colonel Vasil'ev likewise felt that his office had ascertained no political criminal activities. Ultimately Procurator Nimander agreed, as did the Council of Ministers in its early 1913 report. As early as July 1912 Nimander recommended that all arrestees, except for several with political convictions, be released. By early 1913 he had ended all criminal prosecutions and ordered the release of the entire cadre of strike leaders, including those with past records.[39] Thus came to a close the government's involvement with the Lena goldfields strike and massacre. No advanced plan had existed; no criminal political involvement had taken place; and no worker criminality had occurred. Their admitted moral reprehensibility aside, neither Treshchenkov's nor Lenzoto's actions met Nimander's test of criminality, nor that of the Council of Ministers.[40] Still the dead and maimed bore mute witness.

VOICES AND DISCOURSES FROM THE LENA

The idea of examining various voices and discourses about the Lena events reflects insights from Kurosawa's film *Rashomon* and from Bakhtin's concept of polyphonic voices in human events. The dual insights from these two sources are by no means identical. The experiences of the principal characters in *Rashomon* attest to the daunting subjectivity and, it follows, ambiguity of human observation. People know events through the traces they leave in human memory and record. Yet memory and record are never simply factual representations of other previous facts (events) but rather are shot through with predispositions, fallible impressions, conscious and unconscious motivations, and other imponderable and often unmeasurable factors. For example, several thousand mine workers marched to Nadezhdinsk on 4 April 1912 with petitions aimed at releasing arrested strike leaders. On seeing a small line of troops in front of the People's Center, they had certain reactions. Survivors' recollections of the shooting differed utterly from those of the vastly outnumbered soldiers, goaded by their officers and other authorities. The troops and the miners had witnessed the same strike, the same negotiations, the same uneasy confrontations, and on 4 April, the same physical convergence of two groups of human beings, one large and one small. Still, although of similar social background, their recent preconditioning to perceive the 4 April events had diverged widely. Their relative spatial positioning and ultimate actions on the fourth would also perforce drive a further cognitive wedge between them. This is but one example of the "*Rashomon* effect." Use of worker and soldier accounts might well simply lead to a historiographical impasse.

The "Bakhtin application" aims at recapturing the various voices (attitudes, languages, understandings) that make up an event, in this case interpreted as the entire Lena strike and massacre. The *Rashomon* effect discloses the difficulty of knowing a concrete event in any easy objective fashion. It raises the problem. The Bakhtin application concedes the problem and seeks to overcome it by analyzing the bases of the difficulty. It seeks to delineate the various voices and how they interacted to create the event. Workers started out with a set of attitudes and needs, elected and listened to their leaders, and witnessed interactions over time with company and state agents. Out of this collective experience—a melange of hopes, happenings, and interpretations—arose the mistaken idea that the soldiers would not shoot. Vastly outnumbered soldiers, forced on several previous occasions to retreat, saw a huge mass of workers, were told that the workers were hostile and potentially violent, and were ordered to shoot. The intersection of two dynamic mind-sets, each informed by numerous experiences and discrete discourses, produced the event of 4 April. Bakhtinian analysis based on polyphonic voices urges us to see the event in its real human dimensions, without, it should be added, sacrificing ultimate moral judgment. For Bakhtin, morality inheres in the act at the moment of the act, which expresses human intention. In this case, it is necessary to search back into the ideas and languages of the groups and people involved, on the one hand, those who led the workers' demonstration and, on the other, those who represented the company, the police, and the troops. Language reveals not only differing outlooks and experiences but, conceivably, blithe indifference to consequences, misinformation, poor judgment, carelessness, self-deception, outright malign intent, or their opposites, all as way stations to the event. Ferreting out outlooks, experiences, and intentions at the level of verbal expression and suggesting how they contributed to certain results are the crux of this section's analysis.

For the purposes of this discussion, a discourse is a mutually compatible set of terms and expressions used within a certain time frame by a collection of people about a recognizable set of circumstances or events. The people who operate within the particular discourse interpret and understand the given circumstances and events by means of these terms and expressions. They too express themselves in analogous terms, thereby extending and expanding the discourse. Even more crucially, they act accordingly. They also reject opposing discourses; highly criticize differing evaluations and the actions arising out of them; and may take countermeasures. In this usage, discourse does not in any sense displace the empirical world of action and experience. It is simply a contributory factor, an element of the real.

Two very general discourses are discernible from the generous fund of available expressions of opinion from those directly associated with the Lena events. One discourse was proworker and anticompany, whereas the other was procompany and antiworker. Were this all there were to the matter, it would hardly deserve further attention. The reality was altogether more intriguing and surprising. Personages from various institutions and groupings were involved at various stages of the affair. These groups and institutions included the company, branches of the government (civil and police authorities), the church, officers and soldiers, simple workers, socialist activists and exiles, and various uninvolved bystanders. To some extent, group and institutional affiliations predict where individuals would show up on the proworker and antiworker spectrum. For example, company officials at all levels tended to evaluate worker behavior in negative terms, as did military officers. Meanwhile, workers, activists of all kinds and, more interestingly, some low-level company employees, almost all uninvolved onlookers, and the local priests portrayed the company in dark terms and exonerated the workers. Various state officials—police and civilian—were much more difficult to categorize. For instance, at the local level procurators, justices, and police officers tended to a disciplinarian view that brooked no tolerance of worker strikes or violations of perceived proper order. Nevertheless, Police Inspector Galkin and Justice Rein had distinctly proworker attitudes. As regards representatives of the mining administration, the opposite configuration was true. Chief Mining Engineer Tul'chinskii and the Irkutsk mining administers defended the workers' position and deeply criticized the company, whereas Assistant Mining Engineer Aleksandrov had a distinctly reserved attitude toward workers. Moving up the chain of command, in Irkutsk Governor Bantysh joined with the mining administration officials to defend the workers, whereas Irkutsk police officials wished to repress the worker "disorders." Further up, in Petersburg, the workers' cause got short shrift, with several involved ministers and the head of the police all occupying staunchly procompany stances. Middle- and lower-level state officials tended to split along affiliational lines, with police and military officers mostly opposing the workers, and civilian officials mostly supporting them. Observers associated with neither the company nor the state overwhelmingly supported the workers.

The proworker discourse had roots in eras long predating the 1912 strike and shooting. Earlier chapters recount nineteenth-century attempts of reforming bureaucrats and even an occasional company manager to address and redress obvious inadequacies in the miners' hiring, living and working conditions. As noted in chapter 3, the Blagoveshchensk church chronicle for 1904 narrated in starkest terms the pitiable state of affairs for workers and the companies' culpability. Finally, for two years prior to the 1912 events Governor Bantysh and Chief Engineer Tul'chinskii issued a series of dire warnings about the potential for disorders because of Lenzoto's blatant violations of workers' legal and human rights. At the strike's outbreak observers across the board perceived it as peaceful in character and economic in origin. In his very first message about the strike, Teppan informed the Petersburg management that through talks with workers he had ascertained that "the chief motive of dissatisfaction . . . is the receipt from the [company] kitchen . . . of horse meat." Mining Inspector Galkin's first telegram to Governor Bantysh on 3 March noted the "economic causes" of the strike and the absence of "disorders." Likewise his telegrams of 12 and 14 March to Irkutsk authorities emphasized the "peaceful character" of the continuing strike: "no disorders have occurred" and "no disorders or violence have taken place." On the fifteenth a joint message from Galkin and Aleksandrov to the Irkutsk police again noted "no disorders." In his 14 March deposition, Lenzoto employee Gorinov reported that after the 8 March breakdown of worker-company negotiations the strike leaders, despite their frustration, "issued no calls for violent actions." On 20 March, Justice of the Peace Khitun, who did not sympathize with the workers, emphasized the "complete absence of any advance agitation" for the strike. It was a "complete surprise" even for the workers and its "cause is connected with the conditions of labor; [it is] purely economic and all succeeding demands have been economic." On this basis, Governor Bantysh's messages to high Petersburg authorities consistently characterized the strike as "peaceful and quiet," but, asserted the governor, "if disorders occur, I will comply with plans" to suppress them.[41] One might call this the original narrative of the strike's outbreak and progress. This narrative, it so happens, also fits most existing evidence about these events. The strike lacked advanced planning; its causes were economic, that is, connected with living and working conditions; and it progressed without violence or disorders.

Adherents to this version always referred to the elected strike leaders as *vybornye* (elected deputies), tended to discount reported worker violations as routine, minor, and nonthreatening, and emphasized workers' orderliness, restraint, and peaceful intentions. They were aware of incidents when workers became angry, used heightened language, and showed a willingness to defend their interests. They evaluated these as human reactions under remarkably stressful conditions. They characterized Lenzoto's attitudes and actions as provocative, illegal, and implicitly and explicitly aimed at forceful repression of the strike. They attributed these same faults to military and some police and judicial authorities. The arrest of strike leaders was uncalled for, they felt, and had the potential to disrupt the peace. Under extreme pressure from above and from Police Captain Treshchenkov on the spot, some proworker officials reluctantly agreed to limited arrests.

The indiscriminate arrests that instead ensued caused the 4 April worker demonstration, which according to people of this tendency, was also peaceful and nonthreatening in intention. The shooting was unjustified.

A very different narrative of the strike quickly supplanted the original one in certain circles. For several reasons, the procompany-antiworker discourse requires closer attention than the proworker one. First and foremost, people of this tendency brought about the arrest of strike leaders and made decisions that led to the shooting of hundreds of miners. In addition, questions of motivation more obviously arise in this case. Company administrators had a vested interest in ending the strike as rapidly as possible, preferably without potentially costly concessions to workers. High government officials, who were invested with responsibility for state economic and financial welfare and who in many cases had a financial stake in the company, experienced an obvious confluence of motivations with entrepreneurial interests. Police, military, and judicial officers responsible for societal order and hierarchically subordinate to higher authority also had virtually predetermined motives permeated with self-interest. Consequently, real differences existed between people of procompany and proworker cast. Low-level Lenzoto employees, police and mining officials such as Galkin and Tul'chinskii, and highly placed state appointees such as Governor Bantysh had nothing to gain and much to lose by opposing the official line. This required, as Bantysh pointed out, "civil courage." Civil courage does not adhere to the actions of those who support higher authority or act out of self-interest, although at the distant Lena mines some physical courage may have been required. Regardless, the procompany discourse should not be discounted out of hand.

From the outset Acting Manager Teppan's messages to higher company and authorities had mentioned the "taking out of workers" to join the strike. He soon began to use the phrase "forcible taking out" associated with verbal and physical threats (cursing, brandishing of clubs or tools). A very thin line separated legally permissible persuasion to strike and illegal forcible methods. Rumors about forcible incidents did spread, and that at certain points prostrike agitators violated strict legality in trying to bring about full strike compliance, an obviously desirable aim for strikers, cannot be ruled out. Most direct witnesses, including even company employees, and subsequent investigations by the Manukhin Commission did not confirm serious violations of legality. Still, Teppan, managing in the absence of the crude Belozerov and stuck with awesome responsibilities to higher management and stockholders, may well have succumbed to the belief that serious violations of legality were occurring. Some workers, notably those who began reporting to the police, portrayed the strike's rapid spread in this light. Later incidents, when workers searched a mining area police station and a train in hopes of finding elected deputies rumored to have been arrested, were also susceptible to an interpretation of illegality.

Regardless, Teppan's messages to St. Petersburg certainly created an impression sharply at odds with the ones sent by Galkin and elaborated on by Bantysh. Recipients on high of Teppan's messages would likely have comprehended the strike as economic in origin but characterized by potentially illegal worker aggressiveness in spreading and maintaining the strike and protecting its leadership. Thereafter further suspicious circumstances compounded the matter. It became clear that much of the strike leadership consisted of people with political pasts. Several leaders were not miners or workers or even Lenzoto employees but lived in the area illegally. The extreme discipline and organization of the striking workers, plus the addition to strike demands of the eight-hour day and strike leader immunity, created an impression of knowledgeable agency outside the simple mining workers' capacity. Late tsarist officialdom routinely perceived demands for an eight-hour day as "political." The plank on strike leader immunity in fact reflected prior experience. By an odd twist, the messages that the minister of the interior received from the Galkin-Bantysh nexus were more exculpatory than those transmitted through entrepreneurial channels to the minister of trade and industry. The latter, of course, also received mining administration missives that condemned and blamed the company for the whole matter.

When Galkin insisted on the sheerly economic and peaceful nature of the strike, this flew in the face of accustomed thinking patterns and the accumulation of countervailing, evidently reliable information. It was at that point that higher authorities began to doubt the validity of assessments by Galkin and Bantysh. The police generated a report that suggested that in 1909 Galkin had in some way been implicated in a case having to do with the SRs. Thus it was that the Petersburg ministers and other officials began to feel that they were not hearing the "real causes" of the strike. They sent additional troops to Bodaibo, arranged to send a known hard-liner, Treshchenkov, to the mines in order to ascertain the "real causes" and suppress the strike, and determined to arrest politically oriented strike leaders. The arrival of Treshchenkov sharply altered the story line of the messages going up the interior ministry communications chain. Messages received in Irkutsk and Petersburg from both Teppan and Treshchenkov insisted that the strike was disorderly and that the arrest of strike leaders would quickly end the entire affair. The subtext for this version averred secret, criminal political involvement. Tul'chinskii's accounts, which coincided with the already discredited Galkin-Bantysh evaluations, never achieved credibility anywhere higher than Bantysh. The Petersburg ministers ensured that the actual chain of command and exchange of information bypassed Bantysh-Tul'chinskii-Galkin in favor of the Irkutsk police chief and Treshchenkov. This "reliable" informational channel ascertained the "real causes" and opened the way for real action to end the long, costly but so far nonviolent work stoppage.

During the last days before the shooting, Treshchenkov and the military officers comported themselves in a confrontational manner. Orders from above, reflecting data transmitted by Teppan and Treshchenkov, supported repression, first in the form of arrests of strike leaders and then, if workers resisted, in the use of arms. Workers' entry into the Nadezhdinsk area on 4 April undoubtedly frightened the police captain and military officers. After all, hardly a hundred people, albeit armed, stood between them and potential reprisals from thousands of miners who had good reason to be angry. Still, testimony from many observers suggests that something other than fright spurred the orders to shoot. Treshchenkov had confidently predicted, indeed insisted, that the initial arrests would end the strike. Instead, the miners had taken the strike onto a new, still peaceful but even more effective level. At the suggestion of Justice Preobrazhenskii, they were massively delivering individual, carefully worded petitions to free the arrestees. Although Treshchenkov claimed not to have known this, testimony reveals that local mining foremen had telephoned this information to him. Those who had promoted the arrests had nothing but damaged reputations awaiting them if they did not ratchet up the level of control measures. High officialdom all the way to Petersburg was demanding an end to the strike, instead of which the strike continued and the strikers were observing strict legal punctilio in delivering individual petitions.

One can only imagine Treshchenkov's incipient panic about the possibility that the workers might turn violent and sheer dismay at the position he was about to find himself in if they did not. Treshchenkov's entire self-created public image was as a police officer not to be trifled with. High authority had sent him to take things in hand and end the strike. The latest worker démarche left open only two possibilities for a rapid end to the strike: genuine company concessions or some sharp violent action. Were the strike to continue or the company forced to make concessions, his reputation as problem solver would be lost. Galkin, Tul'chinskii, and Bantysh, on whom he had showered contempt, would be proven correct. The workers had upped the ante in a most galling way. He and the army officers made snap decisions with the well-known sanguinary results.

One might preliminarily conclude that, whatever people on the spot such as Teppan and Treshchenkov really thought, high-level recipients of their messages might well have had good reason to suspect legal violations that justified repressing the strike. On one plane, one might characterize this position as tough but not outside the realm of justifiable possibility. After all, in Russia, radical oppositionists had helped organize and lead innumerable strikes and demonstrations with barely concealed or unconcealed political motivations. On another plane, this approach quickly wears thin. High-level authorities, state and entrepreneurial, consistently refused real concessions to what seem to have been realistic and legal workers' demands. They ordered Teppan to take a hard line and then deliberately dispatched Treshchenkov to end the strike. Internal messages emphasize the latter's task as finding out the "real causes" of the strike and bringing it to a close. Treshchenkov did not originate the idea of arresting the main strike leaders; it was transmitted to him. Likewise, the authorities had already decided on the "real causes" before sending Treshchenkov. From him, they wanted confirmation.

What about the possibility that they really believed in the "real causes," code for political agitation and leadership? Here, direct evidence of bad faith exists. Minister of Trade and Industry Timashev, supposedly a more sympathetic character than Minister of the Interior Makarov, rejected a suggestion from Baron Alfred Ginzburg that an objective observer be sent to Bodaibo to find out what was happening there. He did so because reports from Bantysh had characterized the strike as peaceful. He then shot off an order to send additional troops because force might be necessary! Also of interest is 1917 testimony from tsarist officials that Ministry of Trade and Industry administrators later destroyed many of its documents pertaining to the Lena affair.[42]

As regards officialdom at the Lena mines, similar evidence of bad faith exists. For example, Treshchenkov, Preobrazhenskii, and Captain Sanzharenko insisted that the workers had carried objects that constituted weapons and later submitted to the Manukhin Commission a rather pitiful collection of metal rods, bricks, coal, and wooden items supposedly gathered at the spot of the massacre. Yet Treshchenkov and Preobrazhenskii both forbore to testify that they personally had seen such items in the hands of the workers. Why then did they order the shooting? During the hours after the massacre, Treshchenkov blocked off the entire area, preventing even the transport of the wounded. He seized and destroyed the negatives of the photographs of the shooting, knowing as a policeman their enormous value as evidence. Finally, he insisted that everyone involved in the shooting coordinate stories. None of this speaks well for his motivations. This and other evidence resulted in Manukhin's request that criminal charges be brought against

Treshchenkov rather than against any strike leaders. Without resort to melodrama, one may assert that Treshchenkov was hardly an unwitting weapon in the hands of the top-level ministers and entrepreneurs, nor were they in any way his victims. They specifically chose him, precisely because of his prior reputation, to act the way he did. They willed a certain way of dealing with the striking miners and not another. When no other way to end the strike offered itself, they inflicted violence on the workers and justified it by accusing them of criminality and force. They prepared the groundwork for these accusations long before the shooting. They willfully ignored all reports of the workers' peaceful intentions and took to heart only information of the opposite tendency. What happened was self-fulfilling prophecy.

The dual discourses wended their way down through six weeks of a strike to full-blown tragedy. The sharp divergence in the two ways of understanding the strike, coupled with mistakes on all sides, rendered inevitable some form of confrontation. Still, the shooting was not foreordained, even when the workers filed along the narrow Nadezhdinsk road. The workers and their leaders and advisors seem to have acted with better faith, greater wisdom, and more restraint than the supporters of law and order. Company, state, and military officials who operated within the company's discourse felt that they had reason to doubt the legality of the strike and its leadership. They incessantly swapped information back and forth that only reinforced the analysis of the strike as illegal. Even so, outright bad faith from Petersburg ministries down to the police and military officers facing the worker demonstration on 4 April caused the shooting. The discourse predisposed those participating in it to discount workers' claims and in some unspecified way deal with them harshly. It did not, however, require a slaughter. Bad faith dispatched Treshchenkov and military reinforcements to the mines instead of an objective observer. Minister of Trade and Industry Timashev received a perfect opportunity to step out of his accustomed discourse by responding to Ginzburg's suggestion to obtain an objective report. He refused. Bad faith launched Treshchenkov's order to shoot. He could have accepted the workers' petitions, agreed to pass them to the proper authorities, and advised the workers to return to their places of residence to await further disposition. He could have done all this while standing with his line of soldiers to give his words weight. To paraphrase Bakhtin, morality arises at the moment of the act that expresses human intention. Historical analysis does not normally linger over questions of personal morality. It does seek to fix responsibility. The available evidence cannot establish exactly what Treshchenkov thought as he unleashed the soldiers' firepower on the miners, but the modes of analysis employed here do fix direct responsibility on him. Those who sent him bear even greater responsibility precisely because they were responsible officials, whereas he was their lackey. For all the factors that weigh on us, we choose to act, on the basis of intention, one way or another.

Regardless of its origins, the Lena strike and shooting entered the realm of politics. The massacre dealt a powerful blow to and irremediably damaged late tsarist state-society relations. The protest wave threatened to decouple the government even from its accustomed right-wing support, a grave matter indeed. Police officials conceded the likely absence of planning or organized ties on the part of socialist parties in the origins or leadership of the Lena strike. Nonetheless, they described the strike as *in its essence* political in character. They described a socialist-oriented oppositionist culture that, without any organized plan or structured political organizations, was capable of producing results, even out in the distant Siberian mining regions, highly unpleasant for the government. This line of analysis places these tsarist police officials in advance of most political or historiographical commentary down to this day. It also best fits the entire chain of evidence about the Lena events. Perhaps most important of all, this approach and what it portended had the deepest significance for the Russian Empire as a whole.

Chapter 6

Unexpected Consensus in Russian Society

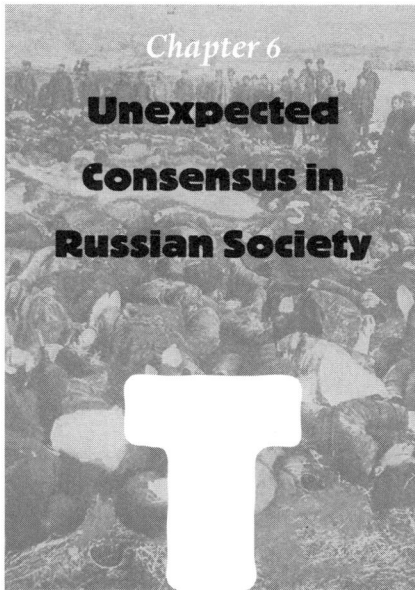

The early months of 1912 seemed to promise nothing remarkable in the life of the empire. The workers' strike movement, although somewhat revived from its 1909–10 nadir, was still at low ebb. The economy was expanding in virtually all areas. Newspaper editorials for 1 January 1912 had been upbeat. The Progressist *Russkoe slovo* (Russian Word) had described the previous year (1911) as not "grey or monolithic." With unusual energy and consensus, the two legislative branches were working on meaningful legislative projects.[1] Words such as "constitutional" and "parliamentary" dotted the pages of *Russkoe slovo* and other newspapers as the nation prepared for upcoming State Duma elections. Newspapers expressed a sense of forward movement in the life of the nation, of progress toward normalcy, which then, as now, reflected west European and New World models. Confidence seemed the watchword. Only the extreme right-wing press paid much attention to autocracy or the monarch.

Into this deceptive calm burst the news of the Lena shooting. The Lena massacre quickly became the empire's major story, supplanting even the sinking of the *Titanic* that occurred at the same time. For weeks thereafter, newspapers provided detailed coverage of the Lena events. Editorials inveighed against those guilty of the shooting. Interviews with ministers and Lenzoto officials, telegrams from Lena workers, and concerned commentary filled the pages of the nations' newspapers. Readers of the press could hardly avoid attaining detailed knowledge of the issue. The State Duma plunged into a heated discussion, as several political parties offered angry interpellations filled with accusations against the government. Reportage of these tumultuous

Duma sessions also filled newspapers' lead pages. The press reported a strike movement, on a scale not seen since 1905–1907, in sympathy for the Lena workers and in protest of those responsible. Secret police reports, the newspapers, and speakers in the Duma and at public gatherings all noted acute public agitation. Russian society reacted furiously and, in a certain way, unexpectedly to the slaughter on the distant Lena River.[2]

During recent decades, historians of late tsarist Russia have emphasized fragmentation among the empire's social elements. They have also tended to portray the post-1905 reforms as ineffective in ameliorating the grave problems facing the nation.[3] A virtual given in historical analysis of Russia, this view hardly requires discussion or, indeed, overt assertion. The evidence presented here indicates a quite different approach. A wide range of information about various aspects of the empire's social and political groups during 1912, with special reference here to the Lena massacre, suggests the need for reopening the discussion.[4]

SOCIETY'S REACTION TO THE MASSACRE

News of the massacre launched a wave of strikes. Contemporary police reports registered the first appearance of revolutionary leaflets on 5 April. Protest meetings in connection with the shooting began on 6 April in Petersburg and many other places. The first strikes broke out in Kharkov and Nikolaev on 9 and 10 April, followed by Odessa and Kiev (12 April), Saratov and Elizavetsgrad (13 April), Riga and Ekaterinoslav (14 April and following days), Petrograd (15 April and thereafter), Nizhnii-Novgorod (16 April), Arkhangelsk and Warsaw (18 April), and so on. During the height of the movement (15–20 April) huge street demonstrations of workers and students marched in Petersburg and many other cities. Afterward, according to police, the number of strikes and protests in Petersburg, Moscow, Sormovo, Lugansk, and Nizhnii ebbed somewhat, although they continued there and elsewhere and eventually merged into even larger waves of strikes and demonstrations for May Day, which clearly received a great impetus from the massacre.

The whole matter is interestingly framed by daily comments from the police. On 10 April, the Special Section of the Department of Police wrote, "the Lena events have caused a frightful tumult in Russia." On the eleventh the police commented that in "left-progressive circles, the SD and Trudovik actions in the Duma are causing great joy. When the country finds out what right-wing elements are doing [unclear reference], it will unify around the leftists. About 90 percent of the Petersburg workers are genuinely interested in the Lena events." On following days, police noted strikes, demonstrations, and student activities in support of the workers from all over Russia. For example, on 12 April the Moscow chief of police reported that "among printers and tailors in Moscow the Lena events are an active topic of conversation. Leather workers and woodworkers are also joining in. Meetings take place at the Society of Aide [and other cultural associations]." Contrarily, on 19 April one agent's report claimed that Petersburg printers and tailors "were reacting weakly to the Lena events . . . [and] were not inclined to support the strikes and demonstrations." Of note is the meticulous care the authorities devoted to the outlooks of each segment of society and each subsegment of the working class. Police reports repeatedly counted strikes and strikers in Petersburg, Moscow, Kiev, and Nizhnii-Novgorod and, on various occasions, in Riga, Grodno, Tver, Brest-Litovsk, Helsinki, Arkhangelsk, Perm, Tiflis, Kaluga, Chernigov, Baku, Warsaw, Ekaterinburg, Poltava, Tomsk, Tersk, and so forth. In related activity, the final session of the Petersburg metalworkers' union, which had just been closed down by the police, passed a resolution protesting the massacre and directed it to the socialist Duma fractions. The labor union journal *Metallist* hardly exaggerated when it stated: "In every corner of Russia, workers one way or another protested the shooting of their comrades on the Lena." On the seventeenth a report about south Russian mining regions commented about "energetic mass agitation" in association with the Lena massacre and, as counterpoint, the peacefully concluded "recent English coal-mining strikes."[5]

On 17 April the Moscow Okhrana (tsarist secret police) attempted to summarize the reaction to the Lena shooting: "In society constant discussion of the Lena events is taking place. Such a heightened atmosphere has not occurred for a long time, along with which one is forced to listen to challenges to the government expressed in the sharpest form. Many are saying that the Lena shooting is reminiscent of the 9 January [1905] shooting . . . at the Winter Palace. Under the influence of the Duma interpellations and speeches, the mood in society is sharpening." According to the Moscow secret police, the speeches of the SD deputy G. S. Kuznetsov inspired special sympathy from the public. Besides the one-day strikes, "all social gatherings [and] sessions, academic, literary, professional and so forth, are honoring the memory of the Lena victims." According to the report's compiler, society had also met "news of the rapidly expanding strike movement, as before, with the greatest sympathy." Isolated individuals who cautioned against the political repercussions of continued demonstrations, bemoaned the police, "drown in a sea of voices that insist precisely on the value of the political . . . strikes as a warning . . . to the government."[6] The police also noted a sharp response among Russian émigrés in western

Europe. Meetings, often sponsored jointly by the SDs and SRs, in Paris, Heidelberg, Geneva, and other cities condemned the shooting and set up collections to support the survivors and the families of those who had died.[7]

The government quickly adopted an aggressive stance toward Lena protest demonstrations. Internal police reports enumerated round after round of arrests among workers and students in Petersburg, Kiev, Riga, Nizhnii-Novgorod, and many other localities. For example, on 15 April police arrested eighty-four men and thirty-nine women for demonstrating on Petersburg's Nevskii Prospekt. On 21 April the police reported a "peaceful demonstration" in Nizhnii, during which "the leaders were arrested and later freed." At midmonth, according to the police, "some were saying that . . . if the strikes continued until the May Day celebration they could constitute an outright threat to the government." Such considerations undoubtedly motivated the government to arrest peaceful demonstrators, a potentially risky tactic given society's tumultuous state. Government harassment contributed to some slackening of strikes by the last week of April. As regards May Day itself, police reports commented almost in awe on the demonstrations, which in size and scale exceeded anything seen in recent years. On 2 May, the chief of the Nizhnii gendarmes worried that "the legal press is now causing a problem. . . . A distinct worker solidarity [has arisen]. This phenomenon must be taken seriously since a good deal is being done by nonparty workers. Even a slight revival of revolutionary organizations will have a great effect."[8] The police carefully monitored messages from workers and other groups to the Duma fractions. One report listed numerous Lena-connected messages to the SD Duma fraction under headings such as "from 116 conscious workers of the Donets-Iur'ev metallurgical plants," "from 300 Jewish workers of Bobruisk," "from 143 workers of the Arkhangel'sk lumber plant Ekonomia," and "from forty workers of the Khar'kov engine plant."[9] However one evaluates them, government policies and opinions highlight the scale and duration of workers' anger at the Lena shooting. In addition, they suggest broad social support for the workers.

WORKERS AND THEIR ALLIES

Statistics on strikes quantify impressions culled from police documents and the press. For example, the Factory Inspectorate counted 46,623 strikers during 1910, 105,110 during 1911, and 740,074 during 1912 (other counts provide somewhat higher but analogous numbers for all three time periods). The figures for the first three months of 1912, when figured in conjunction with data about strikes in preceding years, ad-

Table 6.1

NUMBER OF STRIKE PARTICIPANTS, JANUARY–MARCH 1911 AND 1912

	1911	*1912*
January	5,373	5,554
February	1,855	9,383
March	4,674	4,852
Total	11,902	19,789[a]

Source: Svod otchetov fabrichnykh inspektorov za 1912 god (St. Petersburg, 1913), lxxviii.
[a]Counts that covered all industries provided a figure of 41,000 strikers during January–March 1912. The lower figure excluded mining, metallurgy, and the railroads.

umbrate the strike movement as it might have developed, without a major incident during the balance of 1912. Summary data about strikes for 1910, 1911, and the first three months of 1912 indicate a distinct proportionate expansion of the strike movement (see table 6.1), which might have resulted in perhaps 200,000 to 250,000 strikers for all of 1912. Prior to the massacre, however, nothing indicated a grandiose expansion of worker protest. As things turned out, during the balance of 1912 after the Lena shooting, the conservative figures of the Factory Inspectorate counted more than 2,000 strikes with roughly 700,000 participants. The Moscow Society of Factory Owners' figures ran considerably higher, showing almost 3,000 strikes and well over a million participants. The society's figures also showed more than 1,000 political strikes (strikes with overtly political aims and slogans) with 360,000 participants in April 1912 alone.[10] Strike waves of this magnitude, on the order of four- to sevenfold over likely projected expectations, testify to the shock wave effect of the shooting. The post-Lena 1912 strikes had a second notable characteristic in that they often registered sympathy with other workers and otherwise expressed political motivations rather than localized economic or other problems (see table 6.2). (The categories of "economic" and "political" strikes, although later misused in some historical commentaries, played a role in contemporary usage and are deployed here in the contemporary senses to categorize general tendencies.) Less than 10 percent of recorded strikes during 1911 and early 1912 had overt political content, whereas 80 percent of 1912 strikes after the Lena massacre did. Even the post- Lena 1912 economic strikes (those that registered only local economic complaints) doubled the record for all strikes during the previous year. Furthermore, the post-Lena Russian strike movement did not abate until the outbreak of

Table 6.2

STRIKE PARTICIPANTS BY TYPE, 1911 AND 1912

Type of participant	1911	1912
Economic	96,730	207,720
Political	8,380	855,000
Total	105,110	1,062,720[a]

Source: Obshchestvo zavodchikov i fabrikantov Moskovskogo promyshlennogo raiona v 1912 godu (Moscow, 1913), 19; *Svod otchetov fabrichnykh inspektorov za 1911 god* (St. Petersburg, 1912), lxxxvi.

[a]Compare data for 1912 in table 6.3. Figures from the Moscow Society of Industrialists (*Obshchestvo zavodchikov i fabrikantov Moskovskogo*) were consistently higher, and more accurate, than those of the Factory Inspectorate (*Svod otchetov fabrichnykh inspektorov*), which excluded mining, railroad, and other industries not within its scope.

World War I (see table 6.3). Strikes during 1913 continued at the same expanded pace as during April–December 1912 and then, during the first half of 1914, exploded again to a rate approaching 1905. All this confirms already existing impressions that the Lena massacre heavily spurred the barely revived post-1910 workers' movement.

The archival record of close police observation of the Lena strike movement discloses additional significant data. Under the title "On Unrest among Workers in Connection with the Events of 4 April 1912 at the Lena Mines," the Petersburg police director Beletskii collected information on the strikes from all over the empire, including leaflets released by various groups. The reports from local gendarmes trace the outbreak and spread of the strikes beginning in Kharkov, Nikolaev, Kiev, and Odessa, and then spreading to Petersburg, Moscow, Warsaw, Riga, and on to the Volga, Urals, and Siberia. Local officials, by long habit and at Beletskii's specific request, strove to ferret out information about political involvement in the outbreak of the local strikes. On the whole, their efforts did not yield especially impressive results.

For example, on 7 April the Kharkov police, in response to Beletskii's 6 April warning to be on the alert for local reactions to the massacre, agreed that disorders could break out among the city's eighty thousand workers. The Kharkov gendarmes especially worried about the SRs, whose organization the police had recently "liquidated," inadvertently leaving intact, however, an underground group led by a certain Bulakova. This group was "extraordinarily dangerous in view of [its] potential agitation among workers," including distribution of

Table 6.3

NUMBER OF STRIKE PARTICIPANTS, 1905–1914

Year	No. of participants
1905	2,863,173
1906	1,108,406
1907	740,074
1908	176,101
1909	64,166
1910	46,623
1911	105,110
1912	725,491[a]
1913	887,096
1914	1,327,406[b]

Source: *Svod otchetov fabrichnykh inspektorov za 1913 god* (St. Petersburg, 1914), lxxii.
[a]Compare data for 1912 in table 6.2.
[b]For Jan.–July only.

leaflets. Although the local police considered it "highly desirable" to liquidate the SDs as well, they had canceled plans to do so out of fear "that the results would be no better than with the SRs." The following day the Kharkov police sent a clarification to explain that "no SD organization as such" existed in Kharkov city or province. What existed were "individuals capable of carrying out SD propaganda." This highlighted a situation throughout Russia in which small socialist groups and activists closely tied to factories, schools, and other institutions inevitably survived when the authorities destroyed structured socialist organizations. These low-level groups and even individuals constituted the chief danger everywhere in fomenting strikes. For one example, on 11 April, during a meeting at the Kharkov Locomotive Plant, individuals known to the police, including three SDs, one SR, and several others, made the principal speeches that led to the factory's one-day strike. No information developed by the Kharkov police during the subsequent wave of sympathy strikes went beyond this. Leaflets appeared calling for a one-day strike; factory meetings occurred; speakers recommended a one-day strike; the workers voted for the strike, which usually occurred the next day; and the workers resumed work the following day without further incident or disorders.[11] This was also the universal template for the empire's Lena sympathy strikes, as local police reports reveal with sparkling clarity.

Examination of very detailed police reports from Kiev, Petersburg, and Moscow only slightly expand upon this picture. On 9 April a meeting of South Russian Machinery Plant workers in Kiev voted for a one-day strike after hearing "two [unidentified] orators who called for workers to express their sympathy by means of a one-day strike." On April 11 police noted copies of an SR-SD leaflet calling for Kiev students to carry out a two-day protest strike.[12] A Moscow gendarme report of 13 April identified the city's Society for Aiding Peoples' Education and Entertainment as the place where workers of all sorts exchanged information and coordinated plans for strikes and demonstrations. Printers, who had received a visit from a Petersburg printer, were especially active in "suggesting a one-day strike to fulfill the request of the representative of the SD Duma fraction" (perhaps referring to the Petersburg printer who had visited) and were planning to issue a leaflet. Voluminous reports from Petersburg indicate that an extensive list of Petersburg plants participated in the strikes. The police also devoted considerable attention to SD-SR student coalition groups in encouraging and organizing worker and student demonstrations in the center of the city.[13]

Several themes emerge quite clearly from the empirewide police reports. The strikes were peaceful, orderly, and entailed no demands or issues other than sympathy for the Lena workers. Within each industrial center, the strikes had a rolling character. Strikes began in each industrial center at one or two concerns, followed on succeeding days by other factories, until virtually all concerns had struck, a process that took from one to two weeks. Police reports make clear that locally published leaflets from a range of parties and orators (some identified, some not) proposed the idea of the one-day strike. A third important factor was the newspapers. For example, on 10 April the manager of the Kharkov Locomotive Plant made the rounds of the plant's sections, asking workers about their reason for striking. When he reached the assembly plant, one worker, with newspaper in hand, answered, "Are you aware of what the newspapers are saying about the Lena shooting?" after which he began to read in a loud voice from the paper. Later at a plantwide meeting, a worker (presumably the same one) read from a newspaper. Police in Riga, Tambov, Nizhnii-Novgorod, and other places noted the role of newspapers in spreading the idea of the one-day strike, that is, when newspapers reported one-day strikes in Kharkov, Kiev, or Moscow, activists in other places picked up and carried out the idea as well.[14] In unconventional ways, modes of communication and coordinated action had emerged for the oppositionist movement. The degree of coordination throughout the empire, still not entirely explained in the sources, commands attention.

Whatever occurred at other times, the 1912 strike movement in response to the Lena shooting had a definite characteristic. It did not occur in social isolation. From all corners came commentaries about the degree to which the shooting infuriated Russian society. It also became clear that many social elements resolved to provide moral and practical support to the Lena victims and the workers' cause in general. One police report claimed that every social gathering and session of academic, literary, and professional life addressed the question. A very broad range of newspapers and Duma fractions expressed support in no uncertain terms. The police recorded information about a special conference of Irkutsk lawyers called on 19 May to discuss methods of defending the rights of Lenzoto workers. Moscow and Petersburg advocates also organized support for the Lena workers. In Baku the employees and printers of two local newspapers set up a collection to support those injured in the shooting and the families of those who died. Students of the Kiev Commercial Institute and of Iur'ev high schools, Russian students of Heidelberg University, employees of the Baku Technological Institute, administrators of the Gomel printers' union, and Gomel office clerks channeled messages and funds to Lena workers, as did Baku oil industry office employees. In Moscow, employees of the Economic Society of Officers struck in support of the Lena workers. In retaliation for support of the Lena workers, the Lugansk police raided the city library, the savings bank, the cooperative store, the zemstvo hospital, all labor union offices, and the offices of the newspaper *Donetskaia zhizn'* (Donets Life), where it arrested employees and journalists.

Police reports sometimes emphasized workers and intelligentsia, including most obviously students, as the elements most involved in the wave of protest and support. As suggested in part by data from the press, the Duma debates, and other sources, the matter went much further than the radical intelligentsia. By late April and early May the government began closing down professional and cultural organizations in many cities for their involvement in the protest movement. Among these were the Vitebsk Old Believers' Union, the Moscow German Association for Education in South Russia, the Odessa Union of Office Workers and Accountants, and the Petersburg Society of Gravurists. Entrepreneurial organizations and personages also responded in supportive ways. The Ekaterinoslav Rutchenkovskii Mining Company sent funds. A wealthy Siberian merchant remarked to the press, "It's true, in the past [Siberian] workers did not live well, but at least no one slaughtered them." Remarkably, the Petersburg, Moscow, and Riga Societies of Factory Owners voted to refrain from imposing fines on workers who participated in the one-day protest strikes. In reaching these decisions, the industrial entrepreneurs referred to the "extraordinary circumstances" of the strikes in response to the Lena shooting and the "remarkable concerted elevated mood of the workers' during the May Day Strikes." Entrepreneurial largesse, of course, had its limits as suggested when the Petersburg and Moscow societies declined to pay workers for strike days so as "not to encourage unrest in the workers' milieu and serve as an undesirable precedent."[15] In a plaintive response to Minister of the Interior Makarov's remark "thus it has always been, thus it will always be," a *Vestnik Evropy* (Messenger of Europe) writer captured society's most basic response to the injustices inflicted on workers. "Will it really always be like this?" queried the journal author, "Should it really be like this?"[16] The empire's population resoundingly answered No!

Students

The workers' closest allies in this case were indisputably the students who helped launch the Lena protest movement. Police reports and press accounts noted the constant meetings at educational institutions, as well as the numerous students accompanying workers during street demonstrations. Student collectives printed leaflets on a broad scale. Indeed, the first proclamations protesting the shooting came from socialist student organizations in Kiev, Petersburg, Moscow, and other cities. Packets of proclamations compiled by the police all contained multiple documents of student origin and orientation. The earliest Lena proclamation in any of the collections appeared on 5 April under the signature of the "Autonomous Group of SRs" for distribution at St. Petersburg University: "To students! Yesterday on the Lena a terrible evil took place. . . . The tsarist regime again revealed its horrible face—murderers! . . . We summon you to struggle." On 9 April the Kiev University SR organization's proclamation advised students of that city, "The tsarist armed forces inflicted unheard of cruelty on the workers at the Lena mines. . . . Support the 10 April strike! Show that revolutionary studenthood still exists!" On 13 April SRs, SDs, Ukrainian SRs and SDs, and Polish Socialists of the Kiev Polytechnical Institute issued a proclamation: "Comrade polytechnical students! On 4 April they massacred workers. . . . All students support the country-wide call!" On the fourteenth, the Petersburg General Student Coalition Committee distributed a leaflet at the university, the Psycho-Neurological Institute, and the Women's Advanced Courses.[17]

Ivan Menitskii's recollections about the Lena protest movement among Moscow students expands this picture. When news of the shooting arrived in Moscow, a special student organization (the equivalent of the Petersburg Student Coalition Committee) arose to lead demonstrations. On 9 April it issued a proclamation that stated: "Comrades! Russian society is deeply outraged by the latest events at the Lena mines. . . . Active protest is necessary. . . . Gather at meetings to decide the form of protest." On the seventeenth an SR student organization issued a leaflet calling for a one-day strike. On the nineteenth student leaders collected money for Lena victims during lectures at Moscow University. That same day a "committee of student activists" issued a leaflet that spoke of "meetings and strikes at educational institutions of Petersburg, Riga, Kiev and Ekaterinoslav. . . . The affair of the Lena workers is also the affair of all society in the struggle against political violence." Meanwhile, according to the police, that same day a Moscow University student, a certain Nikolaev, known as a socialist, organized a collection at Shaniavskii University. During a meeting at this institution, one student proclaimed: "Everyone is aware of the damage the Lena events have inflicted on the working class." According to Menitskii, these activities and the appearance of many additional proclamations provoked incessant arrests beginning on 19 April at the Agricultural Institute, Moscow University, and other educational establishments.

Even so, student agitation and an agitated mood among Moscow students did not fade away quickly. On 1 May a proclamation appeared at the Moscow Technical High School that called for a one-day strike in memory of those slain on the Lena. According to the recollections of the mining entrepreneur and Progressist politician Sergei Chetverikov, during the campaign for the Fourth Duma several weeks after the shooting, the Constitutional Democratic leader A. I. Shingarev addressed an election rally at the Historical Museum. After his speech, Shingarev called for an open debate, during which a railroad machinist gave a rousing speech about the Lena shooting. The hall, packed with students and other citizens, rang with outraged shouts against the perpetrators: "Vampires! Exploiters! Executioners!" When police monitors showed signs of shutting down the meeting, Chetverikov quieted the hall and the meeting continued.[18]

The situation hardly differed elsewhere. On 14 April a meeting of six hundred students at the Psycho-Neurological Institute in Petersburg voted for the Student Coalition Committee's sternly worded resolutions. That same day numerous Petersburg students marched with workers in the streets and many were arrested, as police noted the "heightened mood" of workers and students. Agents intensified their observation of SR and SD student circles, but concluded, perhaps prematurely, that arrests during February had weakened these organizations so that they "could not lead the protest movement." The very next day, the Petersburg Student Coalition Committee issued a leaflet addressed to Petersburg students. On the seventeenth police reported the arrest of several members of the Coalition Committee on the Nevskii Prospekt. That same day, a student leader, P. A. Vinogradov, tossed leaflets to crowds of demonstrators at the Kazan Square. Later in the month, student meetings at the Women's Higher Courses and the Technological Institute voted to strike on 24 April in protest of the Lena shooting. When students at the Riga Polytechnical Institute attempted to hold a protest meeting on 18 April, police intervened to break up the gathering. The same occurred at the Kiev Polytechnical Institute on the twenty-first. The future well-known literary critic Marc Slonim, at the time an Odessa gymnasium student and SR workers' circle leader, later recalled the Lena protest strikes and confirmed students' active role in the Odessa movement.[19]

The sheer intensity and longevity of the student reaction to the Lena events are of interest even now, just as they captured the attention of the police then. By nature of their elite status and the location of their institutions, students had easy access to central urban areas. In the case of the Lena demonstrations (and many others), student activists helped organize marches and demonstrations and swelled their size and cohesion. Through their schools, they also had access to copy devices, which accounts for the exceptionally large number of leaflets produced by student collectives. Their return to massive activism at the time of the Lena massacre was almost as important as the rebirth of the workers' movement. Little noted as it has been, direct student involvement in the 1914–17 antiwar and antitsarist movements that led to the February Revolution found its first solid basis in the organized Lena protests.[20]

Socialists

Prior to the massacre, nothing suggests that the socialists were sharply attuned to the potential of the Lena strike to turn into a history-making event. The 5 April 1912 issue of the Petersburg Bolshevik newspaper *Zvezda* (Star), which evidently had gone to press before news of the shooting, contained two routine notices about the strike with no hint of the extraordinary. Likewise, an edition of the SR newspaper *Znamia truda* (Banner of Labor) appeared just as news of the massacre broke, drawing a complaint from some SRs living in Paris about the failure of the paper to prepare its readers.[21] In truth, part of the "bourgeois" press, rather than the socialist, first honed in on the special potential for government violence on the Lena.

Nonetheless, when the revolutionary parties first received news of the Lena massacre they promptly turned to the task at hand. Socialist newspapers and journals—the Bolshevik *Zvezda, Pravda* (Truth), and *Sotsial-Demokrat,* the SR *Znamia truda, Trudovoi golos* (Voice of Labor), *Zavety* (Legacy), and the Menshevik *Rabochaia gazeta* (Workers' Newspaper) and *Nasha zaria* (Our Dawn)—all quickly focused on the Lena events. Party organizations issued incendiary proclamations, denounced the government and capitalist entrepreneurs for indifference to workers' lives, took part in organizing strikes and demonstrations, and in general attempted to use the tragic event to bring about the desired result—that is, revolution. Revolutionary organizations and leadership at every possible level, every imaginable locale, and of every conceivable orientation, sensing that this was indeed an issue that counted, moved to an active stance. Beginning on 5 April and continuing until May, printed proclamations began to appear all over the country from the SDs, the SRs, the Bund, the Jewish Zionist Revolutionary Party "Paolei-Tsion," the Anarcho-Communists, and the Armenian Dashnaks, not to mention various subdivisions such as the Ukrainian SDs and SRs. Conveniently for historians, the police compiled whole packets of confiscated Lena protest leaflets. The packets had titles such as "List of Proclamations Issued in Connection with the Lena Events by Unidentified Parties and Organizations of Obvious Revolutionary Tendency" or "List of Leaflets of the Party of Socialist Revolutionaries in Connection with the Lena Events," "List of Social Democratic Leaflets," and so forth. One combined packet compiled especially for the Manukhin Commission contained, in rough chronological order beginning 5 May, several SR leaflets, several leaflets issued jointly (SDs, SRs, Bundists, etc.), one from the Anarcho-Communists, several each from the Bund and the RSDRP, and several unidentified leaflets, covering, so to speak, all the ground. Cities of origin included among many others Kiev, Baku, the Baltic area, Warsaw, and Kharkov.[22] Although individual party groups issued most leaflets and proclamations, some appeared under joint authorship. For example, the SR and SD organizations in Paris issued a joint proclamation. Soon thereafter the SD and Trudovik Duma fractions entered a joint interpellation aimed at provoking a Duma debate, and the Trudovik fraction, with SD support, entered a resolution for legislation to provide financial and other support for Lena victims and their families. On 13 April a coalition group in Kiev, including the SRs and SDs, their Ukrainian branches, and the Polish Socialist Party, issued a joint proclamation aimed at students of the Polytechnical Institute, as did similar socialist coalition committees at Petersburg University and other educational establishments.[23]

All the proclamations and resolutions expressed solidarity with the slain and wounded Lena workers and scorn for the regime and Lenzoto, coupled, in the case of proclamations, with general revolutionary slogans. A few quotations will provide the flavor of their content. A leaflet issued on 5 April by the Autonomous SR Group at Petersburg University stated: "Yesterday on the Lena a terrible evil occurred. . . . The armed forces fired into an unarmed hungry crowd. The tsarist government again displayed its murderous character. . . . We call you to struggle." The joint party leaflet from Kiev dated 13 April urged people not "to remain silent . . . [in the face of] the massacre of hundreds of workers. A new stage in the history of the revolutionary movement is at hand. . . . Such beastliness is possible only on the part of Autocracy." On 25 April a Bund proclamation told workers that "not one workers' strike can take place in the mines without the interference of armed force. To struggle! To protest!" During April the Kiev Committee of the RSDRP called for a "one-day strike. Into battle, comrades! . . . What has occurred in distant Siberia is terrible. Eternal memory for the victims of this gruesome act."[24] Naturally, the leaflets' compilers tied the specific event to general political messages and slogans. For example, an Anarcho-Communist leaflet proclaimed: "Down with the government!"; an SR leaflet began with the words "Long live the struggle against capital!"; and an SD document ended with the slogan "Down with capitalism!"[25] The composite message was simple: autocracy had again done its worst to unarmed workers, the only answer to which was for concerned people to join the dual struggle to overthrow the regime and capitalism.

Meanwhile, the police closely observed the various parties' responses and activities. An agent's report from Petersburg on 10 April noted that "SD organizations . . . were astounded" by the extent of the workers' response to the shooting. "SD agitators have endlessly stirred up the workers. . . . [But] if the strikes don't spread, the prestige of the SD organization will fall. Much depends on Moscow and Warsaw." (As a matter of fact, the strike movement did spread, presumably leaving unscathed SD prestige.) A few days later, the police claimed that the SD and SR groups at Petersburg University "had been weakened by arrests during February and could not provide leadership for the movement." This evaluation missed the mark since student groups in the capital and elsewhere issued numerous leaflets and took part in street demonstrations. On 12 April the Poltava secret police reported on information that the SR Central Committee Abroad was sending agents to a special conference in Russia with the goal of "using the Lena events as a basis for building the organization inside Russia."[26] That the Lena massacre spurred recruitments and contributions, giving the revolutionary movement a new lease on life, is beyond question. In this regard, the police noted that "90 percent of Petersburg workers are really interested in the events on the Lena. They feel strongly that the Lena tragedy is not a '[passing] episode' . . . [but that] a repetition of 'Lena' is possible anywhere."[27] Naturally, this sharp awareness on the part of workers, coupled with widespread outright support from students and sympathy from society as a whole, could only strengthen revolutionary organizations. The police worried about "even a slight revival of revolutionary organizations" and concluded, in evaluating the post-Lena protest movement, that the socialist campaign about the shooting had wrought "brilliant results."[28]

The socialists responded not with foresight but aggressively to the Lena episode. Even after social unrest in direct response to the shooting had waned somewhat, the socialists continued a steady drumbeat of criticism and commentary. Indeed, in subsequent years the Lena massacre joined Bloody Sunday (5 January 1905) as a defining event in antitsarist and anticapitalist agitation, as testified to by innumerable leaflets, articles, and retrospectives. In the weeks and months after the shooting itself, socialist leaders of every stripe used the Lena events in their analyses. In the journal *Nasha zaria,* the Menshevik Evgenii Maevskii noted that "the events on the Lena rivet general attention and will long continue to do so." The shooting and the government's response to it indicated "the special purely Russian situation as regards the workers' question." The shooting, concluded Maevskii, placed "the workers' question on the agenda of the day." In *Sotsial-Demokrat,* Lenin observed that the "Lena shooting most acutely reflected the *entire* regime . . . [and] had inflamed the masses with a revolutionary fire." Fedor Dan prognosticated that "the grandiose political strikes in connection with the Lena tragedy . . . indubitably demarcate a turning point not only in the Russian workers' movement but in the political fate of the country." In a detailed deconstruction of the government's version of the Lena strike and shooting, Kerenskii characterized the prestrike Lena mines as a "capitalist utopia," which the Lena workers' strike had helped bring to an end.[29] Indeed, the strike and its tragic results had won even greater victories for the Russian workers' movement in terms of popular support and widespread distrust of the government. Furthermore, little noted by historical commentators, the government was forced to respond to public opinion.

THE RUSSIAN PRESS AND THE LENA TRAGEDY

Prior to the 4 April shooting, Russia's press paid scant attention to the Lena strike. By 7 March, more than a week after the strike's outbreak, only *Birzhevye vedomosti* (Stock Exchange Gazette) and one or two other Petersburg and Moscow papers had mentioned the strike. Subsequent to these first reports, only *Birzhevye vedomosti*, perhaps because of the strike's economic implications, pursued the story over the next weeks. Contrary to expectations, *Birzhevye vedomosti*, the Russian equivalent of the *Wall Street Journal*, took a neutral stance and even expressed quiet sympathy for the miners. In its 6 March article, it also first hinted at problems if the government sent additional troops to the Lena mines. In a 10 March discussion of the vast English coal-mining strikes then under way, the stock market newspaper continued to play on this theme. The journalist remarked pointedly that a Russian reader's "head fills with questions [about] how many police and soldiers have been dispatched to quell the [English] strike, how many [strikers] have been beaten, wounded and brought to court and imprisoned?" In reply, the paper answered, "not one soldier, not one person."[30] Perhaps too sanguine about strikes abroad, *Birzhevye vedomosti*'s commentary cleverly and presciently highlighted the potential for violent responses to large Russian strikes.

On 23 March, well before most of the press had even acknowledged the strike, *Birzhevye vedomosti* adopted a clear critical stance. "Informed sources," asserted the newspaper, "feel that Lenzoto is mistaken in not engaging in negotiations with the workers about [the latter's] substantive demands." In its postshooting analysis, *Birzhevye vedomosti* condemned Lenzoto's role as "all-powerful dictator" of the Lena mining region and noted the "extraordinary agitation in society" because of the "excessiveness of the measures taken . . . [at the mines] by any rational calculation, let alone conscience." After chronicling Lenzoto's abuses, the daily pointed out that the government had long known of "the possibility of unrest if nothing were done [to improve the situation] at the mines."[31] Other prominent business papers, such as the Moscow *Kommersant* (Merchant) and the Petersburg *Torgovo-Promyshlennaia gazeta* (Trade and Industry Newspaper), also quietly aligned themselves with predominant public opinion. *Torgovo-Promyshlennaia gazeta*, which even featured a regular and quite sympathetic series devoted to "the workers' question," reprinted the Duma debates that so strongly established joint government-Lenzoto culpability and the workers' helplessness.[32] These influential newspapers offered no help to the state and the company, although they clearly yielded to *Birzhevye vedomosti* in their coverage of the Lena events.

Birzhevye vedomosti's reportage and analysis were doubly remarkable for being very quick off the mark and, in tandem with that of the Progressist *Russkoe slovo* a little later, serving as a virtual template for subsequent Russian press coverage. Whether in direct imitation or not, the conservative (Nationalist) *Novoe vremia* (New Times), the liberal

(Constitutional Democratic) *Russkie vedomosti* and *Rech'* (Speech), the Octobrist *Golos Moskvy* (Voice of Moscow), and many regional newspapers of varying tendencies underwent a similar evolution about the Lena events. This manifested itself as, first, strained neutrality (leavened by barely concealed sympathy for the workers), quickly supplanted by growing suspicion of the government and Lenzoto, and then, as damning evidence poured in about the shooting, unconcealed outrage and condemnation.

The press's responses to the Lena massacre are not easily categorized along a simple right-left spectrum. Quite liberal newspapers, such as those of the Petersburg and Moscow Constitutional Democrats, lagged in acknowledging the affair's significance. Meanwhile, the centrist *Russkoe slovo* eventually surpassed even *Birzhevye vedomosti* in the cogency of its ongoing critical analysis. Like many Russian newspapers, early in 1912 *Russkoe slovo* reported heavily on the coal-mining strikes abroad and on labor-oriented questions at home. From its first notice of the strike on 20 March, the Moscow Progressist paper provided serious coverage of the Lena crisis. On 22 March the paper described Lenzoto's dictatorial hold over its workers, an approach that became a staple in Lena newspaper commentary. When the company requested additional troops, noted the correspondent, the government quickly complied. On 24 March the paper characterized Lenzoto's behavior as "frightful" (*strashnoe*) and the workers' demands as "real and not caprice as a result of agitation." On 3 and 4 April *Russkoe slovo* reported the failure of all efforts to resolve the strike. On 5 April the editors ignored the official government press release about the massacre in favor of an article under the title "Gold" that focused on the intertwined issues of Lenzoto's prominent backers and the horrible conditions at the mines. *Russkoe slovo*'s specialty became successive exposés about the backgrounds of Belozerov and Treshchenkov, the former of which it singled out for blame. About the "gendarme" (Treshchenkov), it posed the more basic question: "Who sent him?" A 7 April editorial posed the eternal Russian question "Who is to blame?" On this and following days, it squarely placed equal blame on Lenzoto and the government. The editors also demanded Interior Minister Makarov's resignation.[33] That *Birzhevye vedomosti* and *Russkoe slovo*, both deeply rooted in Russia's entrepreneurial classes, took highly critical stances before most newspapers had even mentioned the strike and that they continued a barrage of devastating analysis after the shooting is noteworthy.

Meanwhile, flagship Constitutional Democratic (Kadet) newspapers such as the Petersburg *Rech'* and the Moscow *Russkie vedomosti* either failed to notice the strike (*Rech'*) or reported it with caution

(*Russkie vedomosti*). A first note of direct criticism crept into *Rech*'s daily analysis only on 11 April, when the editors implied that the government was underreporting the casualties of the shooting. "It is clear," claimed the Petersburg Constitutional Democrats, "that the government knows nothing and receives its data from persons directly involved in the tragedy." The very next day the editors took a sharply different tack: "We were mistaken. We thought the government lacked information. . . . The government was fully informed about conditions at the mines before the tragedy." *Rech*'s 12 April editorial also characterized as "abnormal" the situation in which the people responsible for the shooting were conducting the investigation. Later editorials asserted that "we now know that the workers presented no threat" and that the "decision to arrest the strike committee was reached at the center [i.e., by the government in Petersburg]."[34] These last two comments constituted elements of an accusation of criminal government culpability. *Russkie vedomosti* chided the government on 7 April for intervening in the strike solely for the benefit of Lenzoto. In an affair that "in no way effects the government," claimed the liberal newspaper, "it summons police and soldiers to defend Lenzoto's shareholders' interests by means unheard of to the English government." As regards the authorities' characterization of the workers' demands for an eight-hour day as "political," the Kadet newspaper wrote scornfully, "If the eight-hour day in the mines is politics, then the [habitual] six-hour day in Petersburg ministries must be full socialism."[35]

In the timing and character of its reportage, the right-centrist (Octobrist) *Golos Moskvy* adhered closely to the Kadet newspapers. This newspaper widely reported labor problems at home and abroad with cautious sympathy for workers. It did not, however, stand out in its reporting of the Lena strike and shooting. A first skeptical note arose on 7 April when, in reference to the government's statement that "as is known, the strike began in late February," the Octobrist editors queried (disingenuously?): "To whom was it known? Who knew about this?" Still, they continued, "[we want] to believe that the government has a clear conscience." The newspaper's following issues established that its wish was in vain. Despite the minister of the interior's characterization of the strike as political, available data made clear that it was economic, noted the Octobrists. A 13 April article, "Full Circle," that linked the Lena events to 1903 and 1905 massacres, lamented that the government has "returned to shooting workers":

> *Sober people who value the development of the Russian economy and industry insist that the entire Russian people without class distinction interrogate the government. We can go full circle but we cannot close the*

circle. At the heart of worker legislation is the principle that the contract between the worker and the entrepreneur cannot be left to the free sphere of negotiation. The law must intervene [to establish] labor norms. The specter of social revolution is a threat to our culture, . . . [but open] struggle . . .is appropriate only if [the socialist movement] widens the gap between classes.

The Octobrists, often characterized as virtual reactionaries, offered as a solution the Western model of a state compromise with workers and socialists on the one hand and with capitalism on the other in the form of state-sponsored welfare legislation.[36]

Regional papers picked up the story shortly before or, more commonly, after the shooting. Of special interest are the Tomsk and Irkutsk newspapers because of their proximity to the Lena Region and their long-term focus on the mining industry. The Tomsk daily, *Sibirskaia zhizn'* (Siberian Life), in its first report of the strike emphasized its "completely peaceful" and economic nature. The company, the editors noted, had rejected legitimate demands and "summoned troops." Later commentaries accused the company of exercising "feudal rights" in the region. "All local functions are in the hands of Lenzoto's administration . . . [and] all government functionaries are virtually . . . hired Lenzoto employees." After the massacre, *Sibirskaia zhizn'* highlighted the "indignation" displayed in the nations' newspapers "right and left" and praised the peaceful settling of the English coal miners' strike as opposed to the violence on the Lena. The paper concluded, "none of this would have happened if the authorities had . . . responded appropriately to the workers and not resorted to harsh measures."[37]

The Irkutsk daily, *Sibir'*, took a sterner line, as befit its status as principal news outlet for the major city nearest to the gold mines and the site of numerous state and private mining offices. From its first 1 April report, it blamed the company for the strike's outbreak and everything that followed. In its criticism of the government, the Irkutsk paper even accused the mining officials Tul'chinskii and Galkin of failing to defend the workers with sufficient energy. In a 12 April editorial, the newspaper found "the Lena tragedy to be a result of a distinct plan to break the strike, which had been proceeding without excesses. . . .The authorities acted hand in hand with the [Lenzoto] mining administrators. . . . Company officials cynically made concessions deliberately designed to be turned down . . . and thus necessitate resort to more decisive measures."[38] Of all the newspapers, *Sibir'*, with the best access to inside sources, made the clearest case for criminal government-Lenzoto collusion.

Other regional papers commented in a similar fashion. The

Arkhangel'sk editorialized that "[Lenzoto's] criminal activities were prolonged and well known to the authorities. And then no sooner had the
workers spoken out for their rights, then those very authorities . . . at
once evaluated this . . . as something revolutionary and arrested the
strike committee." *Vostochnoe pomor'e* (Eastern Seaboard) wanted "the
closest investigation" of what had occurred since "on the eve of the
shooting the workers offered to go back to work on certain conditions." *Ufimskii vestnik* (Ufa Messenger) commented that as "[Lenzoto]
earned millions . . . local workers got [a pittance and] were helpless if
they became unable to work. This sad reality underlay the workers'
unrest." *Ural'skaia zhizn'* (Ural'sk Life) saw "Lenzoto's contempt for the
workers as the cause of the strike." *Saratovskii listok* (Saratov Page)
remarked that in England no one thought of "arresting instigators of
a strike of 2,000,000 workers," whereas in Russia a "strike of 6,000
summons extreme measures."[39]

The responses of conservative newspapers are perhaps the most
surprising. The Nationalist *Novoe vremia* actually became a source of
information and commentary about the Lena events when other newspapers began to pick up its substantive pieces. A 6 April article, "In
Ginzburg's Kingdom," accused the company administration of "obsti-
nately striving . . . to give the strike a tendentious political coloration. . . . In the eternal struggle between labor and capital a peaceful
solution is reached when normal social relations exist." The Lena ab-
normality, for *Novoe vremia,* consisted of the actions of "Jewish administrators, greedy for Russian gold [but] indifferent to Russian blood."
Difficult to sustain in this case because of Lenzoto's many impeccably
Russian, elite administrators and investors, this anti-Semitic twist was
Russian conservatism's hallmark. Much of *Novoe vremia*'s subsequent
reportage and commentary eschewed overt anti-Semitism, although it
did not resist an occasional thrust.[40] On 11 April *Novoe vremia* criticized
the Duma fractions of various parties (SDs, Trudoviks, Constitutional
Democrats, Octobrists, and Nationalists) for focusing on "trivialities"
rather than "looking for deeper causes. . . . Lenzoto is only one of
many companies. Whence its [sacrosanct] position?"[41] Here the conservative *Novoe vremia* trod on sensitive ground since Lenzoto's elite
status and the state's interest in gold were the real keys to its influence.
The newspaper's ongoing discussion posited state, national, and popular interests higher than those of business and the reputations of
elevated personages, heady stuff for a conservative Nationalist newspaper. Minus the anti-Semitism, *Novoe vremia*'s analysis would receive
high marks for genuinely citizen- and statesmanlike views of the
nations's welfare.

Extreme right-wing newspapers combined variations on already noted themes with noxious ritualistic anti-Semitism. *Russkoe znamia* (Russian Banner), the official paper of the Union of the Russian People, condemned the "unprincipled use of force." Quickly abandoning the high road, it then described the Lenzoto administration as consisting "entirely of kikes [*zhidy*]. . . . When will kike violence cease?" Regional reactionary papers followed suit. The Odessa *Russkii golos* (Russian Voice) declared that "at the Lena mines a catastrophe occurred that cost the lives of half-frozen Russian workers. . . . The guilty parties [are] the kikes and their stooges, the Russian liberators [liberal and socialist intelligentsia]." The compendious list of villains, however, did not include Russian workers or soldiers: "They are not guilty. Guilty are those who . . . spread the idea that disobedience would go unpunished . . . [and] the Lenzoto administration [for] deliberately creating the terrible conditions for workers. . . . The richest mines," lamented *Russkii golos,* "fall into the hands of foreign and Jewish capitalists." The *Tverskoe povolzh'e* (Tver on the Volga) mostly worried about how the Lena shooting would be used by foes of the existing order and noted that the "government's declarations [about the strike and shooting] serve as excellent propaganda against the government."[42]

As one aspect of the Lena press coverage, newspapers widely and, on the whole, sympathetically reported on the protest strike movement that seized the empire for weeks after the shooting. Only the reactionary papers fretted about the connection between the strikes and the revolutionary movement.[43] The press response to the protest and sympathy strikes, like its analysis of the massacre itself, calls into question the idea that the various segments of Russian society were hopelessly at odds with one another. It is doubtful that anyone reading the press coverage of the Lena events then or now without prior knowledge of the fragmentation theory would guess at its existence or find it adequate.

THE THIRD STATE DUMA AND THE LENA MASSACRE

Less than a week after the shooting, the State Duma plunged into its stormy deliberations about the Lena affair. Newspaper reportage of the sensational debates that opened on 9 April and continued until the twenty-fifth became a major portion of the Lena press coverage. Some newspapers, perhaps too timid to speak out editorially, highlighted the positions they would have liked to take by featuring excerpts from the Duma sessions.[44] During the first session, five Duma fractions entered interpellations (official questions to responsible government ministers). The Constitutional Democrats, the SDs and Trudoviks acting jointly, the Octobrists, and the Nationalists all introduced formulaic questions. Each interpellation began with a version of the Lena events as motivation and finished with sharply worded "questions" that were virtual accusations laid to the responsible government ministers.[45]

The Constitutional Democratic interpellation asked the interior and justice ministers whether they were "aware that . . . with the goal of serving the interests of the entrepreneurs, persons intervened in a peacefully proceeding strike. . . . If aware, what measures do the ministers suggest to bring the guilty parties to justice?" The SD-Trudovik bloc posed the following question: "Are the chairman of the council of ministers and the minister of the interior aware that on 4 April 1912 at the [Lenzoto] mines . . . for participation in an economic strike . . . workers were fired upon resulting in 270 deaths . . . and 250 wounded?" The Octobrist interpellation asked: "Is the minister of the interior aware that during the disturbances among workers at the Lenzoto mines firearms were used unlawfully . . . [for] insufficient cause? Is the minister of trade and industry aware that Lenzoto's relations with the workers at the mines were illegal?" Finally, the Nationalists queried the ministers of the interior and trade and industry: "Did it in fact take place . . . that local authorities long delayed in fulfilling lawful demands of the workers at the Lenzoto mines? And if [so], what measures will the ministers undertake to disclose the degree of guilt of the local authorities and to fulfill the workers' lawful demands?" The official "motivations" that accompanied the queries revealed the thinking of the various political groups and, with some differences in nuance, covered the same ground. All agreed that the workers were innocent and the guilty parties should be brought to justice. The joint socialist interpellation laid the greatest emphasis on the responsibility of high government circles, whereas others implied this and the Nationalists avoided the question entirely. Even so, the newspapers of all the groups that entered interpellations unhesitatingly accused the government of malfeasance. Consequently, the Duma interpellations, plus the various parties' public stances, constituted a potential basis for consensus about proposed Duma measures. This potential, however, soon fell victim to traditional Duma infighting.

After the introduction of the interpellations, and then again in four other sessions until 25 April, Duma debate raged about the Lena episode. On the floor of the Duma, the stormy discussion wended its way down somewhat different paths than in the press or even in the various party interpellations. Political groups inevitably maneuvered for position, sought allies, and attempted to promote one or another general political agenda within a specific institutional context, that is, the lawmaking body of the nation empowered to take actual steps. In this environment, traditional political alignments and commitments, not to mention modes of speech and address, reasserted themselves. The free and doubtlessly sincere expressions that prevailed in press pronouncements and other public venues now yielded to political reality. Some politicians may even have experienced relief at stepping back into established roles. Even so, two principal lines of discussion arose in the Duma debates: general criticism of the government and Lenzoto for the entire tragic episode, about which consensus survived; and intense squabbling, along traditional political fault lines, about measures to be taken. As one might expect, on this latter question the Constitutional Democrats, SDs, and Trudoviks constituted the activist left; the Octobrists, the center; and the other conservative parties, the right, with the Octobrists maneuvering in such a way that ultimately no measures were undertaken. The politics of action (or inaction) did not so much shatter consensus as supercede it. Nevertheless, much transpired in the Duma before the anticlimax.

During the first day of debates, party tribunes such as N. V. Nekrasov and A. A. Skorokhodov for the Constitutional Democrats, A. I. Guchkov for the Octobrists, and G. S. Kuznetsov for the SDs entered the fray with the shooting's perpetrators as the common objects of attack. Even so, Duma custom at once prevailed so that "applause [or] noise from the left [or] right [or even] center" and other vocal signs of approbation or disapprobation dotted the session minutes, as did the chair's disciplinary bell and voice: "I ask you to stop making noise. I ask you not to speak from your places." The chair also warned Kuznetsov "not to touch upon the actions of the highest power [the emperor] [and] not to touch upon the army," clearly demarcating the limits of the possible in public discussion as prescribed by law.

Nekrasov's opening speech doubted that socialists were responsible for the strike, although he readily conceded the role of "socialist ideas." Guchkov agreed that the use of force had been unjustified. In refusing, however, to support the socialist interpellation, he did not rule out a direct socialist role and commented that "Social Democracy hovers around social ulcers and economic decay." This gratuitous remark set off the first fireworks of the Lena deliberations. The next speaker on the agenda was the Menshevik-SD Kuznetsov, who immediately scorned Guchkov's "points of view." The Menshevik then ridiculed the Octobrist proposal for a government investigation of the Lena affair. He then listed the guilty parties, including Lenzoto, the government, and even the Duma itself for inaction. Kuznetsov concluded by summoning workers "not only to replace . . . the entire regime but to elect a Duma that will really serve their interests on the basis of general voting rights until the Constitutional Assembly." This somewhat implausible mix of muted revolutionism and voting within the system perhaps symbolized some of the prospects and problems for moderate socialism in post-1905 Russia. The final speaker, the Constitutional Democrat Skorokhodov, strove, in vain, to smooth out the differences between potential allies by pitching his remarks at a high moral and emotional level. Russia faced "elemental forces" that he characterized as "unbridled administrative tyranny." Skorokhodov then quoted Mephistopheles' curse, "People will perish for metal" and ended with accusations evocative of Zola's "J'accuse!": "guilty are the ministers . . . and guilty is the premier-minister [who fail to deal with] the hunger, violence, mass murders and executions that reign in this country." Skorokhodov's eloquence notwithstanding, the initial Octobrist-SD clashes probably ended any real possibility of Duma action. A successful proposal would require a coalition of socialists, liberals, Octobrists, and Progressists against the rightist parties whose artificially swollen ranks reflected Stolypin's 1908 electoral laws. The opening speeches destroyed the possibility of an Octobrist-socialist rapprochement, a judgment perhaps clearer in retrospect than it was then.

The 10 April Duma session, which featured lesser stars of the Duma firmament, still operated under a consensual atmosphere, as suggested by the quick approval of a fast track for moving the interpellations forward. When a Trudovik deputy proposed that the Duma create its own Lena investigatory commission, the chair refused the motion on the basis that the law gave no such power to the Duma. The State Duma then approved the Constitutional Democratic and Octobrist interpellations and rejected the socialist (on a vote of 96 to 76) and Nationalist ones. Regardless, the two approved interpellations still provided the possibility of stern Duma action.

The very next day, Minister of the Interior Makarov and Minister of Trade and Industry Timashev appeared to answer the Duma's angry queries, a promptness that indicates the government's sensitivity about the Lena affair. Both ministers characterized the Lena events as "sad" and "sorrowful." After assuring the deputies that the government fully shared society's feelings, Makarov noted that it was his "duty to help you [members of the Duma] to analyze this sad affair." He denied that the government had known about problems at the Lenzoto mines and then provided a lengthy account of the strike, the arrests, and the shooting that reflected quite darkly on the workers' actions and intentions. The interior minister questioned the peacefulness of the strike, hinted that it may have lain outside the protection of the statute on strikes, and emphasized the political nature of the strike leadership. In essence, he propounded the Lenzoto-Treshchenkov version in all details. As the speech continued, voices from the left interrupted with indignant shouts: "Disgusting! Unbearable! Insulting!" drawing countershouts from the right: "Kick out the hooligans!" The chair's bell tried in vain to bring about order.

The interior minister probably did not intend to express himself quite so confrontationally as he now did. Unfortunately, the superheated atmosphere as he proceeded to describe the actual 4 April demonstration and the shooting set the stage. In describing the shooting, Makarov simply repeated Treshchenkov's version that the workers acted in a threatening manner. Fearing that the workers might charge and possibly disarm the soldiers, the commander gave the order to shoot. "What would you say here, gentlemen, if [the shooting] had not taken place and a crowd of several thousand persons had surrounded and disarmed the soldiers?" The rightist V. M. Purishkevich replied from the floor, "They would say there is no government!" Makarov then quoted from a telegram from an unnamed source, to the effect that "the entire affair on 4 April had the goal of seizing the soldiers' weapons, running over them, and destroying the mines." This raised new cries from the left: "Who signed the telegram?" to which someone suggested "Treshchenkov!" Now Makarov, provoked beyond endurance, responded with pathos, "The fighting man [*voin*] and his weapon are inseparable! The loss of a weapon is shameful for the warrior. . . . When an irrational crowd, under the influence of evil agitators, throws itself on the armed forces, the armed forces can do nothing else but shoot" (voices from the right, "Bravo! How true!"). Then Minister of the Interior Makarov mouthed the words that should never have been spoken, "Thus it has always been, thus it will always be!" (drawing the instantaneous response from Kuznetsov, "As long as you are in power!"). Makarov's one phrase, reflecting a moment of extreme frustration and tension, hopelessly compromised the government's attempts to defend itself in the eyes of society. On the floor of the Duma, it drew cries of "Vampires!" after which prolonged tumult ensued, punctuated by the frenzied ringing of the chair's bell. Makarov's hapless attempts to end the speech in a dignified manner met more shouts ("The vampires are celebrating!"), whistling, hissing, and imprecations in all directions.

This was a hard act to follow. Nevertheless, Minister of Trade and Industry Timashev shouldered the unenviable task of smoothing outraged feelings. The mining inspectorate, Timashev conceded, had reported severe Lenzoto violations in its 1911 report and the company, in violation of the law, had lagged in responding to the ministry's pressure to carry out improvements. In fact, Timashev's remarks thoroughly undercut Makarov's formulations, provoking, according to the minutes, discomfort on the right. This and other contradictions induced *Novoe vremia* to wonder whether government ministers "even talked to one another on the telephone."[46] Even so, Timashev improbably claimed government ignorance of grave problems at Lenzoto and urged the Duma to await a full investigation since "much was still unclear" about the shooting.

In a bitter speech, Kuznetsov noted that Makarov's speech was "better [propaganda] than any socialist proclamations," drawing shouts from the right: "What nonsense! The gall! Impudent fellow!" Kuznetsov concluded sarcastically: "We thank Mister Makarov in the name of the working class for the best speech we could have expected. He confirmed what we have always said, that the workers have always been shot and will always be shot." The only remedy: "Begin organized struggle for the destruction of the present regime and for the establishment of the socialist order" (applause from the left). The verbal onslaughts of Makarov and Kuznetsov further crowded the limited space for Duma consensus. People at the political antipodes employed rhetorical strategies—whether deliberately (Kuznetsov) or haplessly (Makarov)—aimed at achieving goals other than consensus building.

Despite the pyrotechnics on previous occasions, the following session provided a taste of what might have been. On 18 April the centrist N. A. Maklakov (soon to be the new interior minister) wondered why it was that "Russian state power, which was hardly noninterventionist . . . did not defend the workers . . . in just the situation where they most required care." The archconservative (Union of Russian People) N. E. Markov (II) took the government to task for failing to enforce legally required standards as regards workers. Exacerbating government delinquency, in his view, was its longstanding knowledge of Lenzoto's illegality. These and other speeches brought into sharp relief the fact that the Octobrists, Nationalists, and the Far Right, groups usually supportive of the government, drew from their quivers arrows aimed directly at the government and the company. In this way, they demonstrated de facto consensus with left-of-center parties such as the Constitutional Democrats, Trudoviks, and SDs.

The combined effect of Makarov's maladroit speech and the surprising breadth of criticism from within the Duma and in society at large induced the conciliatory Minister of Trade and Industry Timashev to return to the floor with a suggestion. The minister now promised a new law that would fully protect gold mining workers in the future ("especially from shootings," cried someone from the left). Greeted with some skepticism by the left of center, this measure clearly had the aim of preventing any censure from the State Duma. The speeches earlier that day had clearly revealed the continued potential for majority support for a censorious motion.

A week later, on 25 April, the Third State Duma met to decide on

Duma responses to the Lena events. Although officially "dissatisfied" with Makarov's approach, the Octobrists suggested that, on the basis of Timashev's suggestions, the Duma move to new business pending a full report from the government investigative commission. The SDs wished to continue the debate, whereas the Trudoviks suggested accepting the Octobrist plan with the proviso that the Duma constitute its own investigative commission, a motion again slapped down by the chair. The Trudovik speaker then accused the Duma, including the chair, of showing "solidarity with the Lena murderers."

The Nationalist A. Motovilov then addressed the Duma with an analysis that in a sense summarized the entire Duma experience with the Lena tragedy. The Nationalist fraction, he claimed, had severe doubts about the government's account of the Lena shooting. "Minister Makarov's explanation . . . suffered from . . . one-sidedness." The leftist speeches, continued Motovilov, intensified those doubts considerably, except in the other direction, at which point he blasted the leftists, for whom he recommended "dogs' muzzles," for "brazenness and gall." After listening to them, he concluded, the Nationalists decided that "it was necessary to await the results of the government's promised detailed investigation."

Ultimately, the Octobrists, SDs, Trudoviks, Progressists, and the Constitutional Democrats offered motions that expressed variously "dissatisfaction" or "outrage" as regards the government's handling of the Lena matter. When the voting came, none of the motions summoned a majority since parties to the left, right, or center variously peeled off in sufficient numbers to defeat each version. Holding the voting balance in the Duma, the Octobrists helped defeat all the motions. The Duma chair finally proclaimed the question "exhausted." The Third State Duma therefore expressed no opinion about the Lena massacre, a result that betrayed everything that had transpired. This was anticlimax with a vengeance. A Trudovik deputy had the last word as he quipped from the floor of the adjourning Duma: "From this evening on we have a muzzle: a good name for the Octobrists."

The Lena events, including the vast protest strikes, caught the socialists by surprise, a factor that highlights a problem in worker-socialist relations. The parties propagandized, urged, and maneuvered, yet workers, not to mention peasants, were not malleable clay. They reacted according to their own schedules. Exhausted by the tumult of 1904–1908, workers began to awaken in 1911, only to be galvanized in 1912 by the horror inflicted on the Lena miners. As participants in strikes, who themselves had faced police, soldiers, and Cossacks, Russia's workers apprehended the nature of the threat, even if the threat rarely came to fruition. The socialists responded very quickly to news of the Lena shooting with leaflets and proclamations that called for strikes. The strikes occurred because the workers identified with the Lena miners' cause sufficiently to undergo the economic and personal hazards of striking and demonstrating.

The discipline of the strikes, including their prolonged timing is noteworthy. Beginning a few days after the shooting, the strike movement peaked on 18 and 19 April, a full two weeks after the shooting, at a time of persistent, critical press coverage. At factory-level protest meetings that began the day after the first news reports of the shooting, the one-day strike achieved almost universal status as an appropriate measure. Here the still-opaque realm of socialist-worker interrelations helped determine what happened and what did not. From the outset, many socialist leaflets specified the one-day strike as an appropriate measure. At factory, district, and citywide meetings and demonstrations, worker activists, often members of oppositionist parties that issued the leaflets, addressed the meetings and recommended the one-day Lena sympathy strikes. Still, the parties could no more order a one-day strike than they could order a strike at all. Workers heeded activists who transmitted party-originated recommendations as fellow workers, who, in concrete cases, said things that made sense.

The discipline of the empirewide strike movement replicated the discipline of the Lena miners in their strike, as noted with alarm by hostile witnesses. Press coverage of the sympathy strike movement specifically noticed the restrained, organized nature of the empirewide worker protest movement. Launched in the midst of maximum public attention, the movement consisted of rolling one-day strikes that ultimately involved a very large number of plants and workers in any single locality, not on any one day but over a period of several weeks. The final effect was achieved when these one-day strikes rolled over into massive May Day demonstrations, a touch not lost on observers. As Fedor Dan remarked, "One is struck by the organization and discipline of the enormous movement. . . . And [this] in the almost total absence of solid organizations!"[47] This signified the rebirth of the workers' movement after the 1908 Stolypin repression. It also signified a new type of workers' movement, still dimly understood by most historians.[48] Even in such distant places as the Lena mines, workers displayed an impressive maturity. This maturity reflected fruitful interactions with socialist activists of multiple party organizations, a matter that suggests research opportunities for historians. This issue also highlights the continued dominance among historians of a Leninist concept of the Russian workers' movement that portrays all important impulses as coming from the top down.

Socialists responded quickly to the news of the shooting, as demonstrated by the flood of leaflets distributed as early as 5 April. As shown by the long list of organizations of every imaginable socialist and anarchist alignment in every conceivable corner of the empire that produced leaflets and proclamations, by 1912 the organized revolutionary movement in the Russian Empire had survived and begun a distinct revival. The parties also realized that the massacre and society's sharp reaction to it offered unparalleled opportunities for furthering organizational and revolutionary goals. Although workers' indignation was highly significant, the reactions of students and the intelligentsia were also important. In view of the massive numbers of activists and leaders languishing in imprisonment or exile, new recruits from the cultured intelligentsia were a sine qua non of organizational success. Revived student activism was an especially propitious signal for the organized revolutionary movement.

As the debacle in the Duma revealed, harnessing social dissatisfaction into a single movement or even in favor of a single resolution was not possible. Indeed, in what nontotalitarian society are such things possible? Still, the massive wave of anger against the government for its handling of the Lena question objectively unified, even against their will, normally nonallied social elements. The remarkable thing was not the failure of a joint program of action but the fact of the actual social consensus. As of 1912 the empire's social and political elements, from the far right to the left, agreed that laboring people required a better deal than they were getting.[49] They also agreed that the mere quest for profit did not outweigh the right to life and that the government at all levels was delinquent as regards workers.

This agreement did not arise in a vacuum. Surveys of the press during the years before World War I suggest a broad basis of support for substantial amelioration of societal tensions.[50] The press widely reported strikes abroad, including the early 1912 coal mining strikes in several nations. Commentators from various viewpoints pointedly emphasized the peaceful nature of state responses to these massive strikes. The Russian labor union movement and Russian strikes received respectful coverage. Newspapers, including these representing big business, criticized the government for repressing the labor unions and universally displayed awareness of workers' legitimate, unfulfilled rights. Broad support, including from entrepreneurial organizations, arose for a worker insurance law. Fortuitously, this law project reached the Duma several months before the shooting and passed into law several weeks afterward. In other words, utterly unnoticed in histories, a context of shared values in industrializing, modernizing Russia had come into existence well before the Lena massacre. This reality explains society's shared responses to the specific events. These shared values did not extend to a thoroughgoing political program for reshaping the state. They did lay a realistic basis for ameliorating the workers' plight and mending state-society relations, matters fraught with potential significance for the future. During the period under discussion, the State Duma also passed laws opening institutions of higher learning to women and had under serious discussion a law for compulsory, free, state-sponsored universal education for children. The prevailing atmosphere explains why the shooting itself and top-level officials' perceived callousness, as symbolized by Makarov's dastardly phrase, hit such a sour note in the press, in the Duma, and in society.

For all its obtuseness, the government was not impervious to popular opinion. In a highly hostile atmosphere, the ministers came to the Duma to account for themselves, as required by law. In the person of Timashev, the government offered concessions in respect to new laws and a real investigation. Naturally, the left harbored deep suspicions about the "senatorial commission" created to carry out the investigation. Yet the published Manukhin Commission Report did not whitewash the Lena tragedy, as anyone can ascertain by consulting it. Furthermore, the government dropped charges against all arrested strike leaders, a result that reflected a healthy respect for public opinion. One may also surmise that Makarov's maladroit handling of his report to the Duma played a role in his replacement before year's end as minister of the interior. His successor, N. A. Maklakov, had used his 18 April Duma speech specifically and pointedly to criticize the government for not defending the Lena workers.

The recollections of V. N. Kokovtsev, chairman of the Council of Ministers, shed some light on these matters. Kokovtsev claimed that he personally had been unaware of any impending crisis before the shooting. On 4 April, after he saw a special edition of a newspaper about the Lena shooting, he consulted with Minister of the Interior Makarov, who professed complete surprise as well. Makarov told his superior that leftist members of the Duma, including Kerenskii, already had received telegrams informing them that more than two hundred workers had been killed (a figure not contradicted by Kokovtsev in his 1933 memoirs, although the tsarist government never admitted to such a total). Outraged Duma deputies had entered interpellations to which Makarov preferred not to respond before the expiration of the current Duma. Kokovtsev insisted that he go at once, with the infamous result. Makarov's speech, recalled Kokovtsev, was like "pouring fuel on fire." The Duma "forgot about Rasputin, forgot about its current work, all committees ceased working, [and] everyone focused on the 'Lena massacre.'" In order to quiet the situation, Kokovtsev sent Timashev back to the Duma with an offer of a real government investigation and recommended former justice minister Manukhin for the task. The emperor approved this choice, recalling Manukhin as "a big liberal but indisputably honest. . . . If I send an Adjutant-General," continued Nicholas, "no one will believe him [and everyone] will think that he is covering up for local officials. Send [Manukhin] off as soon as possible." Kokovtsev recalled that he "did not hide from the Emperor that he looked on Duma developments with great alarm and begged the Emperor for His help."[51] The days were gone when the emperor and his appointed officials could proceed without concern for the elected parliament and society.

Since the 1960s prominent historians have underscored factors that were allegedly driving wedges between Russian institutions, social groups, and political alignments. For historians of this tendency, the Lena massacre constituted yet another nail in the coffin of the late tsarist polity. Although true in a sense, this tendency overlooks the atmosphere that surrounded the shooting, society's reaction to it, and even the government's need to make concessions. Perhaps historians have overdetermined past reality in order to fit convenient, popular, and influential theories and accounts. A new working hypothesis for analysis of the interwar era of late tsarist history (1908–14) should be social consensus rather than fragmentation. The new hypothesis should emphasize the growth of civil society on the basis of individual and group self-definition, as suggested by some new studies of the era. Perhaps current analysis's "social fragmentation" merely represented normal political, social, and economic conflict in a rapidly developing society.

Conclusion

Occurring in the far Siberian taiga at the very outposts of Russian consciousness, the Lena goldfields massacre quickly seized a central place in news reportage, in public discussion, in the Duma, in the government, and among innumerable people and institutions. Why did the shooting of several hundred humble mining workers in a distant place resonate in Russian society? At all ascertainable levels, society reacted with outrage, a not entirely surprising outcome. Only fanaticism, abject fear, or a thirst for revenge spawns indifference to bloodshed on that scale. Work or nonwork along the upper branches of the Vitim River hardly impinged upon the functioning of the Russian polity. Even so, expectable, appropriate indignation at wanton injury and death by no means exhausted the response in this case. The initial spontaneous outbreak of anger became systemic when the broadest circles raised pointed questions about underlying causes.

The searching public inquiry about the nature of a social, economic, and political order that could produce such results did not restrict itself to radical and liberal circles. They already decried the existing order as incompetent, immoral, and anachronistic. That it was guilty of unforgivable malfeasance in this instance went without saying, although oppositionists reiterated this truth in every forum in a multitude of ways. The consensual perception of the Lena shooting as unjustified massacre provided the opposition with renewed concrete justification for its very existence. Makarov's verbal reprise merely enhanced an already richly textured oppositionist discourse. Of perhaps greater analytical import is that centrist, moderately conservative, and even reactionary opinion raised many of the same questions as the oppositionists. The Nationalist *Novoe vremia,* the archreactionary Markov II, and the more moderately conservative Maklakov, soon to be interior minister, all accused the government of failing to protect workers. They all blamed this failure on the network of ties among powerful entrepreneurs, prestigious stockholders, and high-level government officials. This accusatory element enabled the Lena events to strike such a deep chord in Russian society.

The Lena strike and massacre are susceptible to analysis from several perspectives. From one viewpoint, the gold miners' strike reflected an aspect of modernization, with the shooting as an unfortunate by-product along the path of development. The nineteenth-century rise of Siberian gold mining and especially the working of its rich eastern veins constituted a part of a larger picture in which the empire finally initiated exploitation of the vast region's natural riches. By the late nineteenth century, the initial rough-and-ready era of individual prospecting and easy strikes had yielded to intensive large-scale entrepreneurial activity. The government's firm resolve to exert total control over gold, by 1897 the basis of Russia's currency, inexorably tipped the balance toward big business. On one end of the gold business, private prospecting was illegal and, on the other, the metal could be marketed only to the state. The state's intervention in the person of multiministerial administrative commissions produced minute regulation that further hastened the tendency toward large-scale industry. Enterprises of this type then required a larger labor pool than the scant local population could provide. In larger and larger percentages, the miners came from strike-prone European Russia, where their previous experience, however harsh, did not match the cold reality of the Lena taiga.

State Bank loans and the emperor's favors for one company, Lenzoto, lay the foundations for total monopolization. The frontier atmosphere faded in favor of orderly, if not commodious, company towns and facilities. Telegraph and telephone lines, seasonal steamship systems, and local railroad communications, with plans for national Irkust-Bodaibo-Amur connections, all signaled the area's entry into the modern era. Unfortunately, this path to modernization contributed little to microeconomic development. From the outset, the gold industry deforested the hills and polluted the rivers. Gold-mining firms built for the moment and restlessly moved on from site to shoddy site, leaving each the worse for wear. The large companies, eventually unified into one giant entity, purchased inexpensive foodstuffs in quantity from distant Irkutsk and Iakutsk, entirely bypassing local agriculture. Except for purloined gold nuggets that filtered through the untaxed, unmeasured black market, mining left no trace on the local economy. Lenzoto eventually monopolized all trade and services. All income from economic activity, except for workers' paltry unspent wages at work year's end, channeled its way as profits to Irkutsk, Petersburg, or London. Bereft of local noncompany support infrastructure, the miners found themselves in a bind and finally reacted, with poor results. The workers' plight and the undeveloped microeconomy were obverse sides of the same coin, aspects of a modernization project solely for state benefit.

A second way to view the strike and massacre is as local or Siberian history. The descriptions of the rise of gold mining in the Olekminsk region in chapters 1 and 2 constitute the chief elements of the region's nineteenth- and early twentieth-century economic, social, and administrative history. During this period, mining, labor in the mines, and miners' lives while they resided there, not to mention the strike and massacre, occupied extensive space, real and metaphorical. Yet this is local history manqué. State interests and policies so overwhelmed all local considerations, initiative, and endeavor as to blot out all regional perceptions. That the intrusion of the modern world doomed Iakut, Tunguz, and local Russian peasant mores was one layer of reality. That the bright glare of gold entirely whited out their history and experience was another. As for the Lena gold miners, their lives and, in 1912, deaths existed in radical disjunction from the local population and environment. The fate of a population that customarily arrived and departed with dispatch lay lightly on the history of the region as local history. Today the 1912 event known as the "Lena goldfields massacre" vaguely evokes a place. Yet the locality's topography and other characteristics have no delineation. On the one hand, the 1912 strike and shooting cannot be extracted from their spatial environment without obliterating all concrete understanding of what occurred. The isolation and desolation of the place inform and shape the entire story. On the other hand, the episode finds its real historical place, its historicity, only in the story of the Russian Empire, that is, the Russian state. In local history, local and national factors are often in tension, whereas in the history of Lena gold mining and the Lena goldfields massacre the national consumes and transmogrifies the local in a rapacious dialectic.

A third mode of interpretation refers to labor, industrialization's inevitable concomitant. In the remote East Siberian gold mines, inadequate indigenous labor sources necessitated supplement with and then replacement by workers recruited from afar. Their difficult adaptation, or better, maladaptation, to harsh local conditions transformed the labor problem into an endemic labor crisis. A comparative framework may be useful. The nature of the Lena strike at a single large, monopolistic, remotely located enterprise, in which, furthermore, the state had a driving vested interest, renders it unusual on the Siberian, Russian, and for that matter, international scene. Earlier strikes in the Siberian gold mines, in the presence of multiple companies, did not differ substantially in their outcomes from those in other Russian industries or locales. During the Lena-area strikes of the early 1900s, state and company officials often summoned Cossacks as a supplement to the armed guards and police. When faced with company intransigence and armed force, striking workers often backed down and returned to work. For their part, companies routinely made token concessions that sometimes mollified the workers. On some occasions, companies made substantive concessions that brought certain strikes to a successful close for workers. Only rarely did the authorities resort directly to force. The number of deaths during all the gold-mining strikes of 1900–1906 had been exceedingly small. This was equilibrium strike politics, with a light threat of violence.

To put the matter in deeper perspective, since roughly 1890 Russian industries had experienced innumerable strikes quantitatively and qualitatively similar to the 1912 Lenzoto strike, minus, of course, extreme geographical isolation and the ultimate massacre. By 1912 a rich historical experience of strikes existed in Russia. This experience suggested a range of likely responses, of which extreme violence was but a rare possibility. As Governor Bantysh pointed out in one of his commentaries, breaking a strike by force was a possible measure for dealing with economic strikes, whereas it was the principal method recommended by tsarist practice for political strikes. Even so, most of the empire's political, let alone economic, strikes ended peaceably. Furthermore, in tsarist practice breaking a strike did not signify shooting. It meant the arrest of strike leaders, aggressive crowd control, manhandling by police, and even charges by mounted police and Cossacks. These harsh methods intimidated and physically traumatized the strikers, and on occasion killed someone. But they differed substantively from mass shooting. Even the last resort of shooting had delimiting procedures in tsarist practice, as became clear during the investigation of the Lena shooting.

This web of procedures and accumulated experience resulted in the peaceful resolution of the vast majority of Russia's strikes. Friedgut has noted the ritualistic nature of the exchanges between Donbas strikers and officialdom so that by the 1900s strikes there routinely ended quietly.[1] The Lena equilibrium reflected a national one. When commentators about the Lena massacre accused the regime of habitually using the extremes of force against strikes, they engaged in hyperbole. The regime clearly did not like strikes and, even after its own 1905 legislation had legalized strike activity, regularly joined with entrepreneurs in trying to break them. Massacres were, however, rare exceptions. Shootings occurred in the Urals during 1903, during 1912 at the Lena mines, and during World War I at Kostroma and Ivanova. The infamous Bloody Sunday (9 January 1905) involved a huge political demonstration rather than a strike. Given the vast number of strikes in Russian industries between 1900 and 1917, these four heinous incidents do not establish a propensity for extreme force against strikers. They suggest instead an unfortunate potential for violent measures when existing procedures came under radical stress. The shootings represented systems breakdown rather than system.

As regards labor, useful comparisons and contrasts can be drawn with other industrial nations such as Britain, Germany, and the United States. In Germany just prior to World War I, worker-state relations took a decided turn for the worse with new restrictions on union and strike activities. For instance, the new laws criminalized picketers' harassment of strikebreakers with verbal taunts or rude noises. As widely reported in the Russian press, during March 1912 Germany's Ruhr coal miners struck over wage issues, essentially shutting down German coal production and threatening the entire national economy. The disorders and violence that took place came mostly from the strikers, as conceded even by the German Social Democrats. In reprisal, the authorities arrested more than a thousand strikers, brought numerous criminal charges against strike leaders and unruly participants, and even shot to death at least one worker.[2] For all its raucous nature, the 1912 Ruhr coal-mining strike had little direct bearing on the Lena question. The German state had forged the way in developing welfare for workers. Labor unions flourished, and the German Social Democratic Party, with its huge worker constituency, was the single largest party in the German parliament. The tsarist regime's post- 1908 crackdown on labor activism found a pallid reflection in German labor policy between 1912 and 1914.

In Britain, labor-state relations were quite stormy for several decades before World War I. One 1911 clash between transport workers and the authorities even earned the epithet "Bloody Sunday" because of the deaths of two workers and the injuries of others. Still, British labor relations operated in the penumbra of the 1819 Peterloo massacre, in which eleven peaceful political demonstrators perished and hundreds more were injured. Afterward, the government at times used force, but cautiously and very selectively. The British case, like that in Germany, differed substantially from the Russian one in that the British union movement had achieved a high degree of organization. By the end of the nineteenth century, the unions had begun to coalesce into the Labor Party, which by 1910 was the political wing of the entire union movement. British coal miners, like the German coal miners and the Lena gold miners, also struck during the early spring of 1912. Labors' improved status helped the coal miners win a distinct victory when the parliament passed a minimum wage for British coal miners.[3] Russian commentators perceived the British coal-mining strike's resolution in legislation rather than suppression as a veritable model for Russia. In both Britain and Germany, labor had an institutional status and political weight that delimited the possibilities for extreme violence. In Russia, the institutional framework for labor, although developing, was still weak, as was labor's direct political clout.

Perhaps the most useful comparison is with the United States, where significant antilabor violence did occur. The 1894 Pullman strike, the 1912 textile strike in Lawrence, Massachusetts, and the extraordinary 1914 Ludlow massacre in the Colorado coal mines are cases in point. Although only the last resulted in mortalities, antiworker animus and actions reached improbable levels in all three strikes. The 1914 Colorado mining strike that culminated in the Ludlow massacre had the greatest structural similarities to the Lena case. The strike, which arose over issues of union recognition, pay, company stores, and the excessive use of armed guards at the mines, pitted recently unionized coal miners against an enterprise owned by John D. Rockefeller. Rockefeller believed local company officials who painted misleading pictures of Ludlow area life and work. One commentator to the contrary wrote that the region's coal-mining "imposed a degree of vassalage . . . inconsonant with the American ideal of freedom." The company sent hired armed forces and the state militia against the strikers, who angrily reacted with murder, arson, and dynamiting. (Of course, the Lena workers notably refrained from doing anything of the sort. Even had they done everything Lenzoto accused them of, it all would have paled before the Ludlow workers' violence.) By the end of the Colorado strike, more than two hundred people on both sides had died. The most terrible event was the 20 April machine-gun attack on the workers' temporary camp, with armed men and their wives and children inside, followed by the kerosene torching of the tent city. By the end of the day twenty-four people in the workers' camp had perished, including two women and eleven children in the conflagration.[4] Only sheer chance kept the death toll that low.

Parallels between the strikes and massacres at Ludlow and Lena go far beyond the mere scale of the number of deaths, in each case more than two hundred. Both strikes involved the mining industry with mines located in very distant, isolated places; both involved unlimited company control over every aspect of workers' lives; and both companies had ties with extraordinarily influential people. In both cases, top officials relied on local personnel for, as it turned out, tendentious and highly deceptive information. In both cases, after lengthy, desultory negotiations and confrontations the armed forces finally lost patience and went on the attack. A comparison of the Ludlow and Lena events suggests a more violent society in America than in Russia. On the Lena, as in many Russian strikes, the workers actively maintained discipline and avoided any appearance of force. The authorities had genuinely convinced themselves that the arrest of strike leaders would diffuse the entire affair. Even the armed force sent to uphold order was minimal for the task, a factor that probably contributed to a half-panicky spur of the moment decision to shoot. In the American case, one has a sense of no-holds-barred on all sides. Europe, even in its far eastern outposts, was not America.

At least publicly, Rockefeller remained unrepentant even after the tragedy, as did Lenzoto. At congressional hearings summoned to investigate the Ludlow events, Rockefeller maintained an absolute right to exclude unions from his plants as a condition of employment. The American courts up to and including the Supreme Court consistently upheld the owners' right to exclude unions from their premises. Despite public sympathy for brutalized workers, the courts of the land and Rockefeller in essence stated "thus it has always been, thus it will always be."

Comparative analysis of the Lena goldfields strike and shooting with labor disputes in other countries yields interesting results. The status of labor in Britain and Germany created a certain degree of protection for strikers. Universal male suffrage further precluded unlimited violence. The U.S. situation had peculiarities in some ways curiously evocative of the Russian case. In the United States, as in Russia, strikes and unions had not yet acquired the full protection of the law. For its part, the Russian autocracy had not reconciled itself to living strictly within its own laws, which after 1905 formally legalized strikes, unions, and political parties. Furthermore, after the 1908 reaction the government was not particularly wary of the Duma, elected, as it was, on bases that discriminated against the laboring classes. Despite U.S. political democracy, American courts had as yet refused to guarantee workers the full right to protect their interests collectively. Thus, for somewhat different reasons and within different contexts, the potential for extreme repression of striking workers existed in both countries. Of course, the cases of mass shootings of strikers in Russia between 1900 and 1917 exceeded anything that occurred in the United States. The heightened, but not unlimited, potential for extreme force in Russia doubtlessly helps explain the relative orderliness and discipline of many Russian strikes, including the one on the Lena. Even so, in none of the four countries under comparison could striking workers feel absolutely safe from force. Although the threat of force was greater for Russian than for German and British workers, Russian workers comprehended that adherence to certain rules would normally shield them from violent reprisals. The Lena massacre counted as one of a few exceptions that proved the rule. On these matters, Russia differed only by degrees from other industrialized nations.

The entire discussion of Lena gold mining and the 1912 tragedy with all its repercussions raises in the most acute way the question of state-society and state-labor relations in Russia. This topic too is susceptible to comparison with other nations. Much analysis of the early decades of the twentieth century focuses on the rise of corporatism in industrialized nations. Definitions of corporatism emphasize the replacement of nineteenth-century individualism and laissez-faire by two variant collectivist societal models. Pluralism has the characteristic of associations of collective interests that operate under the state but not under its control. Corporatism consists of hierarchical associations, both entrepreneurial and labor, licensed and to some degree controlled or directed by the state. Both variants, as points on a continuum, aim at collective mediation of interests within the political economy, as opposed to open competition and conflict. The political economy as free-for-all was already falling into discredit by the late 1800s.[5] Most commentators feel that, because of their highly developed biases for individualism, the United States and Britain experienced relatively weak corporatist development. Even so, during and just after World War I many British and U.S. leaders adopted or proposed corporatist approaches to national problems of waging war and reorienting postwar economies. Germany, France, and other industrialized nations witnessed fuller versions of corporatism.

How does Russia fit into this framework? Until well into the nineteenth century, Russian autocracy precluded individualism and laissez-faire. As one participant in the Lena Duma debates pointed out, the Russian state was not (even then) noninterventionist. Capitalism and individualism were indeed developing rapidly by the late 1800s and early 1900s but within a framework of preexisting corporatist conceptions of political economy. One might argue that, especially after the 1905 Revolution, the late tsarist regime's paternalistic corporatism had entered a new phase. Individualism, collectivism of several types, state "licensing" and control of the political economy, and outright autocratic propensities all coexisted in uneasy and unstable equilibrium. Corporatist-autocratic conceptions experienced reintensification during World War I and outright hypertrophy under Communism, with only the brief-lived provisional government as ardent practitioner of corporatism sans autocracy. During the years prior to the First World War, Russia was an interesting potential test case for corporatism of the ideal type. Its development would have depended, however, on the progressive retreat of the autocratic regime and the simultaneous maintenance of collectivist modes of interest mediation, not to mention avoidance of war.

As useful as comparative frameworks are, Lena gold mining and its contingent culmination in a strike and shooting must be evaluated and understood primarily in terms of their place in Russian history. In its role as microcosm, the history of Lena mining and the 1912 tragedy generally track the Imperial Russian State's economic, social, legislative, and political development. From a different perspective, the region's unrelieved sparseness, denuded of amenities and overlapping social interactions, exposed in pellucid clarity the actual social relations in and around the mines. By 1912 this web of relations revealed itself as outmoded, as though locked in the region's permafrost, in comparison to that of the rest of Russian society. The Lena events very precisely delineated the growing gap between state and society. Thus the shock effect in European Russia and settled Siberia. In respect to the shooting, this book's findings confirm, in expanded version, several long-standing analytical tendencies. The vociferous worker and socialist responses to the Lena shooting often noted by historians certainly occurred. Chapter 6 fills out for the first time a picture previously sketched only in outline. This study also supports the observations of numerous historians about the late tsarist government's tendency for bureaucratic infighting and working at cross-purposes, as well as its infamous inability to abandon its autocratic pretensions.[6] Still, the data presented here tend to raise questions about, rather than support, traditional interpretations of the late tsarist polity.

Most striking is the degree of consensus among almost all layers of society and political viewpoints about who the tragedy's perpetrators were and who the victims. Since the guilty were the government and entrepreneurs and the suffering innocents the laborers and those who attempted to protect them, the matter escapes definition as a simple morality play with terms of reference valid for all Russian society. Russian conservatives normally presumed the government's innocence and the workers' (and intelligentsia's) guilt. In this case, analysis from all sides made a similar case for systemic problems that led to abuses against humanity in the person of simple Russian workers. Stark rhetorical variance among the different political viewpoints, including the right wing's chauvinism and anti-Semitism and the left wing's revolutionism, do not conceal the overall sense of agreement. This agreement had two principal aspects. The first held that laborers were getting a bad deal and the second, out of which the first flowed as ineluctable consequence, that an unhealthy coincidence of interest and influence existed between officialdom and entrepreneurship.

This consensus did not suddenly arise as a result of the Lena massacre. Rather, society's response to the shooting of Siberian gold miners demonstrated widespread preexisting collective attitudes toward certain important problems and questions. This study is not the first to notice the phenomenon. In her examination of the Russian press, Louise McReynolds repeatedly raises the issue of waxing broad social support for further political reforms and for a better accommodation with laboring segments of society. In this regard, McReynolds specifically challenges the societal fragmentation theory so eloquently outlined by Haimson and developed by numerous other authors. In place of social fragmentation, McReynolds identifies the principal problem of the late tsarist polity as "the distance widening between state and society." She reiterates this theme by arguing that "the newspapers reflected greater cultural cohesion and a wider basis of support for reformist sentiments" than historical commentary has allowed.[7] McReynolds's approach arises from her study of the entire era rather than from one episode. In a study of Stolypin's politics, Peter Waldron cautiously notes that during the post-1905 era "the path of peaceful change was open" and lays primary blame for the failures on obdurate autocratic policies.[8] Although Waldron does not focus on societal consensus, his findings do suggest Russia's as yet unpredetermined fate between 1905 and 1914.

Naturally, the first stirrings of a counterthesis (or return to a revised earlier one) embodied by McReynolds's book and this study will not sweep all before it. The societal fragmentation theory by this time has deep roots and serried ranks of defenders among several generations of scholars. I counted myself among their ranks until confronted by the data of this study. Support for the "pessimistic" version of Russian history after 1905 remains quite strong, as any perusal of existing literature reveals. Even so, this study's findings suggest the need to reopen the discussion with full consideration of new evidence. One of the unintended but quite unfortunate consequences of the pessimistic view has been the shutting down of interest in those very aspects of late tsarist reality that might have uncovered countervailing evidence. Scholars have devoted most of their attention to factors that brought down the regime. They have added an additional twist by asserting the certitude of a radical denouement embodied by Bolshevism. In this iteration, the alleged total lack of social cohesion prior to World War I virtually ensured this outcome, with the First World War's horrors and the provisional government's failures as mere contributory factors. Only detailed examination of Russian society can confirm or deny such sweeping glosses of complex phenomena. Research already under way, as testified to by presentations at historical conferences, about aspects of civil society, entrepreneurship, and related topics certainly bears on the discussion.

Further study of Russian labor, with new emphases, may also bear results. The Lena mine workers, hardly the elite of Russia's working class, observed superb discipline and order throughout the strike, shooting, and aftermath. They did so in part by advising with and accepting leadership from socialists, with a distinct preference for those who urged caution and, within reason, compromise. Failure of these tactics and the descent into mayhem lay in the hands of the authorities. The Lena case did not exist in isolation. By the post-1905 years, Russian labor operated with modes of understanding and action that allowed for self-restraint and negotiations for achievable aims. At the same time, Russia's middle, upper, and educated classes and the various political groups that represented them were ready to work toward a compromise with laboring Russia. Even the government, for all its obduracy, showed signs of yielding to certain kinds of pressure, such as public opinion expressed through the press and the Duma. Russian society indubitably contained opposing tendencies, especially in view of its postemancipation complexity. This fact, common to all historical environments of the modern era, does not justify focusing entirely on conflicting elements to the utter exclusion of all other tendencies. Striving toward negotiation and compromise for the common welfare had intensified. As a consequence, prewar prospects for noncataclysmic change existed. New evidence and new arguments must reopen the case. In its very broadest parameters, the Lena goldfields history portended the end of autocracy. It did not portend, other than as one of many possibilities, the results of October 1917 and thereafter.

Appendix A

Selected Items from Lenzoto Work Contract for 1911–12

This list is adapted from *Pravda o lenskikh sobytiiakh,* ed. P. N. Batashev (Moscow, 1913), apps., sec. 1, no. 4, 10–13.

1. We, workers, are employed at the mines of the said company located in Vitim and Olekma Mining Region for the period from the start of work until 10 September.

2. During this period, we undertake to fulfill in good faith and accurately any mining, general, and household work at the Lenzoto mines and residences, as well as gold prospecting wherever the administration sends us. In no case, may we refuse the work assigned us or change it on our own for tasks other than those required of us by the mining administration.

3. If any of us were hired as specialists with particular skills, this must be confirmed in writing by hirer. Otherwise, the person will be obliged to fulfill any assigned work. But even hired specialists may be assigned general work at the demand of the administration if he does not display sufficient skills in his specialty.

4. Upon reporting to work, we are obliged to hand in our identification documents, which will be held by the administration until the final payoff. . . .

6. At the mine residences the administration provides free housing, firewood, a bath once a week, and water in those cases where the well is located more than 240 meters [787 feet] from the living quarters. Otherwise, we must carry the water ourselves. When assigned to places where no living quarters exist, we are obliged to build our own quarters.

7. In cases of illness diagnosed by the mining doctor, each of us has the right to free medical care or treatment in the mining hospital. Those treated in the hospital must remain there until discharged. But no salaries are paid during this time. In order to prevent infectious disease, the administration has the right subject us to medical examinations, from which we cannot exempt ourselves or our families.

8. From 1 April until 1 October, the workday must consist of 11.5 working hours and from 1 October until 1 April, 11 hours. Lunch breaks are scheduled by the administration and are not included in the workday.

9. In winter . . . we will receive days off as required by law. During the summer, the administration will assign days off at least twice a month. The schedule must be observed by us and in no case may we assign our own days off. . . . Non-Christians may have days off appropriate to their religious observance but must work on Christian holidays.

10. Upon hiring we receive pay books from the administration. These must be kept clean and in good order. All issues to us of food and money are registered in the pay books. . . . All pay is figured on the basis of the pay books. If lost, pay will be figured from the office notes.

11. Once a month, the administration issues according to our earnings food and supplies according to prices set by the district engineer and money. If we are in debt, the administration has the right to refuse payments. A full payoff occurs only at the end of the contracted work period.

12. When hired, we should arrive at the mines alone and can bring families only with the written permission of the administration. In such cases, the administration has the right to hire women and adolescents, a refusal from which will result in their expulsion from the mines. If the husband, father, or brother objects . . . he can be fired for violating the contract. Women assigned as house servants are paid 30 kopecks a day plus room and board or 60 kopecks without room and board. Women hired for surface mining work will receive ⅔ of men's salaries. Besides paid work, women must clean the floors of the barracks and maintain them in good order without pay. Adolescents assigned to work receive from 50 to 75 kopecks. . . .

15. Any special orders must be made known to us at the beginning of the work period, after which we cannot claim lack of knowledge of these orders, which are obligatory.

16. The administration has the right to fine us according to the law, not more than five rubles per incident, for the following: poor work, absences, disobedience, rudeness, drunkenness, and any other violations of order.

17. None of us has the right to engage in gold transactions at the mines during the contract period and if anyone is found with gold, it will be confiscated by the administration. Any gold we find must be placed in certain containers to be remunerated [at certain rates]. . . .

19. Before the end of the work contract, none of us has the right to ask for a payoff [i.e., to quit work]. The administration has the right to fire us for the following reasons: (a) incompetent work, (b) absence from work three days in a row without appropriate cause, (c) laziness, (d) insolent or foolish behavior, (e) contraction of an infectious disease, (f) for gathering crowds threatening to order and quiet, and (g) for any violation of the work contract on our part.

20. At the end of the work period, the administration will provide us free ship passage from the city of Bodaibo to any occupied place assigned by the administration.

Appendix B

Selected Items from "Our Demands," Submitted to Lenzoto, 3 March 1912

This list is adapted from *Pravda o lenskikh sobytiiakh*, ed. P. N. Batashev (Moscow, 1913), apps., sec. 2, no. 28, 65–66.

1. During the strike, food should be issued by the kitchens as usual.

2. (a) Food should be issued to workers on the same conditions as for administrative employees; all food products should be issued in the presence of a worker deputy . . . ; (b) meat should be divided into two sorts; (c) in summer [kvass] should be issued at the company's expense; rye flour should be sifted; [the issuance of] potatoes should be obligatory; cabbage should be obligatory as a protection from shingles.

3. (a) Expansion of living quarters for sufficient air; (b) free lighting (in barracks); (c) unmarried people should have one room for two people; families should have one room. Separate laundry room.

4. (a) Workers hired as specialists should not be sent to tasks not requiring their skills, and the same for mining workers . . . ; (b) no worker can be fired during the winter; firing must occur during the summer and . . . with free passage to Zhigalovo [a transport site on the Vitim River]; (c) . . . the administration should make the payoff as required by law.

5. Eight-hour workday; on holiday eves, seven hours; on Sundays and holidays work is not obligatory; work on such days . . . should be paid at 1.5 the normal rate; overtime work must be paid: first two hours counted as three hours; each hour after that as two hours. . . .

7. Every day's work should be entered into a table and totaled every month; the tables should be available to workers on a daily basis.

8. Pay should be made fully and on a monthly basis. . . . Amounts should be entered into the tables. . . .

10. Cancellation of all fines. . . .

12. Workers sent to distant mines should be paid at 1.5 the normal rate.

13. Medical aid should be provided at first request; during illness caused by Lenzoto, pay must occur at the normal rate and for other illnesses, at one-half pay.

14. The administration cannot fire on the basis of caprice but only with agreement of a workers commission.

15. No forced women's labor.

16. Polite address on the part of administrators; "you" and not "thou" should be used.

17. Eliminate [various named offensive overseers and administrative employees].

18. During the strike no one should suffer any penalties.

On guarantees for elected deputies: (a) all elected deputies should be given the right during negotiations to use free passage on railroads from Feodosievsk to Bodaibo and on horse; (b) the administration must arrange with the local police [to ensure] that the freedom of the deputies is guaranteed; (c) during the strike, the deputies should be given access to the People's Center; (d) the administrations should not send to work in the mines people not approved by the deputies; (e) we want the strike to be peaceful; and therefore declare: if penalties are employed against our deputies then we call all workers out on strike.

Notes

INTRODUCTION

1. I. Volkovicher, "Otkliki lenskikh sobytii v Moskve," *Proletarskaia revoliutsiia* 3 (1923): 66–91; *Zavety* 5 (1912); *Zvezda* 27–33 (1912); I. Menitskii, "Iz proshlogo Moskovskogo studenchestva (Otkliki na Lenskie sobytiia 1912 goda)" in *Put' k oktiabriu* (Moscow, 1923), 1:143–45; Hoover Institution Archive, Nicolaevsky Archive, Box 629, File 11, Otdel'nyi ottisk No. 3 "Rabochego": (Partii Sotsialistov-Revoliutsionerov) "Zhestokii urok"; *Lenskie sobytiia 1912 goda (dok. i mat.),* ed. V. Vladimirova (Moscow, 1925), 259–60; M. I. Lebedev, *"Lena" (Krovavyi urok): Vospominaniia uchastnika sobytii na Lene v 1912 g. 4-ogo aprelia* (Feodosia, 1923), 17; M. Ol'minskii, *Iz epokhi Zvezdy i Pravdy* (Moscow, 1956), 120–21; and A. Vitimskii, "K lenskomu zaprosu," *Pravda* 53 (5 March 1913).

2. *Gosudarstvennaia Duma. Stenograficheskie otchety. Tretii sozyv. Sessiia piataia* (St. Petersburg, 1912).

3. I. Menitskii, *Revoliutsionnoe dvizhenie voennykh godov* (Moscow, 1925), 139; Zhukov, "Revoliutsionnoe znachenie lenskoi zabastovki," *Proletarskaia revoliutsiia* 87 (1929): 54–83; the quote is from Zhukov.

4. G. A. Arutiunov, *Rabochee dvizhenie v Rossii v period novogo revoliutsionnogo pod"ema, 1910–1914 gg.* (Moscow, 1975), 138–42; V. I. Bonnell, *Roots of Rebellion: Workers' Politics and Organizations in St. Petersburg and Moscow, 1900–1914* (Berkeley, 1983), 352–54, 371; L. Haimson, "The Problem of Social Stability in Urban Russia, 1905–1917," pt. 1, *Slavic Review* 4 (December 1964): 620, 626; *Krizis samoderzhaviia v Rossii, 1895–1917* (Leningrad, 1984), 405–12, 507–508; Tim McDaniel, *Autocracy, Capitalism, and Revolution in Russia* (Berkeley, 1988), 142; R. B. McKean, *St. Petersburg between the Revolutions: Workers and Revolutionaries, June 1907–February 1917* (New Haven, 1990), 88–89; M. Melancon, "'Stormy Petrels': The Socialist Revolutionaries in Russia's Labor Organizations, 1905–1914," *Carl Beck Papers* 703 (June 1988): 32.

5. Outside Russia, only my 1993 journal article "The Ninth Circle" has studied the strike and shooting in detail. See M. Melancon, "The Ninth Circle: The Lena Goldfield Workers and the Massacre of 4 April 1912," *Slavic Review* 3 (Fall 1994): 766–95.

6. Michael Melancon, "Unexpected Consensus: Russian Society and the Lena Massacre, April 1912," *Revolutionary Russia* 2 (December 2002): 1–52, explores society's reaction to the shooting. This chapter summarizes the data from the article and adds new archival material about the workers' responses.

7. Among the works of interest about polyphonic speech are M. M. Bakhtin, *Toward a Philosophy of the Act* (Austin, 1993); *Speech Genres and Other Late Essays* (Austin, 1986); *The Dialogic Imagination* (Austin, 1981); and *Problems of Dos-*

toevsky's Poetics ([Ann Arbor, Mich.], 1973). Useful commentaries are David Danow, *The Thought of Mikhail Bakhtin: From Word to Culture* (New York, 1991); Michael Holquist, *Dialogism: Bakhtin and His World* (London and New York, 1990); Gary Saul Morson and Caryl Emerson, *Mikhail Bakhtin: Creation of a Prosaics* (Stanford, 1990); Tzvetan Todorov, *Mikhail Bakhtin. The Dialogical Principle* (Minneapolis, 1984); Sue Vice, *Introducing Bakhtin* (Manchester, 1997); and Caryl Emerson, *The First Hundred Years of Mikhail Bakhtin* (Princeton, 1997). See also Michael Melancon and Alice Pate, "Bakhtin contra Marx and Lenin: A Polyphonic Approach to Russia's Labor and Revolutionary Movements," *Russian History* 31, no. 4 (Winter 2004): 387–417.

8. *Pravda o lensikh sobytiiakh,* ed. P. N. Batshev (Moscow, 1913); S. S. Manukhin, *Vsepoddanneishii otchet chlena Gosudarstvennogo soveta, senatora tainogo sovetnika Manukhina* (St. Petersburg, 1912); G. I. Kvasha, *Statistiko-sravnitel'nye svedeniia o material'nom polozhenii rabochikh na priiskakh Lensko-zolotopromyshlennogo tovarishchestva* (St. Petersburg, 1912); A. Nevskii, *Lenskie sobytiia i ikh prichiny* (St. Petersburg, 1912).

9. Reginald Zelnik, *Law and Disorder on the Narova River: The Kreenholm Strike of 1872* (Berkeley, 1995); Gerald D. Surh, *1905 in St. Petersburg: Labor, Society, and Revolution* (Stanford, 1989); Samuel Baron, *Bloody Sunday in the Soviet Union: Novocherkassk, 1962* (Stanford, 2001); Diane P. Koenker and William G. Rosenberg, *Strikes and Revolution in Russia, 1917* (Princeton, 1989).

CHAPTER I

1. A. E. Krivolutskii, *V Lenskoi taige* (Moscow, 1958), 7–8; I. I. Gamov, *Ocherki dalekoi Sibiri* (Gomel, 1894), 24.

2. The section about the Lena region's geological, meteorological, biological, zoological, and anthropological characteristics and the region's earliest gold mining reflects data from *Sibirskii sbornik* 1 (1889): 2–5; *Pamiatnaia knizhka Iakutskoi oblasti za 1891 g.* (Iakutsk, 1891), 95–167; Krivolutskii, *V Lenskoi taige,* 8–10, 21–28, 36, 66–69; Gamov, *Ocherki dalekoi Sibiri,* 3–58, 67–77, 88–108; Al. Blek, "Rabochie na lenskikh zolotykh priiskakh," *Trud v Rossii* 4 (1922): 68–70; Manukhin, *Vsepoddaneishii otchet,* 1–20; F. V. Boltunov, "Otchet, . . . Materialy po voprosu o postroike severno-baikal'skogo zhelezno-dorozhnogo puti," *Trudy komandirovannoi po Vysochaishemu povelenniu Amurskoi ekspeditsii. Prilozhenie 1 k vypusku XII* (Khabarovsk, 1911): 21–34; William Blackwell, *The Beginnings of Russian Industrialization, 1800–1860* (Princeton, 1968), 60–61; V. V. Danilevskii, *Russkaia tekhnika* (Leningrad, 1949), 85–89. The section heading "Land of Cold and Gold" (*strana kholoda i zolota*) is borrowed from Gamov, 3.

3. Information about early Lena gold mining is from Blek, "Rabochie na lenskikh zolotykh priiskakh," 79; M. I. Lebedev, *Vospominaniia o lenskikh sobytiiakh 1912 g.* (Moscow, 1957), 8–9; *Lenskie sobytiia 1912 goda: Dokumenty i materialy,* ed. V. Vladimirova (Moscow, 1925), v–vii; V. I. Semevskii, *Rabochie na Sibirskikh zolotyhk priiskakh. Istoricheskoe izsledovanie.* 2 vols (St. Petersburg, 1898), vol. 2: *Polozhenie rabochikh posle 1870 g.* 8–10, 18; Boltunov, "Otchet," 34–36.

4. Susan McCaffray, *The Politics of Industrialization in Tsarist Russia: The Association of Southern Coal and Steel Producers, 1874–1914* (De Kalb, 1996), 15.

5. *Polnoe sobranie zakonov* (henceforth *PSZ*) (1837), vol. 12, no. 10521, 729; (1838), vol. 13, no. 11188, 390–96; no. 11279, 742.

6. *PSZ,*(1831), vol. 6 , no. 4793, 15–17, and no. 5008, 291–95.

7. *PSZ* (1838), vol. 13, no. 11188, 396–401.

8. Ibid., 401–405.

9. Daniel Orlovsky, "Professionalism in the Ministerial Bureaucracy on the Eve of the February Revolution," in *Russia's Missing Middle Class: The Professions in Russian History,* ed. Harley D. Balzer (Armonk, N.Y., 1996), 270–71.

10. Data about early Siberian gold mining and labor can be found in V. I. Semevskii, *Rabochie na sibir'skikh zolotykh promyslakh. Istoricheskoe issledovanie V. I. Semevskogo,* 2 vols. (St. Petersburg, 1898), vol. 1: *Ot nachala zolotoi promyshlennosti v Sibiri do 1870 g.;* "Ob issledovanii chastnoi zolotopromyshlennosti," in *Izvestiia sibir'skogo otdela imperialisticheskogo russkogo geograficheskogo obshchestva* 2, no. 4 (8 November 1871): 48–53; Polkovnik Goffman, "O zolotykh promyslakh Vostochoi Sibiri," *Gornyi zhurnal* (1844): 1–54; and P. V. Latkin, "Ocherki severnoi i iuzhnoi sistem zolotykh promyslov Eniseiskogo okruga," *Delo* 11 (1869).

11. *PSZ* (1842), vol. 17, no. 15515, 35–36; (1844), vol. 19, no. 18514, 835; see discussions of possessional versus free labor in Reginald Zelnik, "The Peasant and the Factory," in *The Peasant in Nineteenth Century* Russia, ed. Wayne S. Vucinich (Stanford, 1968), 176–79; and Boris Gorshkov, "Serfs on the Move: Peasant Seasonal Migration in Pre-Reform Russia, 1800–1861," *Kritika* 4 (Fall 2000): 635–36.

12. *PSZ* (1841), vol. 16, no. 14537; vol. 5, no. 15031, 56–57; (1851), vol. 26, no. 25254, 372–76.

13. *Svod zakonov Rossiiskoi imperii poveleniem Gosudaria Imperatora Nikolaiia Pervogo.* vol. 7, *Ustavy monetnyi, gornyi i o solc,* (St. Petersburg, 1857), 442–3.

14. *PSZ* (1855), vol. 30, no. 29243, 290–91, and no. 29779, 645–46.

15. *Svod zakonov,* 432–40.

16. Ibid., 78, 82, 97, 253.

CHAPTER 2

1. "Zolotopromyshlennost' i priiskovoe parakhodstvo v Iakutskoi oblasti," Pamiatnaia knizhka Iakutskoi oblasti za 1891 g. (Iakutsk, 1891), 122–28.

2. Blek, "Rabochie na lenskikh zolotykh priiskakh," 71–72; L. A. Karpinskii, "O sovremennom polozhenii zolotopromyshlennosti na Olekminskikh priiskakh," *Izvestiia Vostochno-Sibirskogo otdela . . . geograficheskogo obshchestva,* 17, nos.3–4 (1886): 4–11.

3. *Sobranie uzakonenii i rasporiazhenii pravitel'stva, izdavaemoe pri pravitel'stvuiushchem senate* 52 (23 June 1870): 702–11. This legislation can also be found in *PSZ* (1870), vol. 45, nos. 48399, 48400, and 48401, 674–88.

4. *Sobranie uzakonenii,* 713.

5. Ibid., 713–15.

6. Semevskii, *Rabochie na Sibirskikh zolotykh priiskakh*, 2:7.

7. Quoted in Semevskii, *Rabochie na Sibirskikh zolotykh promyslakh*, 2:11.

8. PSZ (1877), vol. 52, no. 57225, 402; (1887), vol. 7, nos. 4291, 105–106, and 4309; *Svod zakonov* (1886), vol. 7, no. 110; L. I. Rozanov, *Svod deistvuiushchikh uzakonenii o chastnoi zolotopromyshlennosti v Rossii* (St. Petersburg, 1883), 5–7, 62–68, 84–94, 102–11; and E. N. Vasil'ev, *Dopolneniie k "Svodu deistvuiushchikh uzakonenii o chastnoi zolotopromyshlennosti v Rossii"* (St. Petersburg, 1892), 1–5, 22–29.

9. Karpinskii, "O sovremennom polozhenii zolotopromyshlennosti na Olekminskikh priiskakh," 15–16.

10. "Rabochii vopros Vitimsko-Olekminskikh sistem," *Sibirskaia zhizn'* 79 (8 April 1912). For discussions of this era's labor legislation, see Gaston Rimlinger, "Autocracy and the Factory Order in Early Russian Industrialization," *Journal of Economic History* 1 (1960) : 67–92, and McCaffray, *Politics of Industrialization*, 11–12. In 1912 the association of industrial and commercial entrepeneurs recognized that the "gold-mining industry occupies a special place in our legislation, has its own organization and unusual lay-out . . . sharply differentiated from other branches of national labor"; "Zoloto-promyshlennost'," *Promyshlennost' i torgovlia v zakonodatel'nykh uchrezhdeniiakh, 1907–1912 gg.* (St. Petersburg, 1912), 385. Early conditions of West Siberian gold miners are described in A. Lopatin, "Zametki o polozhenii rabochikh na Eniseiskikh zolotykh promyslakh," *Izvestiia sibir'skogo otdela imperialisticheskogo-russkogo geograficheskogo obshchestva* 2, no. 4 (8 November 1871): 32–48 (abridged and reprinted from *Delo* 11 (1869).

11. Karpinskii, "O sovremennom polozhenii zolotopromyshlennosti na Olekminskikh priiskakh," 10–12.

12. "Ocherki sovremennogo sostoianiia," 16–20; A. Ia-i, "Ot Stretenska po Shilke i Amuru (iz putevykh zametok)," *Sibirskii sbornik* 1 (1889): 59–60.

13. Ia-i, "Ot Stretenska po Shilke i Amuru," 59–60; M. I. Orfanov, *V dali (iz proshlogo). Razskazy iz vol'noi i nevol'noi zhizni Mishla (M. I. Orfanova)* (Moscow, 1883), 55–63.

14. A. Ia.-I, "Ot Stretenska," 59–60; "Ocherki sovremennogo sostoianiia," 15–16.

15. Karpinskii, "O sovremennom polozhenii zolotopromyshlennosti na Olekminskikh priiskakh," 15–18; "Zolotopromyshlennost' i priiskovoe parakhodstvo v Iakutskoi oblasti," 106–13; "Rabochii vopros Vitimsko-Olekminskikh system," *Sibirskaia zhizn'*; "Ob issledovanii chastnoi zolotopromyshlennosti," 48–53; "Ocherki sovremennogo sostoianiia," 13–15.

16. "Zolotopromyshlennost' i priiskovoe parakhodstvo v Iakutskoi oblasti," 113–16; "Rabochii vopros Vitimsko-Oleminskikh system," *Sibirskaia zhizn'*; "Ob issledovanie o chastnoi zolotopromyshlennosti," 51; Karpinskii, "O sovremennom polozhenii zolotopromyshlennosti na Olekminskikh priiskakh," 18–20.

17. "Ocherki sovremennogo sostoiania," 1:22–25; 2:28–32; Semevskii, *Rabochie na Sibirskikh zolotykh priiskakh*, 2:27, 39, 48, 60–63; "Rabochii vopros Vitimsko-Olekminskoi zolotopromyshlennosti," *Sibirskaia zhizn'*.

18. "Ocherki sovremennogo sostoiania," 1: 22–25; 2: 28–32; Semevskii,

Rabochie na Sibirskikh zolotykh priiskakh, 2:27, 39, 48, 60–63; "Rabochii vopros Vitimsko-Olekminskoi zolotopromyshlennosti," *Sibirskaia zhizn'.*

19. Semevskii, *Rabochie na Sibirskikh zolotykh priiskakh,* 2:12–15; *Irkutskie gubernskie vedomosti* 70 (1871); I. Angarskii, "Vitim," *Sibirskii sbornik* 2 (1899): 42–66.

20. *Irkutskie gubernskie vedomosti* 34 (1877); Semevskii, *Rabochie na Sibirskikh zolotykh priiskakh,* 2:43, 51–54; N. P. Sinel'nikov, "Zapiski senatora N. P. Sinel'nikova," *Istoricheskii vestnik,* 61:44; Karpinskii, "O sovremennom polozhenii zolotopromyshlennosti na Olekminskikh priiskakh," 18; "Zolotopromyshlennost' i priiskovoe parakhodstvo v Iakutskoi oblasti," 112.

21. Semesvkii, *Rabochie na Sibirskikh zolotykh priiskakh,* 2:9–17; *Irkutskie gubernskie vedomosti* 70 (1871); Sinel'nikov, "Zapiski," 61:39–44.

22. *Sibir'* 39–42 (1882); *Tomskie gubernskie vedomosti* 29, 30 (1882); *Vostochnoe obozrenie* 1, 17 (1886); Semevskii, *Rabochie na Sibirskikh zolotykh priiskakh,* 2:9–65.

23. *Irkutskie gubernskie vedomosti,* 1880, nos. 11 and 12; *Vostochnoe obozrenie,* 1882, no. 12, 6–7; Semevskii, *Rabochie na Sibirskikh zolotykh priiskakh,* 2:47, 65.

24. Orfanov, *V dali,* 73, 83.

25. Ibid., 64–65, 86; "Ocherki sovremennogo sostoianiia," 21–22; Sinel'nikov, "Zapiski," 60:697–700, 61:41–44.

26. Sinel'nikov, "Zapiski," 60:700–702, and 61:29, 34, 44; *Irkutskie gubernskie vedomosti* 27 (1876); *Sibir'* 1 (1877); Semevskii, *Rabochie na Sibirskikh zolotykh priiskakh,* 2:19–22, 65, 291, 495–504; Manukhin, *Vsepoddanneishii otchet,* 74–75.

27. For early discussions of the Siberian economy, the gold industry, government and entrepreneurial tendencies, and possible alternatives, see Gamov, *Ocherki dalekoi Sibiri,* 84–87; Orfanov, *V dali,* 82–85; *Sibir'* 5 (1882); Ia-i, "Ot Stretenska," 35–36, 46–47, 59–60; "Ocherki sovremennogo sostoiania," 1: 3–8, 21–22; 2: 48–50, 61–64; and Boltunov, "Otchet," 44–48.

28. See analysis throughout Steven Marks, *The Road to Power: The Trans-Siberian Railroad and the Colonization of Asian Russia, 1850–1917* (Ithaca, N.Y., 1991).

29. The entire discussion in Ia-i, "Ot Stretenska," 27–61, when compared to data about the Olekminsk Region, makes this clear.

30. Boltunov, "Otchety," 103–104.

31. Loranskii, "Nashi zadachi," 7–8.

32. *Svod zakonov,* 1893, vol. 7, nos. 647–706, 116–24; *PSZ* (1895), vol. 15, no. 11591, 92–100.

33. *Prodolzhenie svoda zakonov Rossiiskoi imperii. 1906 goda, chast' tret'ia, stat'i k Tomam VII, VIII, IX i X* (St. Petersburg, 1906), no. 93, 19; no. 166, 25–26; and no. 661, 51. For early 20th century tsarist labor laws, see *Zakony o chastnoi fabrichno-zavodskoi promyshlennosti (izvlechennye iz Ustava o promyshlennosti izd. 1893 g. i po prodolzheniiam i iz drugikh chastei Svoda zakonov)* (Moscow, 1913), pt. 3, 1–168. For commentary about post-1905 gold-mining laws, see *Promyshlennost' i torgovlia v zakonodatel'nykh uchrezhdeniiakh),* 378–86.

34. See Theodore H. Friedgut, "Labor Violence and Regime Brutality in Tsarist Russia: The Iuzovka Cholera Riots of 1892," *Slavic Review* 2 (Summer 1987): 247–48, 263, and his *Iuzovka and Revolution: Life and Work in Russia's Donbass, 1869–1924* (Princeton, 1989), vol. 1, esp. chap. 9, "Organization of Work, Physical Conditions, Wages, and Benefits," 259–326; Robert E. Johnson, *Peasant*

and Proletarian: The Working Class of Moscow in the Late Nineteenth Century (New Brunswick, N.J., 1979), 80–98; and Rose L. Glickman, *Russian Factory Women: Workplace and Society, 1880–1914* (Berkeley, 1984), 105–55.

35. *Vostochnoe obozrenie* 30 (1886); 21 (1894); 22, 23 (1895); 49 (1896); Semevskii, *Rabochie na Sibirskikh zolotykh promyslakh*, 433–35; "Ocherki sovremennogo sostoiania," 2: 27.

36. *Sibir'* 62 (1897); Semevskii, *Rabochie na Sibirskikh zolotykh priiskakh*, 2:436–37; "Zolotopromyshlennost' i priiskovoe parakhodstvo v Iakutskoi oblasti," 116–17; Karpinskii, "O sovremennom polozhenii zolotopromyshlennosti na Olekminskikh priiskakh," 19.

37. Semevskii, *Rabochie na Sibirskikh zolotykh priiskakh*, 2:432–38, 458–59; *Novoe vremia* 7397 (1896); *Vostochnoe obozrenie* 148 (1895); *Pamiatnaia knizhka Iakutskoi oblasti na 1891 g.*, 116.

38. "Ocherki sovremennogo sostoianiia," 2: 55.

39. Semevskii, *Rabochie na Sibirskikh zolotykh priiskakh*, 2:874–75; Blek, "Rabochie na lenskikh zolotykh priiskakh," 1: 77; *Lenskie sobytiia 1912 goda*, vii; Boltunov, "Otchet," 40–41.

40. See production statistics in Boltunov, "Otchet," 38–39.

41. *Sobranie uzakonenii i rasporiazhenii pravitel'stva za 1898*, no. 94, 4548; PSZ (1898), vol. 18, no. 15782, 762; Blek, "Rabochie na lenskikh zolotykh priiskakh," 1:72; *Lenskie sobytiia*, vii–viii; Semevskii, *Rabochie na Sibirskikh zolotykh priiskakh*, 2:455; *Vostochnoe obozrenie* 25 (1895); Manukhin, *Vsepoddanneishii otchet*, 57.

42. Blek, "Rabochie na lenskikh zolotykh priiskakh," 1:72–74; *Lenskie sobytiia*, viii.

43. Manukhin, *Vsepoddaneishii otchet*, app. 5.

44. *Lenskie sobytiia*, ix–xii; Blek, "Rabochie na lenskikh zolotykh priiskakh," 1:73–74; Manukhin, *Vsepoddanneishii otchet*, 56–59; Boltunov, "Otchet," 61–65. In 1911 the railroad engineer Boltunov published his survey of the entire region and recommended building the so-called Severo-Baikal'skii zheleznodorozhnyi put' through Bodaibo.

45. Blek, "Rabochie na lenskikh zolotykh priiskakh," 1:71–75; G. Lelevich, "Lenskii rasstrel," *Proletarskaia revoliutsiia* 5 (1922): 17–18; Manukhin, *Vsepoddanneishii otchet*, 1–2, 56–9; A. V. Piaskovskii, *Lenskie sobytiia 1912 g.* (Moscow, 1939), 9–10, 14–16; *Pravda o lenskikh sobytiiakh*, 4–6, 9–11; A. Tiushevskii, *K istorii zabastovki i rasstrela na lenskikh priiskakh* (Petrograd, 1921), 6–7; K. F. Shatsillo, "Lenskii rasstrel i tsarskoe pravitel'stvo," *Bol'shevitskaia pechat' i rabochii klass Rossii v gody revoliutsionnogo pod"ema 1910–1914* (Moscow, 1965), 368; John McKay, *Pioneers for Profit: Foreign Entrepreneurship and Russian Industrialization, 1885–1917* (Chicago, 1970), 109–10.

46. Blek, "Rabochie lenskikh zolotykh priiskakh," 1:74. For example of one such entirely legal maneuver, imperial tax laws in effect allowed nominal increases in capitalization in order to decrease taxes: corporate taxes were figured on the basis of annual profits as a percentage of capitalization. If capitalization increased, even on paper, annual profits would appear as a smaller percentage of capital and taxes would be lower. For a discussion of this matter as regards the coal and steel industries, see McCaffray, *Politics of Industrialization*, 70.

47. Blackwell, *Beginnings of Russian Industrialization*, 60–61; Boris V. Anan'ich, "Economic Policy of the Tsarist Government," in *Entrepreneurship in Imperial Russia and the Soviet Union*, ed. Gregory Guroff and Fred Carstensen (Princeton, 1983), 137; Peter Gatrell, *The Tsarist Economy, 1850–1917* (London, 1986), 223–26; his *Government, Industry, and Rearmament in Russia, 1900–1914* (Cambridge, Eng., 1994), 92–93, 312–13; Sergei Witte, *The Memoirs of Count Witte* (Armonk, N.Y., 1990), 246–49; McKay, *Pioneers for Profit*, 89, 94–95, 108–109; Theodore von Laue, *Sergei Witte and the Industralization of Russia* (New York, 1969), 138–46, 258; Peter Lyashchenko, *History of the National Economy of Russia* (New York, 1949), 561–63; Paul A. Gregory, "The Russian Balance of Payments, the Gold Standard, and Monetary Policy," *Journal of Economic History* 39 (June 1979): 379–99; his *Russian National Income, 1885–1913* (Cambridge, Eng., 1983), 86, 129, 137, 148; P. V. Ol', *Foreign Capital in Russia* (New York, 1983), 76, 201; Olga Crisp, "Russian Financial Policy and the Gold Standard at the End of the Nineteenth Century," *Economic History Review* 1 (1953): 156–70; Paul Gregory and Joel Sailors, "Russian Monetary Policy and Industrialization, 1861–1913," *Journal of Economic History* 36 (December 1976): 836–51; Haim Barkai, "The Macro-Economics of Tsarist Russia in the Industrialization Era: Monetary Developments, the Balance of Payments and the Gold Standard," *Journal of Economic History* 33 (June 1973): 339–71; I. M. Drummond, "The Russian Gold Standard, 1897–1914," *Journal of Economic History* 36 (September 1976): 663–88. The statement about the gold industry's national significance is in *Sovet s"ezdov predstavitelei promyshlennosti i torgovli. Promyshlennost' i torgovlia v zakonodatel'nykh uchrezhdeniiakh, 1907–1912 gg.* (St. Petersburg, 1912), 378.

48. Semevskii, *Rabochie na Sibirskikh zolotykh priiskakh*, 2:469–73, 894–99; "Ocherki sovremennogo sostoiania," 34–35.

49. McCaffray, *Politics of Industrialization*, 117; Semevskii, *Rabochie na Sibirskikh zolotykh priiskakh*, 2:471.

50. *Vostochnoe obozrenie* 23 (1895); *Pamiatnaia knizhka Iakutskoi oblasti za 1891 g.*, 111; Semevskii, *Rabochie na Sibirskikh zolotykh priiskakh*, 2:469, 733; "Ocherki sovremennogo sostoianiia," 34–35.

51. *Golos Belostoka* 85 (1912), quoted in Piaskovskii, *Lenskie sobytiia*, 18; Manukhin, *Vsepoddanneishii otchet*, 59.

52. *Lenskie sobytiia*, xii; Piaskovskii, *Lenskie sobytiia*, 19; Manukhin, *Vsepoddanneishii otchet*, 59–60.

53. Piaskovskii, *Lenskie sobytiia*, 11–12.

54. Ibid., 28–29; *Lenskie priiski (sbornik dokumentov)*, ed. P. Pospelov, in the series "*Istoriia zavodov*" (Moscow, 1937), 214–15.

55. Manukhin, *Vsepoddaneishii otchet*, 59; Piaskovskii, *Lenskie sobytiia*, 27–29.

56. Piaskovskii, *Lenskie sobytiia*, 16–17; Shatsillo, "Lenskii rasstrel," 375.

57. Manukhin, *Vsepoddanneishii otchet*, 59–60; *Lenskie sobytiia*, 33; Piaskovskii, *Lenskie sobytiia*, 19; "Lenskii rasstrel 1912 g." (Novye dokumenty), *Krasnyi arkhiv* 2 (81) (1937): 160–64.

58. Manukhin, *Vsepoddanneishii otchet*, 59–64; Piaskovskii, *Lenskie sobytiia*, 12, 20–21; *Lenskie sobytiia*, 28.

59. *Lenskie sobytiia*, xxiv; Piaskovskii, *Lenskie sobytiia*, 20.

60. Tiushevskii, *K istorii*, 8; *Lenskie sobytiia*, xiii.

61. GARF, F. 1186, op. 1, d. 1, "Report of Manukhin to Emperor Nicholas," ll. 55–56; Blek, "Rabochie na lenskikh zolotykh priiskakh," 1:75; *Lenskie sobytiia*, xiv; A. F. Kerenskii [A. K-ii], "O tom, chto bylo," *Zavety* 5 (August 1912): 89; Manukhin, *Vsepoddanneishii otchet*, 327–28; Friedgut, *Iuzovka and Revolution*, 71–112.

62. Blek, "Rabochie na lenskikh zolotykh priiskakh," 2:51–52; *Lenskie sobytiia*, xiv–xv; Friedgut, "Iuzovka Cholera Riots," 248.

63. Blek, "Rabochie na lenskikh zolotykh priiskakh," 2:51–56; Manukhin, *Vsepoddanneishii otchet*, 99–107; *Pravda o lenskikh sobytiiakh*, 18–20; G. A. Vendrikh, K.V. Belomestnov and L. S. Sholokhova, *Na Lene-reke* (Irkutsk, 1984), 14; I. Kudriavtsev, *Lenskii rasstrel (vospominaniia uchastnika)* (Kharkov, 1934), 14–17.

64. Glickman, *Russian Factory Women*, 86–87.

65. GARF, F 1186, op.1, d.40, "Doklad pravleniia Lenzoto," l. 7; Blek, 3: 28–29; *Pravda o lenskikh sobytiiakh*, 21; Manukhin, *Vsepoddanneishii otchet*, 107–15; Glickman, *Russian Factory Women*, 107; Friedgut, *Iusovka and Revolution*, 299–316.

66. The 305 days in a work year reflected one day a week rest and the various holidays of the Orthodox calendar. If one uses the figures of between 1.50 and 1.70 per day for most workers, then even workers making the highest figure in this range—1.70 per day—would earn only 518 rubles 50 kopecks, close to the overall average noted by noncompany observers and nearly 100 rubles less than Lenzoto's claimed 617 rubles as its overall average. Difficulties arise for all these figures because of the endless variables associated with fines, days missed for illness or injury, overtime work, and off-time prospecting.

67. "Lenskii rasstrel," *Krasnyi arkhiv*, 176; *Pravda o lenskikh sobytiiakh*, 26; *Lenskie sobytiia*, xviii.

68. Blek, 3: 29–40; Manukhin, *Vsepoddaneishii otchet*, 118–23; *Pravda o lenskikh sobytiiakh*, 28–31; Tiushevskii, *K istorii*, 12; *Lenskie sobytiia*, xvi–xxi. The Iuzvka factory administration used financial policies reminiscent of Lenzoto's, except that by the time period under discussion *talon* payments in the Donbass were declining.

69. Blek, "Rabochie na lenskikh zolotykh priiskakh," 3:34–35; Lebedev, *Vospominaniia* (1957), 20–21; Manukhin, V*sepoddanneishii otchet*, 149–50; *Pravda o lenskikh sobytiiakh*, 12, 26–27; *Lenskie sobytiia*, 43–44.

70. GARF, F. 1186, op. 1, d. 42, ll. 63, 119, Chief Mining Engineer Tul'chinskii's 1910 and 1912 reports; Boltunov, "Otchet," 86.

71. Gamov, 88–89; Manukhin, *Vsepoddaneishii otchet*, 160–66; Nevskii, 53; "Lenskii rasstrel," *Kransyi Arkhiv*, 174–75.

72. Manukhin, *Vsepoddaneishii otchet*, 166–70.

73. GARF, F. 1186, op. 1, d. 3, l. 150.

74. Manukhin, *Vsepoddaneishii otchet*, 166–70.

75. GARF, F. 1186, op..1, d..40, "Doklad pravleniia Lenzoto," ll. 6, 22.

76. GARF, F. 1186, op. 1, d. 40, "Dolkad praveleniia Lenzoto," ll. 22–23.

77. GARF, F. 1186, op. 1, d. 32, ll. 44–45.

78. GARF, F. 1186, op..1, d..32, ll. 44–52; Manukhin, *Vsepoddanneishii otchet*, 137–42; V. Pletnev, *Lena: ocherk istorii lenskikh sobytii* (Moscow, 1923), 20–23; *Lenskie sobytiia*, 41; "Lenskii rasstrel," *Krasnyi arkhiv*, 174–77.

79. GARF, F. 1186, op. 1, d. 40, "Doklad pravleniia Lenzoto," l. 50.

80. GARF, F. 1186, op. 1, d. 43, l. 96; d. 3, ll. 137, 147.

81. GARF, F. 1186, op. 1, d. 3, l. 61; d. 42, l. 2; *Pravda o lenskikh sobytiiakh*, 38, 46–48.

82. GARF, F. 1186, op. 1, d. 42, ll. 2–3, 37, 63, 110–21.

83. Blek, "Rabochie na lenskikh zolotykh priiskakh," 1:78–79; G. A. Vendrikh, *Lenskie sobytiia 1912 g.* (Irkutsk, 1956), 13; *Pravda o lenskikh sobytiiakh*, 16–17; Manukhin, *Vsepoddanneishii otchet*, 76–80, 283. Various reports on the population at the mines differ one from the other by several hundreds in one or another direction without changing the overall picture: a large male working population and a smaller one of women and adolescents, some of whom worked and many of whom were unemployed dependents.

84. Glickman, *Russian Factory Women*, 16–17; Friedgut, *Iuzovka and Revolution*, 247–51; McCaffray, *Politics of Industrialization*, 95–121.

85. The railroad engineer used the term *katorzhnyi trud* in his 1911 report; Boltunov, "Otchet," 80–89; GARF, F. 1186, op. 1, d. 42, ll. 2–3, 37, 63, 110–21; F. 102, 4-oe d. pr. 1912, 23ch.2, Osobyi zhurnal soveta ministrov, 17, 24, 31 ianvaria 1913 g. Po . . . otchetu senatora Manukhina," ll. 56–58; F. 1467, op. 1, d. 518, l. 22; d. 520, ll. 102–104; d. 522, l. 100; Lebedev, *Vospominaniia* (1957), 22–23; Tiushevskii, *K istorii*, 12–15; Piaskovskii, 30–35; F. A. Kudriavtsev, *Dnevnik lenskoi zabastovki 1912 goda. Fakty i materialy* (Irkutsk, 1938), 6–7; *Lenskie sobytiia*, xxii, 9–11; Pletnev, *Lena*, 25; "Lenskii rasstrel," *Krasnyi arkhiv*, 175–77; Blek, "Rabochie na lenskikh zolotykh priiskakh," 2: 54–55, 3:36–40; Manukhin, *Vsepoddanneishii otchet*, 97–106, 192, 284; Shatsillo, "Lenskii rasstrel i tsarskoe pravitel'stvo," 369, 372, 380–81. Some Lenzoto working conditions were similar to those in other mining regions and in Russia's factories in general; others were not. On the one hand, Glickman notes the sexual harassment of women in textile mills and other plants (*Russian Factory Women*, 142–43, 146); the heavy use of fines in Russian industry is quite well known; and Friedgut notes one survey of Donbass mining personnel that counted a supervisor or administrator for every two miners (*Iuzovka and Revolution*, 251). On the other, Lenzoto's facilities had a remarkably makeshift character. Nonetheless, perhaps because of differences between gold and coal mining, the death rate from Lenzoto mining accidents in the one year for which data are available (1911) was significantly lower (fewer than 2 per 1,000 workers) than that reported for 1904–1908 in the Donbass coal mines (2.89 per 1,000 workers) (Friedgut, *Iuzovka and Revolution*, 279).

CHAPTER 3

1. Manukhin, *Vsepoddanneishii otchet*, 183, 191.

2. Semevskii, *Rabochie na Sibirskikh zolotykh priiskakh*, 2:647–52; "Zametki o polozhenii rabochikh na Eniseiskikh zolotykh promyslakh," 32–48; Z. G. Karpenko, "Formirovanie rabochikh kadrov v gornozavodskoi promyshlennosti zapadnoi Sibiri (1725–1860)," *Istoricheskie zapiski* 69 (1961): 222–52.

3. Manukhin, *Vsepoddanneishii otchet*, 184; McCaffray, *Politics of Industrialization*, 135–36; Semevskii, *Rabochie na Sibirskikh zolotykh priiskakh*, 2:653, 688, 719 (this source reports the first strikes as early as 1878).

4. *Lenskie priiski*, 214–15; McCaffray, *Politics of Industrialization*, 98–99.

5. Manukhin, *Vsepoddanneishii otchet*, 183–84; Semevskii, *Rabochie na Sibirskikh zolotykh priiskakh*, 2:689, 718–19; *Vostochnoe obozrenie* 17 (1886); 123, 124 (1894); 24 (1895).

6. *Sobranie uzakonenii* (1874), no. 47.

7. Semevskii, *Rabochie na Sibirskikh zolotykh priiskakh*, 2:719.

8. Manukhin, *Vsepoddanneishii otchet*, 184–85; V. I. Dulov, "Zabastovochnoe dvizhenie na Lene v nachale 1900-kh godov," *Uchenye zapiski Irkutskogo Gosudarstvennogo ped. instituta. Kefedra Marksizma-Leninizma. Kefedra istorii*, 17, no. 9 (1961): 13–19.

9. Manukhin, *Vsepoddanneishii otchet*, 188–90; Dulov, "Zabastovochnoe dvizhenie na Lene," 19–30.

10. Manukhin, *Vsepoddaneishii otchet*, 184–85, 188; Dulov, "Zabastovochnoe dvizhenie na Lene," 8.

11. Manukhin, *Vsepoddanneishii otchet*, 184, 190–91.

12. *Lenskie priiski*, 210–12.

13. Dulov, "Zabastovochnoe dvizhenie na Lene," 20.

14. Manukhin, *Vsepoddanneishii otchet*, 188.

15. Ibid., 190–91.

16. *Lenskie priiski*, 222–23.

17. Manukhin, *Vsepoddanneishii otchet*, 185–86.

18. Ibid., 185; *Lenskie priiski*, 222–23.

19. *Lenskie priiski*, 222–23; Manukhin, *Vsepoddanneishii otchet*, 186.

20. GARF, F. 1186, op. 1, d. 42, ll. 2–3; Pospelov, *Lenskie priiski*, 222–23; Piaskovskii, *Lenskie sobytiia*, 29–30 Manukhin, *Vsepoddaneishii otchet*, 183–91.

21. Manukhin, *Vsepoddanneishii otchet*, 444–45, 459–60.

22. *Vostochnoe obozrenie* 59 (1893): 2.

23. Semevskii, *Rabochie na Sibirskikh zolotykh priiskakh*, 2:461–62.

CHAPTER 4

1. Information in this paragraph and the next from GARF, F. 1186, op. 1, d. 40, "Doklad pravlenii Lenzoto," l. 2; d. 81, "Zapiski o prichinakh zabastovki," unsigned, ll. 1–3; d. 44, 130; Iu. S. Aksenov, *Lenskie sobytiia 1912 goda* (Moscow, 1960), 88; "Lenskii rasstrel," *Krasnyi arkhiv*, 177–78; Manukhin, *Vsepoddanneishii otchet*, 193–94; *Pravda o lenskikh sobytiiakh*, 51, 62–3; *Lenskie sobytiia*, 60–61, 73–74.

2. Manukhin, *Vsepoddanneishii otchet*, 192–95; *Lenskie sobytiia* , 60–62, 74–75; *Pravda o lenskikh sobytiiakh*, 51–55; Aksenov, *Lenskie sobytiia*, 88–89; Kudriavtsev, *Dnevnik*, 15–16; Vendrikh, *Lenskie sobytiia*, 28–30; I. P. Sharapov, *Ocherki po istorii lenskikh zolotykh priiskov* (Irkutsk, 1949), 172–73.

3. GARF, F. 1186, op. 1, d. 32, "Vypiski iz dela Irk. Gub. Zhand. Uprav. 'O Bod. zabastovki,' delo no. 30—1912 g., T. 2," l. 234; d. 40, "Doklad pravleniiia Lenzoto," ll. 2–4; F. 102, Ministry of the Interior, 4-oe d. pr., 1912, 23ch.2, "Zabastovka na priiskakh LZT," T. 1, ll. 1–2; Manukhin, *Vsepoddanneishii otchet*, 194–95; *Pravda o lenskikh sobytiiakh*, 63–64.

4. GARF, F. 1186, op. 1, d. 40, "Doklad pravleniia Lenzoto," l .3; d. 44, ll. 129–

30; P. N. Batashev, *Lenskaia zabastovka. Vospominaniia predsedatelia tsentral'nogo biuro stachennogo komiteta* (Moscow, 1933), 38; Lebedev, *Vospominaniia* (1957), 50–51; *Lenskie sobytiia*, xxv–xxvi; *Pravda o lenskikh sobytiiakh*, 64–67, 149–63, 172; *Lenskie priiski*, 267–69; Kudriavtsev, *Dnevnik*, 19; Manukhin, *Vsepoddanneishii otchet*, 95–96; F. S. Grigoriev and Ia. Z. Shapirshtein-Lers, eds., *K istorii rabochego i revoliutsionnogo dvizhenii e v Bodaibinskom zoloto-promyshlennom raione* (Bodaibo, 1924), app. 12, "Vospominaniia o zabastovke 1912 E. Dumpe," 78–79.

5. GARF, F. 1186, op. 1, d. 44, Account of Justice of the Peace Khitun dated 20 March 1912, l. 128.

6. Manukhin, *Vsepoddaneishii otchet*, 196–200; *Pravda o lenskikh sobytiiakh*, 149–63; Grigor'ev and Shapirshtein-Lers, *K istorii*, app. 12, "Vospominaniia Dumpe," 79–81; Vendrikh, *Lenskie sobytiia*, 28–30; *Lenskie sobytiia*, 75–77; Lebedev, *Vospominaniia* (1957), 51–53, 58–63; Batashev, *Lenskaia zabastovka*, 38; G. V. Cherepakhin, "Kak eto bylo," *Trud* 88 (17 April 1937).

7. GARF, F. 1186, op. 1, d. 44, l. 125.

8. Aksenov, *Lenskie sobytiia*, 91–92; Batashev, *Lenskaia zabastovka*, 8–9, 38; Cherepakhin, *Gody bor'by*, 79; Grigor'ev, Shapirshtein-Lers, *K istorii*, 110–12; M. Gudoshnikov, *Lenskii rasstrel, 1912–1932 gg.* (Moscow and Irkutsk, 1932), 15–17; Kudriavtsev, *Lenskii rasstrel*, 30, 37; Lebedev, *Vospominaniia* (1957), 49–54, 64–65, 71–73; M. Lebedev, *Vospominaniia o lenskikh sobytiiakh*, 2nd exp. ed. (Moscow, 1962), 62, 312–19; *Lenskie priiski*, 268–70, 285–86; Manukhin, *Vsepoddaneishii otchet*, 196–98; V. Nevskii, "K desiatiletiiu lenskogo rasstrela," *Krasnaia letopis'* 2–3 (1922): 360; Piaskovskii, *Lenskie sobytiia*, 58–59; F. A. Kudriavtsev, ed., *Predvestnik revoliutsionnoi bury; istoricheskii ocherk, dokumenty, vospominaniia* (Irkutsk, 1962), 195.

9. GARF, F. 1186, op. 1, d. 43, ll. 31–33; d. 44, Deposition of K. V. Gorinov, 14 March 1912, ll. 123–25; interrogation of worker Borisov, d. 32, l. 175.

10. GARF, F. 1186, op. 1, d. 43, ll. 31–33; d. 44, l. 126; F. 102, "Zabastovka na priiskakh LZT," ll. 7–9; *Lenskie priiski*, 272–74; Grigor'ev and Shapirshtein-Lers, *K istorii*, app. 6, 13–16; *Pravda o lenskikh sobytiiakh*, 65–66; Kudriavtsev, *Lenskii rasstrel*, 33–35.

11. GARF, F. 1186, op. 1, d. 33, l. 3; d. 3, l. 163.

12. GARF, F. 1186, op. 1, d. 44, l. 126; op. 1, d. 43, ll. 5–6; Manukhin, *Vsepoddaneishii otchet*, 205–207; Grigor'ev and Shapirshtein-Lers, *K istorii*, app. 12, "Vospominaniia Dumpe," 81–2, and app. 11, "Iz vospominanii Tul'chinskogo," 25–29; *Lenskie priiski*, 275; *Pravda o lenskikh sobytiiakh*, 67–68, 104–105, 150–51, 158–59, 165; Batashev, *Lenskaia zabastovka*, 38–41; Lebedev, *Vospominaniia* (1957), 60–61; *Lenskie sobytiia*, 178–79.

13. GARF, F. 1186, op. 1, d. 32, ll. 69–70.

14. GARF, F. 1186, op. 1, d. 73, ll. 5–6.

15. GARF, F. 1186, op. 1, d. 33, l. 14; d. 32, l. 238; F. 102, 23ch.2, "Zabastovka na priiskakh LZT," T. 1, ll. 9, 21–22.

16. GARF, F. 1186, op. 1, d. 32, ll. 234–35; d. 44, l. 126; F. 102, 23ch.2, "Zabastovka na priiskakh LZT," T. 1, l. 23.

17. GARF, F. 1186, op. 1, d. 32, l. 238; F. 124, Ministry of Justice, op. 50, d. 259, l. 2.

18. GARF, F. 1186, op. 1, d. 32, ll. 135, 236–39; d. 33, l. 4; d. 44, ll. 141–45; d .73, 36–

38; F.102, 23ch.2, "Zabastovka na priiskakh LZT," T. 1, ll. 24–26, 83–85; T. 4, ll. 146–54; F. 124, op. 50, d. 259, ll. 2–4; Manukhin, *Vsepoddanneishii otchet*, 209–10, 215–20; Grigor'ev and Shapirshtein-Lers, *K istorii*, 135–41, apps. 7–9, 16–19, app. 1, "Vospominaniia Dumpe," 85–87, app. 11: "Iz vospominanii Tul'chinskogo," 29–37; *Lenskie priiski*, 277–84; "Lenskii rasstrel," *Krasnyi arkhiv*, 176–79; *Pravda o lenskikh sobytiiakh*, 59–61, 63–65, 68, 152–53, 159–60, 162–63; Batashev, *Lenskaia zabastovka*, 49–50, 52–53; Lebedev, *Vospominaniia* (1957), 66–72; *Lenskie sobytiia*, 94–97; Kudriavtsev, *Dnevnik*, 30–31; Tiushevskii, *K istorii*, 29–31.

19. GARF, F. 1186, op. 1, d. 32, l. 239; d. 44, ll. 141–42.

20. GARF, F. 1186, op. 1, d. 32, ll. 2–3 "Doklad rotmistra Treshchenkova," l. 236; d. 44, 1. 28; F. 102, 23ch.2, "Zabastovka na priiskakh LZT," l. 24; Grigor'ev, Shapirshtein-Lers, *K istorii*, app. 12, "Vospominaniia Dumpe," 80–81, 83–84; Manukhin, *Vsepoddanneishii otchet*, 216–17; Cherepakhin, "Kak eto bylo."

21. GARF, F. 102, 23ch.2, "Zabastovka na priiskakh LZT," ll. 25–26, 43–50.

22. GARF, F. 1186, op. 1, d. 70, "Vypiski iz doklada Ministra Vnutrennego Dela," l. 29; d. 73, l. 41; F. 102, 23ch.2, "Zabastovka na priiskakh LZT," T. 1, l. 57; T. 2, l. 11; Grigor'ev and Shapirshtein-Lers, *K istorii*, app. 16, 108–11; app. 11, "Iz vospominanii Tul'chinskogo," 38; "Lenskii rasstrel," *Krasnyi arkhiv*, 177–79; Manukhin, *Vsepoddaneishii otchet*, 220–21; *Pravda o lenskikh sobytiiakh*, 65–66.

23. Information is sparse about Tul'chinskii's career prior to his assignment as chief mining engineer in the Olekminsk Region. According to brief biographical remarks in *Russkoe Slovo*, he had successfully fulfilled a very difficult assignment during 1905 in his capacity as mining engineer, when he investigated certain abuses of the North-Eastern Siberian Society (Severo-Vostochnoe Sibirskoe Obshchestvo), a mining concern in Chukota. Subsequently, he received a similar assignment in the Far East, where he achieved heroic status in investigating the affairs of certain mining concessions with holdings in Sakhalin and Vladivostok. He seems to have been a troubleshooter for the Ministry of Trade and Industry's State Mining Administration, a body with oversight functions for the empire's mining industry. If this is the case, he may well have received his assignment to Lenzoto's mines with the task of investigating and ameliorating abuses there, a task that ran afoul of the government's overriding interest in gold production and Lenzoto's superb connections. See *Russkoe Slovo* 82 (8 April 1912).

24. For information about Treshchenkov's previous career, see *Russkoe Slovo* 82 (8 April 1912); 83 (10 April 1912); *Golos Moskvy* 82 (8 April 1912).

25. GARF, F. 102, 23ch.2, "Zabastovka na priiskakh LZT," l. 103; F. 1186, op.1, d.42, l. 9; d.32 "Doklad rotmistra Treshchenkova," ll. 2–14; telegrams of Treshchenkov, ll. 241–53; *Lenskie sobytiia*, 71–72; Piaskovskii, *Lenskie* sobytiia, 62.

26. GARF, F 1186, op.1, d.44, Interrogation of Tul'chinskii on 14 April 1912, l. 209; d.32, l. 241; d.32, "Doklad rotmistra Treshchenkova," ll. 3–4; d.42, ll. 25–27; F. 102, 23 ch.2, "Zabastovka na priiskakh LZT," ll. 121–41.

27. GARF, F 1186, op.1, d.32, l. 239; F. 102, 23 ch.2, "Zabastovka na priiskakh LZT," ll. 62, 67–71, 72, 78; F. 124, op. 50, d. 259, ll. 3–4; Manukhin, *Vsepoddaneishii otchet*, 222–29; "Lenskii rasstrel," *Krasnyi arkhiv*, 179; Grigor'ev and Shapirshtein-Lers, *K istorii*, 148–73, apps. 19–23, 114–22, app. 11, "Iz vospominanii Tul'chin-

skogo," 44–50, 54, 59, app. 12, "Vospominaniia Dumpe," 92–100; Cherepakhin, "Kak eto bylo"; Lebedev, *Vospominaniia* (1957), 71–73; Kudriavtsev, *Dnevnik*, 36–39; Tiushevskii, *K istorii*, 34–35; *Lenskie priiski*, 285–88; Piaskovskii, *Lenskie sobytiia*, 60; *Lenskie sobytiia*, 54–56, 100–102; Aksenov, *Lenskie sobytiia*, 104–105; *Pravda o lenskikh sobytiiakh*, 119–22; Vendrikh, *Lenskie sobytiia*, 79–80; Lelevich, "Lenskii rasstrel," 15; Kerenskii, *Zavety*, 102.

28. GARF, F. 1186, op. 1, d. 42, ll. 25–27; d. 32, l. 241.

29. GARF, F. 102, 23ch.2, "Zabastovka na priiskakh LZT," ll. 121–41.

30. GARF, F. 1186, op. 1, d. 32, ll. 4–5, 239–41; d. 33, "Doklad Bantysha," ll. 6–7; F. 124, Ministry of Justice, op. 50, d. 259, ll. 37–40.

31. *Russkoe slovo* 76 (1 April 1912).

32. GARF, F. 1186, op. 1, d. 42, "Doklad Tul'chinskogo," l. 28; d. 33, "Doklad Bantysha," ll. 6–8.

33. GARF, F. 1186, op. 1, d. 32, "Doklad rotmistra Treshchenkova," l. 5.

34. GARF, F. 1186, op. 1, d. 32, ll. 5–6, 241–42; d. 33, "Doklad Bantysha," ll. 13–15; d. 42, ll. 27–28; d. 44, l. 209; d. 73, telegram of Bantysh' to the Minister of Internal Affairs, dated 5 April, ll. 73–74.

35. GARF, F. 1186, op. 1, d. 32, "Doklad rotmistra Treshchenkova," l. 6; F. 102, 23 ch. 2, T. 4, Report of Captain Lepin, l. 150; Manukhin, *Vsepoddanneishii otchet*, 224–25, 229–34; Grigor'ev and Shapirshtein-Lers, *K istorii*, 170–80, apps., 24–32, 122–29, app. 11, "Iz vospominanii Tul'chinskogo," 50–57; app. 12, "Vospominaniia Dumpe," 103–104; "Lenskii rasstrel," *Kransyi arkhiv*, 179–80; *Lenskie priiski*, 297; Cherepakhin, "Kak eto bylo"; Vendrikh, 80–81; Tiushevskii, *K istorii*, 39–40; *Lenskie sobytiia*, xlviii–l, 55–57, 67–69, 81–82, 148–49; *Zvezda* 26 (5 April 1912): 13; *Pravda o lenskikh sobytiiakh*, 76–78.

36. GARF, F. 1186, op. 1, d. 44, Interrogation of Tul'chinskii, l. 210; d. 42, "Doklad Tul'chinskogo," l. 28; Manukhin, *Vsepoddanneishii otchet*, 234–40; Grigor'ev and Shapirshtein-Lers, *K istorii*, app. 11, "Iz vospominanii Tul'chinskogo," 57–64; *Lenskie sobytiia*, 68–69, 103–104, 170–71; Kerenskii, *Zavety*, 103; *Pravda o lenskikh sobytiiakh*, 80–92, 143–44.

37. Kudriavtsev, *Lenskii rasstrel*, 41; Lelevich, "Lenskii rasstrel," 16.

38. GARF, F. 1186, op. 1, d. 42, "Doklad Tul'chinskogo," ll. 28–30; d. 44, Interrogation of Tul'chinskii, ll. 210–12; d. 32, "Doklad rotmistra Treshchenkova," l. 6; Interrogation of mining guards, l. 215.

39. GARF, F. 1186, op. 1, d. 32, l. 243; d. 73, l. 67.

40. GARF, F. 1186, op. 1, d. 32, "Doklad rotmistra Treshchenkova," ll. 6–8; d. 44, Interrogation of Tul'chinskii, ll. 212–13; d. 42, "Doklad Tul'chinskogo," ll. 30–31.

41. GARF, F. 1186, op. 1, d. 32, ll. 11–12, 15–17; d. 70, l. 68; d. 43, "Iz letopisi priisk. Blagoveshchenskoi tserkvi," ll. 173, 178–79; Manukhin, *Vsepoddanneishii otchet*, 245; *Pravda o lenskikh sobytiiakh*, 89; *Lenskie priiski*, 294–97.

42. *Rech'* 98 (11 April 1912); *Birzhevye vedomosti* 12878 (10 April 1912); *Tverskoe povolzh'e* 485 (15 April 1912); *Sibirskaia zhizn'* (Tomsk) 88 (19 April 1912).

43. GARF, F. 1186, op. 1, d. 32, "Doklad rotmistra Treshchenkova," ll. 8–9; d. 81, "Anonymous notes on the reasons for the strike," l. 7.

44. GARF, F. 1186, op. 1, d. 44, Interrogation of I. M. Dmitriev, 5 May 1912, l. 252.

45. GARF, F. 1186, op. 1, d. 32, l. 8; Manukhin, *Vsepoddaneishii otchet*, 238–46;

Grigor'ev and Shapirshtein-Lers, *K istorii*, 182–85, app. 16, 20, apps. 32–39, 128–37, app. 11, "Iz vospominanii Tul'chinskogo," 66–75; *Pravda o lenskikh sobytiiakh*, 85–92, 145, 177–216; *Lenskie priiski*, 294–97; Cherepakhin, "Kak eto bylo"; Vendrikh, *Lenskie sobytiia*, 4, 93–97; Pletnev, *Lena*, 44–45; Lelevich, "Lenskii rasstrel," 16; "Lenskii rasstrel," *Kransyi arkhiv*, 162–63; Tiushevskii, *K istorii*, 41–45; Kudriavtsev, *Dnevnik*, 41–45; Nevskii, *Lenskie sobytiia*, 66–67; Kerenskii, *Zavety*, 109; Lebedev, *Vospominaniia* (1957), 88–103; Aksenov, *Lenskie sobytiia*, 116–22; *Lenskie sobytiia*, li–lix, 69–93, 103–11.

46. GARF, F. 1186, op. 1, d. 3, l. 59.

47. GARF, F. 124, op. 50, d. 259, l. 140.

48. GARF, F. 1186, op. 1, d. 32, "Doklad Treshchenkova," l. 8; d. 42, "Doklad Tul'chinskogo," l. 31; d. 44, Interrogations of Lepin and Sanzharenko, ll. 184–85; Interrogation of I. P. Pimen, Lenzoto clerk, about photographer Koreshkov, l. 241; Manukhin, *Vsepoddaneishii otchet*, 247–48, 309–18; *Pravda o lenskikh sobytiiakh*, 85–89, apps. 57–58, 77, apps. 205–206, 179–80; Pletnev, *Lena*, 45; Grigor'ev and Shapirshtein-Lers, *K istorii*, app. 33, 129–30; Lebedev, *Vospominaniia* (1962), 313.

49. GARF, F. 1186, op. 1, d. 32, "Doklad rotmistra Treshchenkova," ll. 7–8; d. 42, "Doklad Tul'chinskogo, l. 31; d. 43, "Doklad Sviashch. N. P. Vinokurova," l. 180.

50. GARF, F. 1186, op. 1, d. 3, Manukhin's special report to the emperor, l. 59; d. 73, Manukhin, "Recommendation for Criminal Indictment of Treshchenkov," l. 12; F. 124, op. 50, d. 259, ll. 100–111; Grigor'ev and Shapirshtein-Lers, *K istorii*, app. 39, 135–36; Nevskii, *Lenskie sobytiia*, 66–68; *Lenskie sobytiia*, liv–lv, 116–17; Manukhin, *Vsepoddaneishii otchet*, 244–47, 313; *Lenskie priiski*, 301–302; Pletnev, *Lena*, 48–49.

51. GARF, F. 1186, op. 1, d. 44, ll. 338–39, 348–50; d. 32, 'Doklad rotmistra Treshchenkova," ll. 8–9.

52. GARF, F. 1186, op. 1, d. 76, Manukhin, "Recommendation for Criminal Indictment of Treshchenkov," l. 8.

53. GARF, F. 1186, op. 1, d. 76, ll. 10–11.

54. GARF, F. 1186, op. 1, d. 3, l. 59; d. 32, l. 8; d. 81, l. 7.

55. GARF, F. 1186, op. 1, d. 44, Interrogations of soldiers, ll. 245–47.

56. Cherepakhin, *Gody bor'by*, 87; GARF, F. 1186, op. 1, d. 44, l. 155; d. 32, l. 23, 246–54; *Lenskie priiski*, "Iz vospominanii G. V. Cherepakhina," 293–94.

57. GARF, F. 1186, op. 1, d. 32, l. 71; d. 73, l. 68, ll. 114–16; *Rech'* 96 (9 April 1912); *Sibir'* 83 (10 April 1912); *Ural'skaia zhizn'* 81 (12 April 1912).

58. *Lenskie sobytiia*, 188.

59. Kokovtsev, Count V. N., *Iz moego proshlogo. Vospominaniia, 1907–1919 gg.* 2 vols. (Paris, 1933), 2: 56–63.

60. GARF, F. 124, op. 50, d.259, Messages from Procurator Nimander to the Minister of Justice, dated 15 May and 5 June 1912, ll. 100, 103; F. 102, 23ch.2, "Zabastovka na priiskakh LZT," T. 3; T. 4, l. 210; F. 1186, op. 1, d. 32, "Vypiski iz dela Irkutskogo zhandarmskogo upravleniia, 'O Bodaibovskoi zabastovke,'" T. 2, ll. 242–60; *Pravda o lenskikh sobytiiakh*, pp. 76–102, 127–140; *Lenskie priiski*, 296–330, *Lenskie sobytiia*, 189–94.

61. GARF, F. 102, 23ch.2, "Zabastovka na priiskakh LZT," T. 2, l. 58–70; T. 3; T. 4, ll. 242–49, 254–55.

62. GARF, F. 102, 23ch.2, "Zabastovka na priiskakh LZT," T. 4, ll. 210, 242, 254–55.

63. See Dr. S. A. Bernstein, *The Financial and Economic Results of the Workings of the Lena Goldfields Company Limited* (London, n.d.); and *Documents Concerning the Competence of the Arbitration Court Set Up in Connection with the Question Outstanding between the Lena Goldfields Company, Limited, and the U.S.S.R..* (Moscow, 1930).

64. GARF, F. 102, 23ch.2, "Zabastovka na priiskakh LZT," T. 4, ll. 263–71; F. 124, op. 50, d. 259, ll. 176–84.

CHAPTER 5

1. GARF, F. 1186, op. 1, d. 32, l. 3; F. 102, DPOO, 1912, d. 342, ll. 284–87; F. 124, op. 50, d. 259, "Dopros Treshchenkova," ll. 135–41; Zhukov, "Revoliutsionnoe znachenie lenskoi zabastovki,," 54–57, 82–83; Sh. Levin, "K istorii zabastovki na lenskikh zolotykh priiskakh," *Byloe* 20 (1922): 178–93; Vladimirova, "Vstupitel'naia stat'ia," *Lenskie sobytiia 1912 goda.*, iv–lxxi.

2. Manukhin, *Vsepoddanneishii otchet*, 185–86.

3. Dulov, "Zabastovochnoe dvizhenie na Lene," 12–26.

4. Ibid., 35; Manukhin, *Vsepoddanneishii otchet*, 186.

5. P. Lavrov was a nineteenth-century Russian populist who urged young members of the Russian intelligentsia to live and work among laborers in order to win their confidence and spread socialist ideas on the basis of this trust.

6. E. I., "Pamiati P. M. Anan'eva," *Katorga i ssylka* 5 (1923): 23–40.

7. GARF, F. 1186, Delo Manukhina, op. 1, d. 32, l. 94; N. Rostov, "Novoe o lenskikh sobytiiakh" (po dannym arkhiva Irk. Gub. zhand.), *Byloe* 20 (1922): 164–65; Lebedev, *Vospominaniia* (1957), 27.

8. Lebedev, *Vospominaniia* (1957), 28.

9. GARF, F. 102, DPOO, 1912, d. 342, l. 286; F. 1186, Delo Manukhina, op. 1, d. 32, l. 94.

10. Lebedev, *Vospominaniia* (1957), 40–41; Batashev, *Lenskaia zabastovka*, 29–30; Cherepakhin, *Gody bor'by*, 72–73.

11. GARF, F. 102, DPOO, 1912, d. 242, 5ch.27, ll. 3–42.

12. GARF, F. 102, DPOO, d. 242, 9ch.27B, ll. 1–163.

13. GARF, F. 1186, op. 1, d. 3, ll. 88–99.

14. GARF, F. 1186, op. 1, d. 43, ll. 17, 27; F. 102, 23ch.2, "Zabastovka na priiskakh LZT," T. 4, ll. 204–205; F. 124, op. 50, d. 259, ll. 158–162.

15. GARF, F. 1186, op. 1, d. 32, l. 238; d. 42, l. 27.

16. GARF, F. 1186, op. 1, d. 73, ll. 6–7, 39; Grigor'ev and Shaperstein-Lers, *K istorii*, app. 10, 19; *Lenskie priiski*, 266; *Lenskie sobytiia*, 178.

17. GARF, F. 1186, op. 1, d. 44, ll. 123–31, 143–45; Manukhin, *Vsepoddanneishii otchet*, 198, 206.

18. *Lenskie sobytiia*, 178; GARF, F. 1186, op. 1, d. 44, ll. 141–42.

19. GARF, F. 1186, op. 1, d. 44, "O stachennom komitete," ll. 123–66; F. 102, 23ch.2, T. 4, "Raport prokurora sudebnoi palaty, podpisannyi Nimander," l. 124;

Manukhin, *Vsepoddanneishii otchet,* 210 and 198–248; Vladimirova, "Vstupitel'naia stat'ia," *Lenskie sobytiia,* xxviii.

20. *Svod zakonov Rossiiskoi imperii. Zakony ugolovnye* (St. Petersburg, 1857), vol. 15, 102–103; *Svod zakonov ugolovnykh. Chast' pervaia. Ulozhenie o nakazaniiakh ugolovnykh i ispravitel'nykh* (St. Petersburg, 1885), 274; *Prodolzhenie svoda zakonov Rossiiskoi imperii. Chast' vtoraia. Ulozhenie o nakazaniakh ugolovnykh i ispravitel'nykh* (St. Petersburg, 1902), article 1358.

21. PSZ (1905), vol. 25, 850–52.

22. Manukhin, *Vsepoddanneishii otchet,* 208.

23. GARF, F. 1186, op. 1, d. 3, ll. 117, 287–88; d. 32, l. 3.

24. GARF, F. 1186, op. 1, d. 32, ll. 3, 92–93.

25. GARF, F. 102, 23ch.2, "Raport prokurora sudebnoi palaty," T. 4, ll. 122–32.

26. GARF, F. 1186, op. 1, d. 70, ll. 98–100, 142–51.

27. GARF, F. 1186, op. 1, d. 32, ll. 94–95; F. 102, 23ch.2, "Raport prokurora sudebnoi palaty," T. 4, ll. 127–28; F. 124, op. 50, d. 259, ll. 213–19.

28. GARF, F. 102, 23ch.2, "Raport prokurora sudebnoi palaty," T. 4, ll. 122–41.

29. GARF, F. 1186, op. 1, d. 32, ll. 239–43.

30. GARF, F. 1186, op. 1, d. 32, l. 243.

31. GARF, F. 1186, op. 1, d. 32, l. 6; d. 42, l. 27; d. 44, ll. 213–14.

32. GARF, F. 1186, op. 1, d. 32, l. 6; Lebedev, *Vospominaniia* (1957), 84–95; Cherepakhin, *Gody bor'by,* 81–86.

33. Lebedev, *Vospominaniia* (1957), 72–73; Cherepakhin, *Gody bor'by,* 79–82; Kudriavtsev, *Lenskoi zabastovki 1912 goda,* 21–22; Piaskovskii, *Lenskie sobytiia 1912 goda,* 58–59; Aksenov, *Lenskie sobytiia 1912 goda,* 90–91; Vladimorova, "Vstupitel'naia stat'ia," *Lenskie sobytiia,* iv–lxxi; Zhukov, "Revoliutsionnoe znachenie," 82–83.

34. GARF, F. 1186, op. 1, d. 44, ll. 19–200, 216–17.

35. GARF, F. 1186, op. 1, d. 70, ll. 98–100.

36. GARF, F. 1186, op. 1, d. 32, ll. 76–86; d. 33, l. 13; d. 73, ll. 73–74, 136; *Birzhevye vedomosti* 12850 (22 March 1912).

37. Information in this paragraph and the following one from GARF, F. 102, 1912, d. 342, ll. 284–87; F. 124, op. 50, d. 259, l. 218.

38. GARF, F. 124, op. 50, d. 259, l. 218; F. 102, 23ch.2, "Zabastovka na priiskakh LZT," T. 2, l. 225; T. 4, "Osobyi zhurnal soveta ministrov 17, 24, i 31 ianvaria 1913 g. Po. . . otchetu senatora Manukhina," l. 45.

39. GARF, F. 124, op. 50, d. 259, ll. 196–206; F. 102, 23ch.2, "Zabastovka na priiskakh LZT," T. 3, ll. 65–66; T. 5, ll. 45–46.

40. GARF, F. 102, 23ch.2, T. 5, ll. 46–56.

41. GARF, F. 1186, op. 1, d. 44, l. 128; d. 32, ll. 233–35; *Pravda o lenskikh sobytiiakh,* 63–63.

42. GARF, F. 1467, Extraordinary Investigatory Commission of the Provisional Government, op. 1, d. 523, l. 157; d. 525, l. 131.

CHAPTER 6

1. *Russkoe slovo* 1 (1 January 1912).

2. This chapter is for the most part an abridged version of Melancon, "Unexpected Consensus: Russian Society and the Lena Massacre, April 1912," *Revolutionary Russia,* 2 (December 2002): 1–52. The discussion of the workers' reactions below includes new archival data and therefore expands on the discussion in "Unexpected Consensus."

3. A useful summary of this approach and of the entire historiographical question can be found in Arthur Mendel's "On Interpreting the Fate of Imperial Russia," in *Russia Under the Last Tsar,* ed. Theofanis George Stavrou (Minneapolis, 1969), 12–41. See also Melancon, "Unexpected Consensus," 3–5, and, for a revisiting of the original fragmentation theory, Leopold Haimson, "'The Problem of Political and Social Stability in Urban Russia on the Eve of War and Revolution' Revisited," *Slavic Review* 4 (Winter 2000): 849–50.

4. Also of interest in this regard is Michael Melancon, "Russia's Outlooks on the Present and Future, 1910–1914: What the Press Tells Us," and other selections in *Russia in the European Context: A Member of the Family, 1789–1914,* ed. Susan McCaffray and Michael Melancon (New York, 2005).

5. GARF, F. 102, op. 1912, d. 342, ll. 3, 11–14, 16, 20, 24–31, 37–41, 49, 53–55, 61–63, 69–70, 110; F. DP, 4 d-vo 1912, d. 150, ll. 259; F. 1186, op. 1, d. 70, ll. 49–50; *Zvezda* 30 (15 April 1912); *Metallist* 14 (1912): 7. Interesting Soviet-era discussions can be found in M. Balabanov, *Ot 1905 k 1917. Massovoe rabochee dvizhenie* (Leningrad and Moscow, 1927), 155–93; V. Ia. Laverychev, *Po tu storonu barrikad (iz istorii bor'by Moskovskoi burzhuazii s revoliutsiei)* (Moscow, 1967), 78–95; G. A. Arytiunov, *Rabochee dvizhenie v Rossii v period novogo revoliutsionnogo pod"ema, 1910–1914* (Moscow, 1975), 138–55; A. Ia. Avrekh, *Lenskii rasstrel i krizis tret'eiunskoi sistemy* (Moscow, 1962); L. M. Shalaginova, "Otkliki na lenskie sobytiia v Rossii," *Istoricheskii arkhiv* 1 (January–February 1962): 176–85; K. F. Shatsillo, "Lenskii rasstrel i tsarskoe pravitel'stvo," *Bol'shevistskaia pechat' i rabochii klass Rossii v gody revoliutsionnogo pod"ema ,1910–1914* (Moscow, 1965), 364–88.

6. GARF, F. 102, op. 242, d. 342, l. 98.

7. GARF, F. 102, op. 242, d. 342 (1), l. 3.

8. GARF, F. 102, op. 242, d. 342, ll. 25, 30–31, 69, 75, 98–99, 143.

9. GARF, F. 102, op. 242, d. 342(1), ll. 170–74.

10. *Obshchestvo zavodchikov i fabrikantov Moskovskogo promyshlennogo raiona v 1912 godu* (Moscow, 1913), 19; *Svod otchetov fabrichnykh inspektorov za 1913 god* (SPb, 1914), lxxii. Discrepancies between the two sets of figures and the Factory Inspectorate's regularly smaller numbers represent the latter body's restricted area of responsibility, which excluded mining, metallurgy, and railroads.

11. GARF, F. 102, Ministry of the Interior, 4-oe deloproizvodstvo 1912 g., d. 150, "O volnenii sredi rabochikh po povodu sobytii 4-go aprelia 1912 g. na lenskikh priiskakh," ll. 3–6, 23–24, 35, 38–39, 40–43.

12. GARF, F. 102, d. 150, ll. 28, 31.

13. GARF, F. 102, d. 150, l. 71; ll. 104–18.

14. GARF, F. 102, d. 150, ll. 35, 38–39, 46, 68, 91, 169.

15. GARF, F. 1186, op. 1, d. 70, l. 125; F. R-6935, op. 5, d. 55, l. 1; F.102, op. 242, d. 342, ll. 170–74; Arutiunov, *Rabochee dvizhenie*, 150, 154–55; *Russkoe slovo* 91, 97, 98, 105 (19, 26, 27 April; 9 May 1912); *Saratovskii Listok* 80 (12 April 1912); *Moskovskie gubernskie vedomosti* 36 (9 May 1912).

16. *Vestnik evropy* 5 (May 1912): 391–401, 420.

17. GARF, F. 1186, op. 1, d. 70, ll. 35–37; F. 102, op. 242, d. 342, ll. 16–17, 20–21, 38.

18. Menitskii, "Iz proshlogo Moskovskogo studenchestva (Otkliki na Lenskie sobytiia)," 142–45; GARF, F. 102, op. 242, d. 342, l. 87; Sergei Chetverikov, *Bezvozvratno ushedshaia Rossiia* (Berlin, n.d.), 55–57.

19. GARF, F. 102, op. 242, d. 342 (1), ll. 16–17, 20–21, 31, 38, 62, 69; Shalaginova, "Otkliki na lenskie sobytiia v Rossii," 178, 181; Marc Slonim, "An Autobiographical Fragment: The Birth of a Socialist Revolutionary," *Sbornik* (Leeds) 4 (Winter 1978–79): 59–60.

20. For information about this phenomenon, see Michael Melancon, *The Socialist Revolutionaries and the Russian Anti-War Movement, 1914–1917* (Columbus, Ohio, 1990).

21. *Zvezda* 26 (5 April 1912); *Znamia truda* 42 (April 1912); "Otrytoe pis'mo Ts.K. P.S.R.," April 1912 Paris, Gruppa katorzhan S.R. in Special Collections, Gosudarstvenaia Obshchestvenno-politicheskaia biblioteka, Moscow.

22. GARF, F. 102, op. 242, d. 342, ll. 176–77; F. 1186, op. 1, d. 70, ll. 35–66.

23. GARF, F.. 1186, d. 70, ll. 35–68.

24. GARF, F 1186, op. 1, d. 70, ll. 35–41.

25. GARF, F. 1186, op. 1, d. 70, ll. 47–52.

26. GARF, F. 102, op. 1912, d. 342, ll. 3–4, 16, 76.

27. GARF, F102, op. 1912, d. 342, ll 5–16.

28. GARF, F.102, op. 242, d. 342, l. 26.

29. *Nasha zaria* 4 (April 1912): 50–60; 5 (May 1912): 60–68; *Sotsial-Demokrat* 27 (4 June 1912); *Zavety* 5 (August 1912): 81–116.

30. *Birzhevye vedomosti* 12822 (6 March 1912), 12829 (10 March 1912); *Novoe vremia* 12925 (6 March 1912); *Russkie vedomosti* 55 (7 March 1912).

31. *Birzhevye vedomosti*, 12846, 12847, 12850 (20–22 March 1912), 12856–94 (28 March–19 April 1912).

32. *Kommersant* 790, 802 (27 April; 15 May 1912); *Torgovo-Promyshlennaia gazeta* 76, 80, 83, 86 (1, 6, 10, 13 April 1912).

33. *Russkoe slovo* 66, 68, 70 (20, 22, 24 March 1912); 74–89, 91, 93, 94, 95, 97, 99, 100, 105 (30–31 March; 1–17, 19, 21–24, 26, 29 April; 1, 9 May 1912).

34. *Rech'* 59, 64, 84 , 93–100, 105 (1, 6, 28 March; 6–13, 18 April 1912).

35. *Russkie vedomosti* 80, 82–86, 88, 95–102, 106–108, 111–12, 115, 122 (7, 9–13, 15, 24 April; 5, 10, 12, 16–17, 20, 29 May 1912).

36. *Golos Moskvy* 80, 81, 82, 86 (6–8, 13 April 19012).

37. *Sibirskaia zhizn'* 72–73, 75, 78–80, 83–84, 86, 91–93 (31 March; 1, 4, 8, 10, 13, 17, 22, 24–25 April 1912).

38. *Sibir'* 76, 78, 82–84, 86–87, 94 (1, 4, 8, 10–12, 22 April 1912).

39. *Arkhangel'sk* 78, 80–82, 85–86, 88, 100 (7, 10–12, 15, 17, 19 April; 3 May 1912); *Vostochnoe pomor'e* 40–42, 54 (8, 10, 12 April; 17 May 1912); *Ufimskii vestnik* 77–81 (7–9, 11–12 April 1912); *Ural'skaia zhizn'* 77–84 (7–8, 10–15 April 1912).

40. *Novoe vremia* 12945, 12952, 12954, 12955 (28 March; 4, 6, 8 April 1912).

41. *Novoe vremia,* 12954–59 (6–11 April 1912).

42. *Russkoe znamia,* 78, 80, 81 (7, 10–11 April 1912); *Tverskoe povolzh'e* 485, 487 (15, 29 April 1912); *Russkii golos* 10, 11 (15, 22 April 1912); *Volga* 74, 75, 77, 79–81 (6–7, 10, 12–14 April 1912).

43. For details of this coverage, see Melancon, "Unexpected Consensus," 30–33.

44. Duma debates about the Lena shooting are in *Gosudarstvennaia Duma. Stenograficheskii otchet. Tretii sozyv. Sessiia piataia* (St. Petersburg, 1912), pp. 1659–89 (April 9 session); pp. 1794–1829 (April 10 session); pp. 1945–1963 (11 April session); pp. 2736–52 (18 April session); and pp. 3325–52 (25 April session). Minutes, summaries, or both appeared in numerous central and regional newspapers; see for example, *Novoe vremia,* 8–27 April 1912, and *Russkie vedomosti,* 8–26 April 1912. A slightly abridged version of the pertinent Duma session minutes can be found in *Lenskie sobytiia,* 2: 255–350.

45. For the full texts of the questions and detailed analysis of the motivations, see Melancon, "Unexpected Consensus," 34–36.

46. *Novoe vremia* 12960 (12 April 1912).

47. Fedor Dan, "Posle 'Leny'," *Nasha Zaria* 5 (May 1912): 63.

48. For further information about the new type of workers' movement, see analysis in Alice Pate, "The Liquidationist Controversy: Russian Social Democracy and the Search for Unity," *New Labor History: Worker Identity and Experience in Russia, 1840–1918,* ed. Michael Melancon and Alice Pate (Bloomington, Ind., 2002), 95–122.

49. I thank Susan McCaffray for this observation.

50. Louise McReynolds, *The News Under Russia's Old Regime* (Princeton, 1991), effectively creates a broader framework for this study's findings about this period. See especially pp. 224–25, 248–49, 251, and 286. See also Melancon, "Russia's Outlooks."

51. Kokovtsev, *Iz moego proshlogo,* 56–63, 76.

CONCLUSION

1. Friedgut, *Iuzovka and Revolution,* 96–111, 210–14.

2. Carl Schorske, *German Social Democracy, 1905–1917: The Development of the Great Schism* (New York, 1972), 257–58; Helga Grebing, *The History of the German Labour Movement* (Dover, N.H., 1985), 67–74; Susanne Miller and Heinrich Potthoff, *A History of German Social Democracy from 1848 to the Present* (New York, 1986), 38–54; Stanley Pierson, *Marxist Intellectuals and the Working-Class Mentality in Germany, 1887–1912* (Cambridge, Mass., 1993).

3. E. P. Thompson, *The Making of the English Working Class* (New York, 1966), 684–92; R. Page Arnot, *The Miners: Years of Struggle* (London: George Allen and Unwin, 1953), 90–122; H. A. Clegg, Alan Fox, and A. F. Thompson, *A History of British Trade Unions since 1889,* 3 vols. (Oxford, 1964)1:486; R. A. Florey, *The General Strike of 1926* (London, 1980), 32, 45.

4. Foster Rhea Dulles and Melvyn Dubofsky, *Labor in America* (Arlington

Heights, Ill., 1984), 207; Stanley Buder, *Pullman: An Experiment in Industrial Order and Community Planning, 1880–1930* (London, 1967), 169–89; George McGovern and Leonard Guttridge, *The Great Coalfield War* (Boston, 1972); *Massacre at Ludlow: Four Reports* (New York, 1971); H. M. Gitelman, *Legacy of the Ludlow Massacre* (Philadelphia, 1988).

5. Informative analyses of these questions can be found in Larry G. Gerber, "Corporatism in Comparative Perspective: The Impact of the First World War on American and British Labor Relations," *Business History Review* 62 (Spring 1988): 93–127, "Corporatism and State Theory," *Social Science History* 3 (Fall 1995): 313–32, "Shifting Perspectives on American Exceptionalism: Recent Literature on American Labor Relations and Labor Politics," *Journal of American Studies* 2 (1997): 253–74.

6. Among the many studies that comment on aspects of these problems are Richard Robbins, *The Tsar's Viceroys: Russian Provincial Governors in the Last Years of the Empire* (Ithaca, 1987); Peter Waldron, *Between the Two Revolutions: Stolypin and the Politics of Renewal in Russia* (DeKalb, Ill., 1998); Robert Thurston, *Liberal City, Conservative State: Moscow and Russia's Urban Crisis, 1906–1914* (Oxford, 1987); Richard Wortman, *Scenarios of Power: Myth and Ceremony in Russian Monarchy* (Princeton, 1995–2000); and Steven Marks, *Road to Power: The Trans-Siberian Railroad and the Colonization of Asian Russia, 1850–1917* (Ithaca, 1991).

7. McReynolds, *News Under Russia's Old Regime*, 224–25, 248–49, 251, 286.

8. Waldon, *Between the Two Revolutions*, 186.

Bibliography

PRIMARY SOURCES

Archives

GARF, F. 102, Ministerstvo vnutrennikh del.
GARF, F. 124, Ministerstvo iustitsii.
GARF, F. 1186, Delo Manukhina.
GARF, F. 1467, Extraordinary Investigative Commission of the Provisional Government.
Hoover Institution Archive, Nicolaevsky Archive.

Newspapers

Arkhangel'sk (Arkhangelsk)
Birzhevye vedomosti (St. Petersburg)
Dvukhglavnyi orel (Kiev, Monarchist)
Golos Moskvy (Moscow, Octobrist)
Irkutskie gubernskie vedomosti (Irkutsk)
Kaluzhskie gubernskie vedomosti (Kaluga)
Kazanskaia gazeta (Kazan)
Kolokol (St. Petersburg, Rightist)
Kommersant (Moscow)
Moskovskaia gubernskie vedomosti (Moscow)
Nasha zaria (Social Democratic, Menshevik-oriented)
Novoe vremia (St. Petersburg, Nationalist)
Rech' (St. Petersburg, Constitutional Democratic)
Russkie vedomosti (Moscow, Constitutional Democratic)
Russkii golos (Odessa, Monarchist)
Russkoe slovo (Moscow, Progressist)
Russkoe znamia (St. Petersburg, Rightist)
Saratovskii listok (Saratov)
Sibir' (Irkutsk)
Sibirskaia zhizn' (Tomsk)
Sotsial-Demokrat (Social Democratic, Bolshevik-oriented)
Tomskie gubernskie vedomosti (Tomsk)
Torgovo-Promyshlennaia gazeta (St. Petersburg)
Tverskoe povolzh'e (Tver)
Ufimskii vestnik (Ufa)
Ural'skaia zhizn'

Utro Rossii (Moscow, Octobrist)
Volga (Saratov, Rightist)
Vostochnoe pomor'e (Nikolaev-on-Amur)
Zavety (Socialist Revolutionary, Reformist)
Zemshchina (St. Petersburg, Rightist)
Znamia truda (Socialist Revolutionary)
Zvezda (Social Democratic)

Published Sources

Angarskii, I. "Vitim." *Sibirskii sbornik* 2 (1899): 42–66.

Batashev, P. N. *Lenskaia zabastovka. Vospominaniia predsedatelia tsental'nogo biuro stachennogo komiteta.* Moscow, 1933.

———. *Lenskii rasstrel. Vospominaniia predsedatelia biuro stachennogo komiteta.* Moscow, 1936.

———, ed. *Pravda o lenskikh sobytiiakh.* Moscow, 1913.

Boltunov, F. P. "Otchet .... Materialy po voprosu o postroike severno-baikal'skogo zhelezno-dorozhnogo puti." *Trudy komandirovannoi po Vyso-chaishemu poveleniiu Amurskoi ekspeditsii. Prilozhenie 1-oe k vypuska XII.* Khabarovsk, 1911.

Cherepakhin, G. V. *Gody bor'by. Vospominaniia starogo bol'shevika.* Moscow, 1956.

———. "Kak eto bylo." *Trud* 88 (17 April 1937).

Chetverikov, Sergei. *Bezvozvratno ushedshaia Rossiia.* Berlin, n.d.

"Chto takoe rabochii narod v Sibiri?" *Sibir'* 11 (7 September 1875): 1–2.

Dan, Fedor. "Posle 'Leny'." *Nasha Zaria* 5 (May 1912): 60–68.

Documents Concerning the Competence of the Arbitration Court Set Up in Connection with the Questions Outstanding between the Lena Goldfields Company, Limited, and the U.S.S.R. Moscow, 1930.

E. I. "Pamiati P. M. Anan'eva." *Katorga i ssylka* 5 (1923): 238–40.

Fraktsiia progressistov v 4-oi Gosudarstvennoi Dumy. Sessiia 1, 1912–1913, vypusk 1. St. Petersburg, 1913.

Goffman (Polkovnik). "O zolotykh promyslakh Vostochnoi Sibiri." *Gornyi zhurnal* (1844): 1–54.

Gosudarstvennaia Duma. Stenograficheskie otchety. Tretii sozyv. Sessiia piataia. St. Petersburg, 1912.

Grigor'ev, F. S., and Ia. Z. Shapirshtein-Lers, eds. *K istorii rabochego i revoliut-sionnogo dvizheniia v Bodaibinskom zoloto-promyshlennom raione. Lenskoe "9 ianvaria"—4 aprelia 1912 goda.* Bodaibo, 1924.

Ia-i, A. "Ot Stretenska po Shilke i Amuru (iz putevykh zametok)." *Sibirskii sbornik* 1 (1889).

Karpinskii, L. A. "O sovremennom polozhenii zolotopromyshlennosti na Olek-minskikh priiskakh." *Izvestiia Vostochno-Sibirskogo otdela . . . geograficheskogo obshchestva* 17, nos. 3–4 (1886): 1–25.

———. "Otchet o deiatel'nosti Irkutskago gornago upravleniia v 1890 g." *Gornyi Zhurnal* 4 (1891): 343–54.

"Kartiny priiskovoi zhizni." *Vostochnoe obozrenie* 43 (1888): 9–10.

Kerenskii A. F. [A. K-ii]. "O tom, chto bylo." *Zavety* 5 (August 1912): 82–113.

"Khronika zolotopromyshlennago dela." *Vostochnoe obozrenie* 4 (1888): 7.

"Koe-chto o sibirskoi promyshlennosti." *Sibir'* 14 (28 September 1875): 1.

Kokovtsev, V. N. *Is moego proshlogo. Vospominaniia, 1907–1919 gg.* 2 vols. Paris, 1933.

Krylov, A. N. *Moi vospominaniia.* Moscow, 1984.

Kudriavtsev, I. *Lenskii rasstrel (vospominaniia uchastnika).* Kharkov, 1934.

Kvasha, G. I. *Statistiko-sravnitel'nye svedeniia o material'nom polozhenii rabochikh na priiskakh Lensko-zolotopromyshlennogo tovarishchestva.* St. Petersburg, 1912.

Latkin, P. V. "Ocherki severnoi i iuzhnoi system zolotykh promyslov Eniseiskogo okruga." *Delo* 11 (1869).

Lebedev, M. I. *"Lena" (Krovavyi urok). Vospominaniia uchastnika sobytii na Lene v 1912 g. 4- ogo aprelia.* Feodosia, 1923.

———. *Vospominaniia o lenskikh sobytiiakh.* 2nd exp. ed. Moscow, 1962.

———. *Vospominaniia o lenskikh sobytiiakh 1912 g.* Moscow, 1957.

Lenin, V. I., and I. V. Stalin. *O lenskikh sobytiiakh.* Moscow, 1938.

Lenskie sobytiia 1912 goda. Dokumenty i materialy. Ed. V. Vladimirova. Moscow, 1925.

Lenskie sobytiia (stat'i i materialy). Moscow, 1938.

Lenskii rasstrel. Al'bom. Comp. T. Takonulo. Moscow and Leningrad, 1932.

Lenskii rasstrel, 4–17 aprelia 1912 g. Sbornik statei i vospominanii uchastnikov. Ivanovo-Vosnesensk, 1924.

"Lenskii rasstrel 1912 g." (Novye dokumenty). *Krasnyi arkhiv* 81, no. 2 (1937): 133–206.

Lenskoe zolotopromyshlennoe tovarichestvo, aktsionernoe obshchestvo. Doklad A. G. Ginzburga i P. M. Saladilova. . . Stachka rabochikh na promyslakh. St. Petersburg, 1912.

Lopatin, A. *Dnevnik Vitimskoi ekspeditsii 1865 goda.* St. Petersburg, 1895.

———. "Zametki o polozhenii rabochikh na Eniseiskikh zolotykh promyslakh." *Izvestiia sibir'skogo otdela imperialisticheskogo-russkogo geograficheskogo Obshchestva* 2, no. 4 (8 November 1871): 32–48. Abridged and reprinted from *Delo* 11 (1869).

Loranskii, A. "Nashi zakony o zolotopromyshlennosti." *Gornyi zhurnal* 3 (1872): 476–514; 7–8 (1872): 335–70.

Mansyrov, S. P. "Moi vospominaniia o Gosudarstvennoi Dume (1912–1917)." In *Istorik i Sovremennik*, 5–45. Berlin, 1922.

Manukhin, S. S. *Vsepoddanneishii otchet chlena Gosudarstvennogo soveta, senatora tainogo sovetnikia Manukhina po ispolneniiu Vysochaishee voslozhenago na nego 27 Aprelia 1912 goda razsledovaniia o zabastovke na lenskikh promyslakh.* St. Petersburg, 1912.

Massacre at Ludlow: Four Reports. New York, 1971.

"Nashi zolotye promysla." *Vostochnoe obozrenie* 44 (1888): 10.

Nevskii, A. *Lenskie sobytiia i ikh prichiny.* St. Petersburg, 1912.

"Novye gornye upravlenie v Sibiri." *Vostochnoe obozrenie* 27 (1888): 1–2.

"Ob issledovanii chastnoi zolotopromyshlennosti." *Izvestiia sibir'skikh otdela imperialisticheskogo russkogo geograficheskogo obshchestva* 2, no. 4 (8 November 1871): 48–53.

Obshchestvo zavodchikov i fabrikantov Moskovskogo promyshlennogo raiona v 1912 godu. Otchet obshchestva za 1912 g. Moscow, 1913.

——. *Biulleten'* 16 (1912); 17 (1913).

——. *Izvestiia* 2–3 (August–September 1913).

"Ocherki sovremennago sostoianiia zolotopromyshlennogo dela na Olekminskikh i Vitimskikh priiskakh." *Sibirskii sbornik* 1 (1889): 1–26; 2 (1889): 26–64.

Ol', P. V. *Foreign Capital in Russia.* New York, 1983.

Ol'minskii, M. *Iz epokhi Zvezdy i Pravdy.* Moscow, 1956.

"O prichinakh khishchnichestva zolota." *Vostochnoe obozrenie* 33 (1888): 2–3.

Orfanov, M. I. *V dali (iz proshlogo). Rasskazy iz vol'noi i nevol'noi zhizni Mishla (M. I. Orfanova).* Moscow, 1883.

"O sibirskoi zolotopromyshlennosti." *Sibir'* 5 (27 July 1875): 1.

Otchet pravleniia akstionernogo obshchestva LZT za 1910–1911 gg. i smena na operatsii 1912–1913 gody . St. Petersburg, 1912.

Otchet pravleniia akstionernogo obshchestva LZT za 1912–1913 gg. i smena na operatsii 1913–1914 gody . St. Petersburg, 1914.

Otchet tsentral'nogo komiteta Soiuza 17 Oktiabria o ego deiatel'nosti s 1 sentiabria 1911 goda po oktiabr' 1912 goda. Moscow, 1912.

Pamiatnaia knizhka Iakutskoi oblasti za 1891 g. Iakutsk, 1891.

Petrishchev, A. "Khronika vnutrennei zhizni." *Russkoe bogatstvo* 5 (1912): 59–81.

Polnoe sobranie zakonov. Vol. 6. St. Petersburg, 1831.

Polnoe sobranie zakonov. Vol. 25. St. Petersburg, 1905.

Pravda o lenskikh sobytiiakh. Ed. P. N. Batashev. Moscow, 1913.

Predvestnik revoliutsionnoi bury; istoricheskii ocherk, dokumenty, vospominaniia. Ed. F. A. Kudriavtsev. Irkutsk, 1962.

Prodolzhenie svoda zakonov Rossiiskoi imperii. Chast' vtoraia. Ulozhenie o nakazaniakh ugolovnykh i ispravitel'nykh. St. Petersburg, 1902.

Prodolzhenie svoda zakonov Rossiiskoi imperii. 1906 goda, chast' tret'ia, stat'i k Tomam VII, VIII, IX i X. St. Petersburg, 1906.

Promyshlennost' i torgovlia v zakonodatel'nykh uchrezhdeniiakh, 1907–1912 gg. St. Petersburg, 1912.

"Rabochii vopros Vitimsko-Olekminskikh sistem." *Sibirskaia zhizn'* 79 (8 April 1912).

Rostov, A. "Novoe o lenskikh sobytiiakh" (po dannym arkhiva Irk. Gub. zhand.). *Byloe* 20 (1922): 163–77.

Rozanov, I. *Svod deistvuiushchikh uzakonenii o chastnoi zolotopromyshlennosti v Rossii.* St. Petersburg, 1883.

Shestoi ocherednoi s"ezd predstavitelei promyshlennosti i torgovli. Zhurnaly zasedaniia. Moscow, 1912.

Shipov, D. N. *Vospominaniia i dumy perezhitka.* Moscow, 1918.

Shul'gin, V. V. *Dni.* Leningrad, 1925.

Sinel'nikov, N. P. "Zapiski senatora N. P. Sinel'nikova." *Istoricheskii vestnik* 60 (1895): 373–84, 693–711; 61 (1895): 26–46.

"Skoptsy-zemledel'tsy Iakutskoi oblasti." *Vostochnoe obozrenie* 24 (1888): 6–7.

Slonim, Marc "An Autobiographical Fragment: The Birth of a Socialist Revolutionary." *Sbornik* 4 (Leeds, Winter 1978–79): 59–60.

Sobranie uzakonenii. St. Petersburg, 1877.

Sobranie uzakonenii i rasporiazhenii pravitel'stva, izdavaemoe pri pravitel'st-vuiushchem Senate 52 (23 June 1870).

Sobranie uzakonenii i rasporiazhenii pravitel'stva 3a, 1898, no. 94.

Sovet s"ezdov predstavitelei promyshlennosti i torgovli. Promyshlennost' i torgovlia v zakonodatel'nykh uchrezhdeniiakh 1907–1912 gg. St. Petersburg, 1912.

"Ssyl'nye i Iakuty." *Vostochnoe obozrenie* 19 (1888): 1–2.

Svod otchetov fabrichnykh inspektorov za 1909 god. St. Petersburg, 1910.

Svod otchetov fabrichnykh inspektorov za 1910 god. St. Petersburg, 1911.

Svod otchetov fabrichnykh inspektorov za 1911 god. St. Petersburg, 1912.

Svod otchetov fabrichnykh inspektorov za 1912 god. St. Petersburg, 1913.

Svod otchetov fabrichnykh inspektorov za 1913 god. St. Petersburg, 1914.

Svod otchetov fabrichnykh inspektorov za 1914 god. St. Petersburg, 1915.

Svod zakonov. St. Petersburg, 1886.

Svod zakonov Rossiiskoi imperii. Vol. 7, *Ustavy monetnyi, gornyi i o sole;* vol. 15, *Zakony ugolovnye.* St. Petersburg, 1857.

Svod zakonov ugolovnykh. Chast' pervaia. Ulozhenie o nakazaniiakh ugolovnykh i ispravitel'nykh. St. Petersburg, 1885.

Vasil'ev, E. N. *Dopolneniie k "Svodu deistvuiushchikh uzakonenii o chastnoi zoloto-promyshlennosti v Rossii."* St. Petersburg, 1892.

Vitte, S. Iu. *Vospominaniia (tsarstvovaniia Nikolaia II).* 2 vols. Berlin, 1922.

Vladimirova, V. ed. *Lenskie sobytiia 1912 goda (dokumenty i materialy).* Moscow, 1925.

Witte, Sergei. *The Memoirs of Count Witte.* Armonk, N.Y., 1990.

Zakony o chastnoi fabrichno-zavodskoi promyshlennosti (izvlechennye iz Ustava o promyshlennosti izd. 1893 g. i po prodolzheniiam i iz drugikh chastei Svoda zakonov). Moscow, 1913.

Zhilkin, I. "Provintsial'noe obozrenie." *Vestnik evropy* 5 (May 1912): 391–401.

"Znachenie khimicheskago sposoba obrabotki zolotykh rud v Vostochnoi Sibiri." *Vostochnoe obozrenie* 12 (1888): 11–12; 13 (1888): 12.

SECONDARY SOURCES

Aksenov, Iu. S. *Lenskie sobytiia 1912 goda.* Moscow, 1960.

Anan'ich, B. V. "Economic Policy of the Tsarist Government." In *Entrepreneurship in Imperial Russia and the Soviet Union,* ed. Gregory Guroff and Fred Carstensen, 125–39. Princeton, 1983.

Anderson, Barbara A. *Internal Migration during Modernization in Late Nineteenth-Century Russia.* Princeton, 1980.

Arnot, R. Page *The Miners: Years of Struggle.* London, 1953.

Arutiunov, G. A. *Rabochee dvizhenie v Rossii v period novogo revoliutsionnogo pod"ema, 1910–1914 gg.* Moscow, 1975.

Avrekh, A. Ia. *Lenskii rasstrel i krizis tret'eiiunskoi sistemy.* Moscow, 1962.

———. *Tsarizm i IV Duma 1912–1914 gg.* Moscow, 1981.

———. *Tsarizm i tret'eiiunskaia sistema.* Moscow, 1966.

Bakhtin, M. M. *The Dialogic Imagination.* Austin, 1981.

————. *Problems of Dostoevsky's Poetics*. [Ann Arbor, Mich.], 1973.

————. *Speech Genres and Other Late Essays*. Austin, 1986.

————. *Toward a Philosophy of the Act*. Austin, 1993.

Balabanov, M. *Ot 1905 k 1917. Massovoe rabochee dvizhenie*. Leningrad and Moscow, 1927.

Barkai, Haim. "The Macro-Economics of Tsarist Russia in the Industrialization Era: Monetary Developments, the Balance of Payments, and the Gold Standard." *Journal of Economic History* 33 (June 1973): 339–71.

Baron, Samuel. *Bloody Sunday in the Soviet Union: Novocherkassk, 1962*. Stanford, 2001.

Bernstein, S. A. *The Financial and Economic Results of the Workings of the Lena Goldfields Company Limited*. London, n.d.

Blackwell, William. *The Beginnings of Russian Industrialization, 1800–1960*. Princeton, 1968.

————. *The Industrialization of Russia. An Historical Perspective*. Arlington Heights, Ill., 1970.

Blek, Al. "Rabochie na lenskikh zolotykh priiskakh." *Arkhiv istorii truda v Rossii* 4 (1922): 68–84; 5 (1922): 47–56; 10 (1923): 28–42.

Bonnell, V. I. *Roots of Rebellion: Workers' Politics and Organizations in St. Petersburg and Moscow, 1900–1914*. Berkeley, 1983.

Buder, Stanley. *Pullman: An Experiment in Industrial Order and Community Planning, 1880–1930*. London, 1967.

Carstensen, Fred. *American Enterprise in Foreign Markets: Studies of Singer and International Harvester in Imperial Russia*. Chapel Hill, N.C., 1984.

Clegg, H. A., Alan Fox, and A. F. Thompson. *A History of British Trade Unions since 1889*. 3 vols. Oxford, 1964.

Crisp, Olga. "Russian Financial Policy and the Gold Standard at the End of the Nineteenth Century." *Economic History Review* 1 (1953): 156–70.

Danilevskii, V. V. *Russkaia tekhnika*. Leningrad, 1948.

Danow, David. *The Thought of Mikhail Bakhtin: From Word to Culture*. New York, 1991.

Drummond, M. "The Russian Gold Standard, 1897–1914." *Journal of Economic History* 36 (September 1976): 663–88.

Dulles, Foster Rhea, and Melvyn Dubofsky. *Labor in America*. Arlington Heights, Ill., 1984.

Dulov, V. I. "Zabastovochnoe dvizhenie na Lene v nachale 1900-kh godov." *Uchenye zapiski Irkutskogo Gosudarstvennogo ped. instituta. Kefedra Marksizma-Leninizma. Kefedra istorii*, 17, no. 9 (1961): 13–19.

Emerson, Caryl. *The First Hundred Years of Mikhail Bakhtin*. Princeton, 1997.

Florey, R. A. *The General Strike of 1926*. London, 1980.

Friedgut, Theodore H. *Iuzovka and Revolution: Life and Work in Russia's Donbass, 1869–1924*. Princeton, University, 1989.

————. "Labor Violence and Regime Brutality in Tsarist Russia: The Iuzovka Cholera Riots of 1892." *Slavic Review*, no. 2 (Summer 1987): 245–65.

Gamov, I. *Ocherki dalekoi Sibiri*. Gomel, 1894.

Gatrell, Peter. *Government, Industry, and Rearmament in Russia, 1900–1914.* Cambridge, Eng., 1994.
———. *The Tsarist Economy 1850–1917.* London, 1986.
Gerber, Larry G. "Corporatism and State Theory." *Social Science History* 3 (Fall 1995): 313–32.
———. "Corporatism in Comparative Perspective: The Impact of the First World War on American and British Labor Relations." *Business History Review* 62 (Spring 1988): 93–127.
———. "Shifting Perspectives on American Exceptionalism: Recent Literature on American Labor Relations and Labor Politics." *Journal of American Studies* 2 (1997): 253–74 .
Gessen, I. *Istoriia gornorabochikh SSSR.* 1: *Istoriia gornorabochikh Rossii do 60 gg. XIX veka;* 2: *Vtoraia polovina 19-go veka.* Moscow, 1926.
Gitelman, H. M. *Legacy of the Ludlow Massacre: a Chapter in American Labor Relations.* Philadelphia, 1988.
Glickman, Rose L. *Russian Factory Women: Workplace and Society, 1880–1914.* Berkeley, 1984.
Golder, Frank A. *Russian Expansion on the Pacific.* New York, 1971.
Gorshkov, Boris. "Serfs on the Move: Peasant Seasonal Migration in Pre-Reform Russia, 1800–1861." *Kritika* 4 (Fall 2000): 627–56.
Grant, Jonathan. *Big Business in Russia: The Putilov Company in Late Imperial Russia, 1868–1917.* Pittsburgh, 1999.
Grebing, Helga. *The History of the German Labour Movement.* Dover, N.H., 1985.
Gregory, Paul A. "The Russian Balance of Payments, the Gold Standard, and Monetary Policy." *Journal of Economic History* 39 (June 1979): 379–99.
———. *Russian National Income, 1885–1913.* Cambridge, Eng., 1983.
Gregory, Paul A., and Joel Sailors. "Russian Monetary Policy and Industrialization, 1861–1913." *Journal of Economic History* 36 (December 1976): 836–51.
Gudoshnikov, M. *Lenskii rasstrel 1912–1932 gg.* Moscow and Irkutsk, 1932.
Habermas, Jürgen. *The Structural Transformation of the Public Sphere: An Inquiry into a Category of Bourgeois Society.* Cambridge, Mass., 1991.
Haimson, L. "The Problem of Political and Social Stability in Urban Russia on the Eve of War and Revolution Revisited." *Slavic Review* 4 (Winter 2000): 846–75.
———. "The Problem of Social Stability in Urban Russia, 1905–1917." Pt. 1, *Slavic Review.* 4 (December 1964): 619–42; pt 2, 1 (March 1965): 1–22.
Hildermeier, Manfred. *The Russian Socialist Revolutionary Party before the First World War.* New York, 2000.
Holquist, Michael. *Dialogism: Bakhtin and His World.* London and New York, 1990.
Johnson, Robert E. *Peasant and Proletarian: The Working Class of Moscow in the Late Nineteenth Century.* New Brunswick, N.J., 1979.
Karpenko, Z. G. "Formirovanie rabochikh kadrov v gornozavodskoi promyshlennosti zapadnoi Sibiri (1725–1860)." *Istoricheskie zapiski* 69 (1961): 222–52.
Koenker, Diane P., and William G. Rosenberg. *Strikes and Revolution in Russia, 1917.* Princeton, 1989.

Krivolutskii, A. E. *V Lenskoi taige.* Moscow, 1958.

Krizis samoderzhaviia v Rossii, 1895–1917. Leningrad, 1984.

Kudriavtsev, F. A. *Dnevnik lenskoi zabastovki 1912 goda. Fakty i materialy.* Irkutsk, 1938.

———. *Lenskie sobytiia 1912 goda.* Irkutsk, 1942.

———, ed. *Predvestnik revoliutsionnoi bury; istoricheskii ocherk, dokumenty, vospominaniia.* Irkutsk, 1962.

Laverychev, V. Ia. *Po tu storonu barrikad (iz istorii bor'by Moskovskoi burzhuazii s revoliutsiei).* Moscow, 1967.

———. *Tsarizm i rabochii vopros v Rossii (1861–1917 gg.)* Moscow, 1972.

Lelevich, G. "Lenskii rasstrel." *Proletarskaia revoliutsiia* 5 (1922): 12–24.

Lenskie priiski (sbornik dokumentov). Ed. P. Pospelov. In the series *Istoriia zavodov.* Moscow, 1937.

Lenskii rasstrel. Bibliografiia. Ed. V. I. Nevskii. Moscow and Leningrad, 1932.

"Lenskii rasstrel." *Sputnik kommunista,* no. 14 (1922): 66–72.

Lenskii rasstrel 1912 goda. Moscow, 1923.

Levin, Sh. "K istorii zabastovki na lenskikh zolotykh priiskakh." *Byloe* 20 (1922): 178–93.

Lyashchenko, Peter. *History of the National Economy of Russia.* New York, 1949.

Maevskii, A. "Lena." *Nasha zaria* 4 (1912): 50–60.

Marks, Steven. *Road to Power: The Trans-Siberian Railroad and the Colonization of Asian Russia, 1850–1917.* Ithaca, 1991.

McCaffray, Susan. *The Politics of Industrialization in Tsarist Russia: The Association of Southern Coal and Steel Producers, 1874–1914.* De Kalb, Ill., 1996.

McCaffray Susan, and Michael Melancon, eds. *Russia in the European Context: A Member of the Family, 1789–1914,* New York, 2005.

McDaniel, Tim. *Autocracy, Capitalism, and Revolution in Russia.* Berkeley, 1988.

McGovern, George S., and Leonard F. Guttridge. *The Great Coalfield War.* Boston, 1972.

McKay, John. *Pioneers for Profit: Foreign Entrepreneurship and Russian Industry, 1885–1913.* Chicago, 1970.

McKean, R. B. *St. Petersburg between the Revolutions: Workers and Revolutionaries, June 1907–February 1917.* New Haven, 1990.

McReynolds, Louise. *The News Under Russia's Old Regime.* Princeton, 1991.

Melancon, M. "The Ninth Circle: The Lena Goldfield Workers and the Massacre of 4 April 1912." *Slavic Review* 3 (Fall 1994): 766–95.

———. "Russia's Outlooks on the Present and Future, 1910–1914: What the Press Tells Us." In *Russia in the European Context: A Member of the Family, 1789–1914,* ed. Susan McCafffray and Michael Melancon, 203–26. New York, 2005.

———. *The Socialist-Revolutionaries and the Russian Anti-War Movement, 1914–1917.* Columbus, Ohio, 1990.

———. "'Stormy Petrels': The Socialist Revolutionaries in Russia's Labor Organizations, 1905–1914." *Carl Beck Papers* 703 (June 1988).

———. "Unexpected Consensus: Russian Society and the Lena Massacre, April 1912." *Revolutionary Russia* 2 (December 2002): 1–52.

Melancon, Michael, and Alice Pate. "Bakhtin contra Marx and Lenin: A Polyphonic Approach to Russia's Labor and Revolutionary Movements." *Russian History* 31, no. 4 (Winter 2004): 387–417.

Mendel, Arthur. "On Interpreting the Fate of Imperial Russia." In *Russia Under the Last Tsar,* ed. Theofanis George Stavrou, 12–41. Minneapolis, 1969.

———. "Peasant and Worker on the Eve of the First World War." *Slavic Review* 25 (1966): 23–33.

Menitskii, I. "Iz proshlogo Moskovskogo studenchestva (Otkliki na Lenskie sobytiia 1912 goda)." *Put' k oktiabriu* 1 (Moscow, 1923): 142–45.

———. *Revoliutsionnoe dvizhenie voennykh godov.* Moscow, 1925.

Miller, Susanne, and Heinrich Potthoff. *A History of German Social Democracy from 1848 to the Present.* New York, 1986.

Morson, Gary Saul, and Caryl Emerson. *Mikhail Bakhtin: Creation of a Prosaics.* Stanford, 1990.

Nevskii, V. "K desiatiletiiu lenskogo rasstrela." *Krasnaia letopis'* 2–3 (1922): 201–14.

New Labor History: Worker Identity and Experience, 1840–1918. Ed. Michael Melancon and Alice Pate. Bloomington, Ind., 2002.

Nikolaevskii, B. "Lenskaia stachka 1912 g." *Byloe* 15 (1920): 155–73.

Orlovsky, Daniel. "Professionalism in the Ministerial Bureaucracy on the Eve of the February Revolution." In *Russia's Missing Middle Class: The Professions in Russian History,* ed. Harley D. Balzer, 54–81. Armonk, N.Y., 1996.

Pate, Alice. "The Liquidationist Controversy: Russian Social Democracy and the Search for Unity." In *New Labor History: Worker Identity and Experience in Russia, 1840–1918,* 95–122. Bloomington, Ind., 2002.

Piaskovskii, A. V. *Lenskie sobytiia 1912 g.* Moscow, 1939.

Pierson, Stanley. *Marxist Intellectuals and the Working-Class Mentality in Germany, 1887–1912.* Cambridge, Mass., 1993.

Pletnev, V. *Lena: ocherk istorii lenskikh sobytii.* Moscow, 1923.

Predvestnik revoliutsionnoi buri. Istoricheskii ocherk, dokumenty, vospominaniia. Ed. F. A. Kudriavtsev. Irkutsk, 1962.

Rimlinger, Gaston. "Autocracy and the Factory Order in Early Russian Industrialization." *Journal of Economic History* 20, no.1 (1960): 67–92.

Robbins, Richard. *The Tsar's Viceroys: Russian Provincial Governors in the Last Years of the Empire.* Ithaca, 1987.

Schimmelpennick van der Oye, David. *Toward the Rising Sun: Russian Ideologies of Empire and the Path to War with Japan.* DeKalb, Ill., 2001.

Schorske, Carl. *German Social Democracy, 1905–1917. The Development of the Great Schism.* New York, 1972.

Semevskii, V. I., Rabochie na Sibirskikh zolotyhk priiskakh. Istoricheskoe izsledovanie. 2 vols. , Vol. 1, *Ot nachala zolotoi promyshlennosti v Sibiri do 1870 g.;* vol. 2, *Polozhenie rabochikh posle 1870 g.* St. Petersburg, 1898.

Shalaginova, L. M. "Otkliki na lenskie sobytiia v Rossii." *Istoricheskii arkhiv* 1 (January–February 1962): 176–85.

Sharapov, I. P. *Ocherki po istorii lenskikh zolotykh priiskov.* Irkutsk, 1949.

Shatsillo, K. F. "Lenskii rasstrel i tsarskoe pravitel'stvo." In *Bol'shevistskaia pechat' i rabochii klass Rossii v gody revoliutsionnogo pod"ema 1910–1914.* Moscow, 1965.

Surh, Gerald D. *1905 in St. Petersburg: Labor, Society, and Revolution.* Stanford, 1989.

Thompson, E. P. *The Making of the English Working Class*. New York, 1966.

Thurston, Robert. *Liberal City, Conservative State: Moscow and Russia's Urban Crisis, 1906–1914*. Oxford, 1987.

Tiushevskii, A. *K istorii zabastovki i rasstrela na lenskikh priiskakh*. Petrograd, 1921.

Todorow, Tzvetan. *Mikhail Bakhtin: The Dialogical Principle*. Minneapolis,1984.

Treadgold, Donald. *The Great Siberian Migration*. Princeton, 1957.

Vendrikh, G. A. *Lenskie sobytiia 1912 g*. Irkutsk, 1956.

Vendrikh, G. A., K. V. Belomestnov, and L. S. Sholokhova. *Na Lene-reke*. Irkutsk, 1984.

Vice, Sue. *Introducing Bakhtin*. Manchester, UK, 1997.

Volkovicher, I. "Otkliki lenskikh sobytii v Moskve." *Proletarskaia revoliutsiia* 3 (1923): 66–92.

von Laue, Theodore. "The Chances for Liberal Constitutionalism." *Slavic Review* 25 (1966): 34–46.

———. *Sergei Witte and the Industrialization of Russia*. New York, 1969.

Waldron, Peter. *Between the Two Revolutions: Stolypin and the Politics of Renewal in Russia*. DeKalb, Ill., 1998.

Wolff, David. *To the Harbin Station: The Liberal Alternative in Russian Manchuria, 1898–1914*. Stanford, 1999.

Work, Community, and Power: The Experience of Labor in Europe and America, 1900–1925. Ed. James E. Cronin and Carmen Siriani. Philadelphia, 1983.

Wortman, Richard. *Scenarios of Power: Myth and Ceremony in Russian Monarchy*, 2 vols. Princeton, 1995–2000.

Zelnik, Reginald. *Law and Disorder on the Narova River: The Kreenholm Strike of 1872*. Berkeley, 1995.

———. "The Peasant and the Factory." In *The Peasant in Nineteenth-Century Russia*, ed. Wayne S. Vucinich, 158–90. Stanford, 1968.

Zhukov. "Revoliutsionnoe znachenie lenskoi zabastovki." *Proletarskaia revoliutsiia* 87 (1929): 54–83.

Index

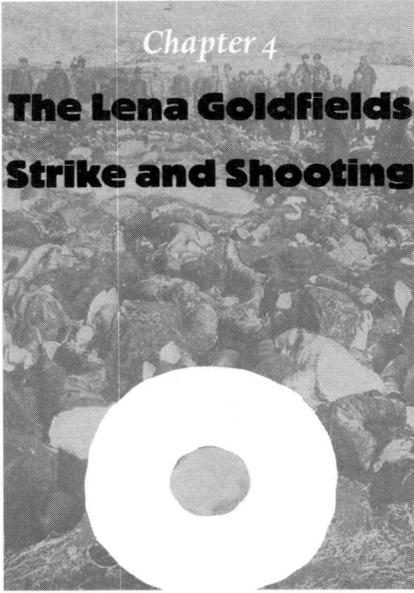

Politics, the Strike Committee, and Competing Discourses

Sormovo, 154
State Duma. *See under* Russian government
strike(s) (movement): Lena, 8, 23, 25–26, 38, 63, 78, 115, 121–23, 139, 141–43, 163, 165, 169, 185, 187, 191, 197; protest against, 121–22, 135, 157–58, 161–65, 179; Irkutsk, 121; Kreenholm, 8; Novocherkassk, 8; in 1917, 8
St. Petersburg, 5–7, 17, 34, 36, 38, 41, 44–45, 47–49, 51, 61, 7–73, 77, 80, 84–87, 89–90, 92, 94–97, 101, 111, 114, 125, 133, 142, 145–46, 148–49, 151, 154–55, 157–69, 186; general student coalition committee, 161–162; mining institute, 38; Psycho-Neurological Institute, 161–162; Society of Factory Owners, 160; Society of Gravurists, 160; women's advanced (higher) courses, 161–62
Surh, Gerry, 8
Sushkin, G. G., 120, 128–29, 131

Tartars, 12, 79
Teppan, A.G., 80–81, 84–85, 87, 92–93, 95, 98, 114–15, 124–26, 129, 145, 147–50
Teptorgo mountain, 10
Tersk, 155
Tiflis, 155
Timashev, S. I., 44, 86–87, 89, 150–51, 175–77, 181
Timiriazev, V. I., 44
Titanic, 153
Tiushevskii, A. A., 6
Tomsk, 33, 155, 169; provincial council, 33
Torgovo-Promyshlennaia gazeta, 167
Trapeznikov, K., 19, 26, 65–66
Traskin (mining police inspector), 75–76
Treshchenkov, N. V., 92–115, 121, 127–29, 133–34, 136, 142–43, 146, 148–51, 168, 175–76
Trudoviks (Duma fraction), 3; role in protest movement, 154, 164; role in Duma debates, 171–73, 175, 177–78
Trudovoi golos, 163
Tul'chinskii, K. N., 50, 56–57, 60–61, 74, 86, 90–95, 97–101, 105–109, 112–13, 124, 128, 131, 134, 140, 145, 147–49, 170

Tunguz people (tribe), 9, 12–13, 187
Turkic language group, 12
Tver, 103, 155, 171
Tverskoe povolzh'e, 103

Ukraintsev, M. F., 90, 126, 129–30, 135–36, 139
Utro Rossii, 123

Viazovoi, V., 81, 125, 130, 132–33
Vasil'ev, N., 115, 136, 141–42
Vestnik Evropy, 160
Vilyuy River, 10
Vinogradov, A. K., 121
Vinogradov, P. A., 162
Vinokurov, Father, 107
Vishnegradskii, A. I., 44
Vitebsk Old Believers' Union, 160
Vitim River. *See* Lena River, tributaries of
Vladimirova, V., 115

Warsaw, 154–55, 157, 164–65
Witte, S. Iu., 44–45
workers (labor, miners): Lena, 6, 21, 26, 30–31, 38, 40–41, 46–47, 57, 60–64, 74, 76–77, 116, 127, 153, 159–61, 164, 179, 187, 189–90, 194; children, 26, 29, 32–34, 37–40, 52–54, 57–59, 62, 92, 104–105, 107, 113; hard-labor prisoners, 34–35, 39; political exiles, 21, 23–24, 35, 39, 61–62, 75; possessional workers (serfs), 23–25, 65; women, 26, 29, 32, 34, 37–38, 40, 53–54, 56, 60, 62, 84
World War I, 8, 114, 157, 180, 188–89, 192, 194

Za narod, 121
Zalogin, A. A., 117
Zavelina, Steppanida, 80
Zelionko, R., 81–82, 100, 125–26, 129–36
Zelnik, Reginald, 8
Zemlia i volia, 122
Zhukov, 114, 136
Zhuravlev-Ivanov, D., 81
Znamia truda, 122, 163
Zvezda, 121, 163